Tight Lines: Ten Years of the Yale Anglers' Journal

TIGHT LINES

Ten Years of the YALE ANGLERS' JOURNAL

Foreword by NICK LYONS   Illustrations by JAMES PROSEK

Preface by JAMES PROSEK and JOSEPH FURIA

Edited by Joseph Furia, Wyatt Golding, David Haltom, Steven Hayhurst,
Joseph Kingsbery, and Alexis Surovov

Yale University Press
New Haven & London

Illustrations by James Prosek reproduced courtesy of the artist and Waqas Wajahat, LLC. 17 East 64th St., New York NY 10021.

Produced by Scott & Nix, Inc.,
150 West 28th Street, Suite 1103, New York, NY 10001.
WWW.SCOTTANDNIX.COM

Printed in China.

Library of Congress Control Number: 2007921825
ISBN 978-0-300-12630-3 (cloth : alk. paper)

A catalogue record of this book is available from the British Library.

The paper of this book meets the guidelines for permanence and durability of the Committee on Production Guidelines for Book Longevity of the Council on Library Resources.

10 9 8 7 6 5 4 3 2 1

THE YALE ANGLERS' JOURNAL
Aaron Alter

THE *YALE ANGLERS' JOURNAL* has thrived on the dedication of its staff and supporters to create and maintain a medium for understanding angling and the natural world. This dedication extends beyond the pages of the journal and of this anthology, capturing a wide spectrum of life's aspects. The diversity of our contributors, staff, supporters, and readers brings out the nature of this dedication. Through literature, the *Yale Anglers' Journal* has become a confluence.

As a confluence, the journal has provided its readers with an array of prose and poetry whose uniqueness sets the journal apart from other publications of its genre. This diversity has developed to go beyond the eclectic list of contributors who are in this anthology and the eighteen issues of the journal to date. Today, the journal's confluence accepts and enjoys contributions and recognition from all around the world. The *Yale Anglers' Journal* staff has worked hard, traveling around the world to expand the pieces that float through its pages.

In this way, the journal has grown up from its impressive roots. While the feel of the pages and their content remains intact, they are now being filled, in part, by those who fish on foreign waters. The success of previous editors and the support garnered from the dedication of the staff and supporters has made this reality possible. It is humbling, much as the quality of this anthology is, to feel the fruit of the journal's success as its seeds are spread on new ground and by new means.

When I assumed the role of editor-in-chief this last semester, I could never have imagined the world that this journal would open up to me. I have experienced a reality that, while plagued by hours behind a desk in the office, goes beyond the angling that the journal's literature covers. Much as the journal itself has grown in ways that one never could have predicted, my world has grown through the confluence of life, of ideas, of angling experiences, and ways of looking at the world that only this journal could have provided.

Maintaining this confluence, created and sustained by the dedication of so many people, as the streams that feed in to it diversify and expand, remains the responsibility that I am honored to share a piece of. This anthology and the growth of the *Yale Anglers' Journal* itself are the fruit that I hope you all continue to enjoy with me.

For more information on the *Yale Anglers' Journal*, please see WWW.YALEANGLERSJOURNAL.COM or write to Editor, *Yale Anglers' Journal*, P.O. BOX 204048, New Haven, CT 06520-4048.

CONTENTS

FOREWORD
Nick Lyons

WHAT A FRESH, varied, and thoughtful anthology this is! It collects the best essays, poems, and stories from the first ten years of the *Yale Anglers' Journal* and is like no other basket of fishing-in-print I know. Perhaps its greatest virtue is that it is consistently entertaining.

There are always new anthologies about angling being published—usually tightly focused on fly fishing or a particular species or locale, some accompanied by coffee-table and luscious photographs or heavily dependent on that great pool of fishing "classics," many of which are in the public domain and thus appear in book after book. Since those "classics" are fine stories, there's no harm in keeping them available to fishermen who like to read or are persuaded by them to read more and thus enhance the fishing experience. But *Tight Lines* is different. For one thing, it is radically more diverse. It includes pieces by such notables as Howell Raines (a wonderful section on love and fishing), Jimmy Carter, Robert Behnke (the most knowledgeable of the trout biologists), the late and brilliant Ernest Schwiebert, the poet John Hollander, W. B. Yeats, hilarious work by Peter Just, Christopher Buckley, and others, and one of those truly exceptional essays, "Marcel Proust and the Art of Fly Fishing" by Yale Professor R. Howard Bloch. There is also more than a smattering of writers whose names will be new to most readers, some of them (I suspect) quite young, perhaps still students at Yale, all of them interesting. As such, this is a truly *sui generis* anthology, in that its generous range includes poetry and prose, early and mature work, great humor, adventure, a broad variety of perspectives, significant brooding about matters piscatorial, and much more.

Starting from the potentially proscribed world of a literary magazine begun by undergraduates at Yale University, its publishers and editors reached out beyond academia with telling effect for what was pertinent and engaging. The magazine from the outset centered on the written word in a variety of its occasions, leaning more toward "literature" than ever toward "how-to" or "where-to," and this in itself was original, as was that original concept of having it emerge from the vision of some students led by James Prosek and Joseph Furia.

I especially like that this is an ample anthology, clear, eminently readable, full of surprise, remarkably not repetitive for a collection of pieces connected in some way to fishing. The quality of the work invariably fluctuates, given that some of the contributors are highly experienced, practiced, and sophisticated writers and some are not. I like this. It adds to the surprise, the sense of discovery, the true scope of the book. It gives a glimpse of young writers who may well become some of the best in the field, and it all helps to provide a significant reading experience for serious fishermen of a variety of stripes.

Graced with James Prosek's fine illustrations and blessed with its great variety and achievement, this is a bold fishing book slated for a long and treasured life.

PREFACE

James Prosek

I ENTERED COLLEGE with an aching passion for trout fishing that began when I was nine-years-old. There weren't many outlets for my yearnings on the urban campus of Yale. I joined the crew team, in part, because it allowed me daily visits by bus to one of my favorite Connecticut rivers, the Housatonic. I rowed most every waking day that the river was ice-free, and often tried to peer at a small dock on the east bank—as our scull of eight sped by—where I caught many perch and eel as a kid.

Sophomore year I quit rowing, and discovered in my new-found time, a world of angling literature in the stacks of Sterling Memorial Library. Dusting off copies of Izaak Walton's *The Compleat Angler*, some of which were over 250-years-old, I felt like I'd found buried treasure. Volume after volume with marbled endpapers like swirling back-eddies, set with beautiful etchings and engravings of fish and the English countryside. I pored through those books and was transported to places I'd never been—the River Dove in the Peak District of Staffordshire and the chalk streams of Hampshire. So, for that moment, I lived my passion through books, and while reading, snow falling outside the neo-gothic windows, I became a kind of Waltonian.

Walton's *Compleat Angler*, originally published in 1653, was the first book to treat angling as a "contemplative man's recreation" (as the subtitle reads), as opposed to solely a means of catching fish for sustenance (though Walton did eat his share of fish). But the book suggested to me, that angling was even more than a recreation; it was a way of life, a spiritual pastime, or a kind of religion (the *Compleat Angler* some say, is in part code for the *Compleat Anglican*). Angling was a way into nature, and for Walton, a way to escape the turbulent civil war of the mid-seventeenth century—a kind of pre-Thoreauvian pastoral fantasy/polemic about how to live with humility and simplicity.

My junior year I applied for a travel fellowship to follow in the footsteps of Izaak Walton through England. As an English major, I told the judges, I would write my senior thesis on Walton, and having convinced the fellowship committee to take the bait, I began preparations, come late-April, to go off across the pond, my head filled with visions of rising trout and chalk streams.

Around that time, I got a call from a friend in my college, Frannie Furia. Her cousin Joe, a high school senior, had been admitted to Yale. Joe had decided, though, to go to Middlebury, because he loved trout fishing and had mapped out a trout stream he could walk to from campus. But his father wanted him to go to Yale. That night I got a call from Joe Furia's father in Seattle—Joe was coming to visit Yale… might I take him around, show him that there are anglers who have survived on campus?

"I'll take him around," I said, "but I don't want to influence his decision."

STUDY TO BE QUIET

Mind you, the book on my mind at that moment, Walton's book, is essentially a book of persuasion and conversion. It begins with a fisherman meeting a hunter on his way to the River Lea, a tributary of the Thames, from Fleet Street in London. The angler, Piscator, is off to fish for trout, and the hunter, Venator, is going shooting for otters. The angler dislikes otters (competition) and so the two are quick friends. In dialog, the Piscator and Venator give arguments in favor of their respective pastimes, and the angler winning, continues by instructing the hunter in his faith.

Joe showed up near my dorm room one early May day, dressed like a cast member from *A River Runs Through It*, plaid shirt, suspenders, canvas pants…or cast out from Walton's pages. He had a knapsack filled with boxes of beautiful trout flies he'd tied himself, and a split cane bamboo fly rod in an aluminum tube. I couldn't quite believe what I was seeing, but was struck by his enthusiasm and zeal… now that I was a jaded college junior, soon-to-be-senior.

Joe came with me, carrying his fishing kit, to a few of my classes. During a slide presentation in my Philosophy of Architecture class, I passed him a note on a scrap of paper, "If you come to Yale we could start an angling journal."

That was it. He took the scrap of paper and over the summer, with submissions from our friends, a tangible publication began to emerge from Joe's Seattle home. The first issue was out that fall.

I think, in part, it's the contemplative nature of angling that prompts people to write about it. Fishing is mostly about time spent in silence and it provides a chance to think about family, friends, what's going on in one's life, nature, making art and writing stories. Fishing is really a catalyst for sharing what you're working out, or to simply tell a good tale. The journal has stayed pretty close to its original vision. It remains an undergraduate publication, run by undergraduates, that encourages submissions from anyone, anywhere around the world. Angling is a universal pastime that can be exercised anywhere there's water, so there is a great diversity of landscapes, places, and characters in the stories. I hope that anyone who picks up this anthology may also find, that angling is a recreation—if one is in the concrete jungle, or where the weather prohibits—that can be practiced in the mind.

Joseph Furia

THE IDEA THAT EVOLVED into the *Yale Anglers' Journal* was born eleven years ago in 1996 when I visited colleges to decide which I would attend the following September. Middlebury, with a trout stream on campus, had the lead. In an effort to tip the scales toward Yale, my cousin, Frannie (Yale '97) conspired with my father to introduce me to James Prosek, whose first illustrated book, *Trout*, was by then a classic. James took me to one of his classes, during which he suggested that I could become the first editor-in-chief of a Yale fishing publication that he and I might co-found. The hook was set.

The next few months were challenging. James was researching his senior thesis and putting together another book, so it was left up to me to set up the publication. The first question was what type of fishing magazine the *Journal* was going to be. To address it, I visited a large local bookstore and found ten literary journals, which had the common characteristics of an uncomplicated design, well-composed articles, poetry and art, and no advertising. That is when the light bulb lit up—the *Yale Anglers' Journal* would not be another "hook and bullet" magazine—it would be a literary publication that explored life through the medium of angling. The great jazz musician, William "Count" Basie, when asked what the secret was to the special sound of his jazz arrangements, answered, "it's not the notes I play—it's the ones I leave out." And so it would be true of the *Journal*.

Other fishing publications were not only full of advertising, but their articles were mostly devoted to gear, technique or fishing destinations, and none of them were run by students. However, the *Journal* would be defined not only by its excellent prose, poetry and art, but also by its complete absence of how-to, where-to, and what-with articles.

The *Journal* would be the why-to of fishing publications defined by three main characteristics: it would be (1) literary, (2) non-commercial, and (3) student-run. *Webster's Dictionary* defines literature as "writing in prose or verse; esp. writing having excellence of form or expression and expressing ideas of permanent or universal interest." The *Journal* would include well-written work, but also work that would have timeless, universal appeal because it would be as much about life as about fishing. Just as a reader does not need to fish to enjoy the alpine fishing scene in Hemingway's *The Sun Also Rises*, so a reader would not have to be an angler to enjoy the *Journal*. Furthermore, the *Journal* would strive to publish artwork that would be equally appreciated by angler and non-angler alike.

Part of establishing the *Journal* included securing undergraduate organization status, an effort for which I received substantial support from then Assistant Dean Philip Greene, who was also instrumental in securing our office, and from our faculty advisor, Professor Nelson Donegan. Among other things, we formalized our non-

profit status and our commitment to remain non-commercial by not including advertising, although we sold issues to cover publishing costs. A positive side effect of excluding advertising was and is that this reinforced the timeless, literary nature of the publication.

Finally, the most unique aspect of the *Journal* would be that Yale undergraduates would run the show, volunteering their time without compensation of any kind. And yet the *Journal* would compete with professional publications outside the University. Of course, inexperienced volunteers would not be perfect (indeed the Journal has published typos, sometime delayed its publication dates and made other mistakes). But the students would be learning and, with each new editorial board, the *Journal* would be invigorated with a fresh perspective.

When I graduated in 2000 the future of the *Journal* was bright. We had published six issues that had received praise from readers both within and outside of the worlds of angling and literature. We had attracted contributions from men and women who had diverse interests outside of angling. We secured submissions from statesman-anglers such as Elliot Richardson and Jimmy Carter, from professional humorist-anglers, such as Christopher Buckley of the *New Yorker*, and from editor-anglers, such as Howell Raines of the *New York Times*. We had a competent staff of undergraduates led by a new editor-in-chief, Alexis Surovov, as well as an advisory board of graduate students, faculty and alumni. And we had held a sold-out first annual fund-raising dinner.

The *Journal*'s accomplishments during these eleven years flow entirely from the students who have sacrificed so much to produce this unique publication. I am humbled by their achievements and honored to be a part of the *Journal*'s legacy as its first editor-in-chief. I hope that all of you who enjoy this anthology will also be encouraged to subscribe so that you will continue to enjoy and support this unique publication in the years to come.

PART I

Backcasts

COASTAL CUTTHROAT TROUT *Oncorhynchus clarki clarki*

PILGRIMAGE
TO HAIG-BROWN

Skip Morris

Here is the opinion that Roderick Haig-Brown forced me to adopt as my own, as he stated it in *Fisherman's Fall*:

> Fishing is not a sport I expect ever to exhaust or abandon.

"Forced" may seem too strong a word, but it's not—the seductive power of *Fisherman's Fall, A River Never Sleeps*, and all his other books that plucked me from my chair and set me in his boots, the current breaking around my legs and riverbed gravel crunching beneath my feet, the power of his books that filled my head with his fascination for fish and water was too great for a boy with fishing in his blood to resist. I knew even as a teenager that I, too, would never exhaust or abandon fishing. Haig-Brown had me hooked, played out, and landed, and I admired him for it. He was, I felt, a master of words, a spell-caster who understood the thrill of the singing reel, the defeat of the broken tippet, and the wonder of peering into a trout pool better than any other writer possibly could, and conveyed them with unmatched clarity and force. The power of his prose had to come in part from his living in the finest little fishing area in the world—I was convinced of that. But how I believed this in spite of the vastness of his Canadian home province of British Columbia with its multitude of rivers and lakes and the great extent of its intricate coastline is now, to me, something of a mystery. There is a wealth of wonderful fishing throughout British

Columbia, of course, but it never even occurred to me that any of it could compare with his little part of Vancouver Island.

So, once he'd got me addicted to fishing, the man's passion for his waters, and the waters that inspired such passion, set me to planning a fishing trip to the country that leapt so appealingly from the pages. Such a trip seemed reasonable to me—our home near Seattle, Washington lay fewer than three hundred miles south of Haig-Brown's farm on Vancouver Island; just a modest drive, I figured. So I began working on Dad. I wheedled. I nudged. I dropped hints to keep the issue on his mind. And all this time I was appealing to Mom, knowing she'd be the easier of the two and that if I could get her to work her own angle, he'd have little chance of holding out. It took some doing, but I wore him down, with Mom's help of course.

My soonest opportunity for such a distant trip would be Easter Break, an escape of around two weeks from the chaos and tyranny of high school. It would be early in April, a difficult time for fishermen, when streams can be high or even flooding from icy runoff or rain or both, and when fish may still be sluggish and unresponsive with blood winter-thick, creeping through drowsy dead-cold flesh. None of this concerned me, of course, or even occurred to me— I was, after all, only fifteen-years-old, an innocent. And anyway, how could fishing ever be less than excellent in Haig-Brown's waters?

Easter Break came at last, and early one brisk April morning my friend Don and I heaped our tackle into the trunk of Dad's big sedan, and then swung wide the doors and hopped into the back seat for the trip. I seemed hardly to depress the car seat, half-floating in the soft mist of anticipation. Don and I chatted openly about fishing and softly in private about girls as we rode the freeway up the Washington coast to the Canadian border just south of Vancouver—as we waited in the long line to get through customs, I could distinctly feel my full weight on the pillowy car seat, and the area of contact was growing uncomfortable. Still, my enthusiasm remained high. We left the border and headed for the ferry terminal. Getting through the ferry line took over an hour, though it seemed more like all day. Even the topic of girls was losing its interest. The ferry left the mainland and plodded across the ribbon of water separating it from Vancouver Island and the small city of Nanaimo, which, on our arrival, seemed dark and industrial; it was reassuring to watch it fade behind us as the road drifted into a magical corridor of dense coastal forest. Within an hour, the promise of Haig-Brown's country had grown much smaller as the distress in my buttocks had grown much larger. What was that car seat made of anyway, stone? But on we continued up the elongated island's eastern side, through a few hamlets, and across a few streams of varied size, the sort I'd normally have strained to examine from the bridges but instead hardly turned my head to notice, and on and on through dull, repetitive, and unceasing forest on my pilgrimage to Haig-Brown. By now my buttocks ached deeply. I was bone-tired, and it showed. Don didn't look too good either. About the time it seemed we'd never reach at our destination, cheerful country yards and houses and side roads, mottled in shadow and low sunlight, began telling encouragingly of the approaching town. I let out a heavy sigh and stretched the stiff, weary muscles down my back.

Roderick Haig-Brown had no idea we were coming—in fact, no idea we even existed. I had neither written him nor told Dad of my intention to meet him. But Dad seemed happy to drive slowly along the road that flanks the south side of the river and watch for a mailbox saying "Haig-Brown." As we crept up the tree-lined side-road, my head filled with bright images from his books, three of which lay beside me on the car-seat: the magnificent Canyon Pool on the Campbell River and the schools of big sea-run cutthroat trout that once milled about it in August, until it was desecrated and murdered by the dams and their penstocks that permanently starved the pool of fresh current; the good run of little steelhead that surprised him by suddenly appearing a dozen years after the dams were installed; his bright, lazy days of three-quarter-pound trout on Buttle Lake, with the always present chance that one of its eight- or ten-pounders would venture up from the depths for his

fly; his failed but joyful mission to really figure out the movements and feeding patterns of sea-run cutthroats in the estuaries. We soon found the mailbox bearing his name and standing before his home and his farm on the banks of the Campbell River in the outskirts of the village named for the river and stretching upstream from its mouth.

He came to us in his driveway in a manner far too casual for the event—Roderick Haig-Brown standing right there was an event!—and asked could he help us. Dad explained that I was a great admirer of his work as I looked down at Dad's shoes. We each shook his hand, and he invited us in.

I cannot trust my memory of Haig-Brown, his home, or what happened there—I was young and overwhelmed by the presence of the man, and, of course, it all happened three-and-a-half decades ago. Nevertheless, this is how I remember it. His den was as elegantly somber as I'd imagined it. There were tall bookcases of dark wood displaying the dark spines of books; narrow windows peered out across a field to the river but allowed in only enough light to disperse a soft glow throughout the room. There was a small stone fireplace, too. A pair of coal-black Labrador retrievers lay in the corner, anxious but in obedient restraint. It was perfect. Well, almost perfect—the tiny table by the window and the fly-tying vise and few tools that lay upon it were a disappointment. I'd expected bins of feathers and hides, racks of floss and thread and bright tinsels, a long row of bright metal tools, certainly much more than the few tools on that insignificant little wooden square for such an important operation.

The dogs rose and came to us together with wagging tails and curious noses. Haig-Brown scolded them gruffly and they moped back to their corner. I knew he'd be stern with them—I knew the man, I felt—but I knew also that they'd have his respect.

Haig-Brown himself seemed entirely perfect, a looming but graceful man built all of long bones—long torso, long arms, long hands and fingers—speaking few but well-chosen and elegantly ordered words, reserved, and with just the right balance of gentleness and firmness. He seemed exactly the man to write of fishing with such passion.

I stood mostly in awestruck silence, but managed to ask about the fishing: Were the lakes going yet? Were the salmon fry out in the rivers and the cutthroats coming up from the salt to feed upon them? He seemed dubious about our chances of finding really good fishing anywhere now, as though, to my surprise, the odds were somehow against us, though we at least had some hope. The Campbell River, he said, would be as good as anyplace to start. He described a pool below an island he said we'd recognize, but he warned us that we'd have to cross to the island and that would be difficult if the river was up. This sounded like just the sort of reasonable put-up-or-shut-up challenge I'd have expected from him. I remembered his telling in *A River Never Sleeps*

how Major Greenhill had made him strip naked and then swim across an icy English river in January after two felled mallards because Greenhill's retriever was too old for the job. Whatever I was up against, I figured it had to be short of that.

There was nothing more to say except thank you, which we did, and then left for the place he had recommended on his river. When we got there, the island he'd described lay across a considerable side channel. The time it took to scramble into my waders and fumble the line and leader up through the guides seemed interminable. As soon as I'd tied on the fly I realized I'd missed a guide with the line, and so had to cut off the fly and repeat nearly the whole operation. I was considering taking up swearing. When finally I charged in, I felt the cold force of the river, and the surprise of it made me hesitate. Then I really looked the channel over for the first time, and it looked tough. But I was determined to make it across, to prove myself worthy of Haig-Brown's country, his rivers, and his fish. A little way out I realized that it was tough wading, felt the fear that comes with dubious control out in strong current, and vaguely recalled a line from his *Fisherman's Summer*. It goes as follows:

> Wading upstream over a bottom of great round slippery rocks—and the Campbell has little else—is bad at any time…

Though I was wading across stream, not upstream as in his line, it seemed about as difficult as you could ask. I pushed on, though impressing Haig-Brown suddenly seemed a minor thing compared with remaining upright. Once out on the island, after the moment of relief had passed, I sensed something familiar. The smell of swollen water, the chill damp air, and the dark, green-tinged current sweeping threateningly by all felt like just another gloomy Washington river in spring. Still, this was Haig-Brown's familiar, gloomy river, so while holding fast to my high expectations I tossed my little wet fly out into the main river and let it swing down into the sheltered and seemingly bottomless eddy below the island. I kept putting the fly out further and further and letting it swing downstream until I felt a tug, followed by nothing. Then I felt another tug, struck, and a couple of dozen feet of line spun off the reel. The current weighed on the line and the fish fought as hard as it should have, so it was a while before I slid him up the gravel bar below the island. He was a splendid sea-run cutthroat of about fourteen inches, thick, silvery, and handsomely spotted—a perfectly suitable fish for the occasion. I killed him with blows from a rock, as I often did back then (though I wouldn't now) and dropped him into my wicker creel.

Nothing else came to the fly, so I waded back across, pretty much forgetting about Haig-Brown again for a little while. Don had stayed wisely with the near, safer shore, but had caught nothing.

It was almost dusk, so we took down our rods and packed

our tackle away into the car. As I cleaned the fish in the river, I had what seemed a wonderful notion: why not give the trout to Haig-Brown? It would be a thank you for his fishing advice, I said, but I knew it was really to show the master that I was a fisherman worthy of his river and his respect. It seemed perfect.

He would come out as before, I imagined; then he'd silently marvel at the wonderful trout when I raised it from the creel. He wouldn't say it, but he'd judge me a fine fisherman. I could picture him hoisting the fish himself and nodding in approval of both it and me.

But when we pulled in, his wife, Ann, came out. She said he was gone right now. I stammered out that I'd met him earlier that day and had brought him a fish from the Campbell. "Did you take it on the fly?" she asked, beaming. I told her yes I had, right where he'd suggested I fish. "Oh, Roddy will be so pleased that you took it on the fly! I'll fix it for him tonight, while it's still fresh." She took the fish, thanked us, and we drove away.

I sat reveling in proud achievement, even though things hadn't gone quite as I'd imagined, and trying to forget I'd heard the great Roderick Haig-Brown referred to as "Roddy." I casually picked up *A River Never Sleeps*, opened it at random, and began reading contentedly. After a couple of paragraphs I came to this line:

I do not fish for fish to eat; having to eat fish is one of the penalties of having been out fishing and with this penalty in mind I probably fish a little less often and less painstakingly than I otherwise would.

FISHING WITH MY DADDY

Jimmy Carter

A FEW MILES NORTH of the Okefenokee was the small village of Hortense, not far from where the Little Satilla River joins the Big Satilla. This was one of my father's favorite fishing spots; he tried to go there every year with some of his associates in the farming, peanut, and fertilizer business. On two occasions he took me with him, when I was about ten- or twelve-years-old. We stayed in a big and somewhat dilapidated wood-frame house on a small farm near the banks of the Little Satilla. The house had been built to accommodate at least three generations of a family, but now there were just a man named Joe Strickland, his wife, Shug, and two daughters, one a pretty girl in her teens named Jessie. Joe was the guide for our group of about six people. The women cooked our meals and plowed mules in the small fields during the day while we were fishing. It was the first time I had seen women plowing, which I found quite surprising, but they all seemed to take it as a matter of course.

The Little Satilla is a serpentine stream in the flattest part of Georgia's coastal plain, weaving back and forth from one bend to another. A number of oxbow lakes had been left behind when the river changed its course. We fished in the area of what was called Ludie's Lake. On the outside of almost every bend of the stream there was a deep hole, often cut into a steep bank, and on the opposite side of the river was usually a sand bar. There were not as many bushes and snags in the water as we had around Plains, and the bottom was sandy and firm.

I had never done this kind of fishing before. We spent our time in the stream, wading halfway across it to fish in the deep water under the overhanging banks, using the longest cane poles we could handle. I wore cutoff overall pants with no shirt, and tied my fish stringer to one of the belt loops. Joe and I were the only ones barefoot; all the other men had on old tennis shoes or brogans to protect their tender feet. We fished with large pond worms and caught mostly "copperheads," which were very large bluegill bream whose heads, when mature, assumed a bronze color, perhaps from the tannin stain in the water.

The group of us would string out along the river, my daddy and I usually fishing within sight of each other. We always had a fairly good idea of what luck each fisherman was having. For some reason I have never understood, the men would shout "Billy McKay!" when they had on a nice fish. The words would roll through the woods as all of us smiled; the enthusiasm of the voices was contagious. Each night after supper I went to bed early, but the men stayed up to play poker and to have a few drinks. Sometimes they made enough noise to wake me up, but I didn't mind. It seemed to make me more a member of the party if they weren't trying to stay quiet just for me. Most often I was tired enough to go right back to sleep.

While we were in the river Joe moved quietly from one of us to another, just to make sure we were properly spaced and to give advice about the water and some of the bypasses we had to take around obstacles. He tried—successfully—to build up a reputation as something of a character and always gave the group something to talk about during the months between our visits to Hortense.

Once we were walking single file along a path toward the river and Joe called, "Watch out for the barbed wire!"

One of the men said, "Joe, you didn't look down. How do you know wire's there?"

Joe said, "My feet will flatten briers or thorns, but I can feel barbed wire when I step on it."

Another time, when we had to cross the river, Joe walked down the bank, entered the water with his pole and lunch over his head, and moved smoothly across toward the other side with the water never higher than his armpits. The next man, whom I called Mr. Charlie, was the oldest in the group, and he stepped off in the water and immediately went down out of sight. He came up sputtering, and shouted, "Joe, how deep is it here?"

Joe replied, "Oh, I reckon it's about fifteen foot." Joe could tread water like a duck, and just wanted to demonstrate his prowess so that none of us would forget.

Then came my most memorable day. Late one afternoon, after a good day of fishing, Daddy called me over and asked

me to keep his string of fish while he went up the river to talk to one of his friends. I tied it on with mine on the downstream side of me while I kept fishing, enjoying the steady pull of the current on our day's catch. It wasn't long before I watched my cork begin to move slowly and steadily up under a snag and knew I had hooked a big one. After a few minutes I had a large copperhead bream in my hands, but as I struggled with it and wondered how I was going to hold the fish while untying the stringer, a cold chill went down my spine. I realized that the tugging of the current on the stringers was gone, as were all our fish! My belt loop had broken.

I threw my pole up on the nearest sand bar and began to dive madly into the river below where I had been standing.

Then I heard Daddy's voice calling my nickname, "Hot," he said, "what's wrong?"

"I've lost the fish, Daddy."

"All of them? Mine too?"

"Yes, sir." I began to cry, and the tears and water ran down my face together each time I came up for breath.

Daddy was rarely patient with foolishness or mistakes. But after a long silence, he said, "Let them go." I stumbled out on the bank, and he put his arms around me.

It seems foolish now, but at that time it was a great tragedy for me. We stood there for a while, and he said, "There are a lot more fish in the river. We'll get them tomorrow." He knew how I felt and was especially nice to me for the next couple of days. I worshipped him.

At Joe's home we ate fish and whatever was in season. Both times I went, our breakfasts consisted of biscuits, grits, green beans, and fried fish. It was the first time I had eaten green beans early in the morning, but soon it seemed like a normal thing to do. With plenty of butter and sugar-cane syrup to go with the piles of hot biscuits, we never got up from the table hungry.

When I left Joe's place to come home, his daughter Jessie told me that she had brought me a going-away present. She then handed me a baby alligator about a foot long, whom I immediately named Mickey Mouse. When I returned to our house I installed him inside a large truck tire, partially buried in the ground and covered with boards. For a number of weeks I fed him earthworms, crickets, wasp larvae, and anything else he would eat. My friends were quite envious of my new pet. Unfortunately, the cats and dogs around the farm were also interested. One morning I went out to feed Mickey and found the boards pushed aside and the little alligator missing. Daddy was very considerate and said he was sure the 'gator had escaped into the nearest swamp. I was not quite naive enough to believe him, but from then on I stayed on the lookout for my 'gator whenever I was fishing or exploring along the neighborhood creeks.

Almost fifty years later, after I left the White House, I stopped by Hortense, Georgia, to try to find the place we used to visit. I couldn't remember the roads or even Joe's last name when I inquired of some folks in the service station. I did recall the pretty daughter, but one of the men told me: "We had a lot of pretty daughters around here." At least I remembered the bare feet, barbed wire, good catches, lost

fish, Mickey Mouse, and green beans for breakfast. When I described some of these things to the postmistress, she said, "You must mean Joe Strickland. Miss Jessie still lives at the same place, but in a new house." I followed her directions and found the cottage in what had been the large yard of the old house, just a few steps from the Little Satilla River.

Miss Jessie responded to our knock on her door, saying, "Won't y'all come in!" even before she knew who we were. We had a good time reminiscing about old times. Both her parents had died long ago, and she was intrigued that I remembered so much about them. She said she remembered my visits: "I told a lot of people while you were in the White House that the President had fished with my daddy."

To which I replied, "When I was in the White House, I told several people the same thing about yours. Many of the most highly publicized events of my presidency are not nearly as memorable or significant in my life as fishing with my daddy and yours when I was a boy."

GREAT UNCLE

Dane Barca

Because sometimes he stands on the edge of the wharf,
his eighty-seven years etched
in the fleshy haloes about his eyes,
and casts into the school beneath the wharf:

Because sometimes he stands barefoot on the pile-ons,
the grass peers through years of cracks,
the blades spun through toes,
his soles bound to the dull weight of this earth:

Because sometimes he stares into the sea,
his truck still hitched to bring the boat to water,
the caulk and pitch still rigged to his hands,
wielding his boat like a weapon,
the diesel that assumes his sighs:

Because sometimes you catch the passing day
in the movement of shadows across his face—
soft as the sea running beneath his skin,
the sun marking time in the spray, his eyes creased with salt
that once held captive the rain,
his skin bent into rent riddles of flesh:

Because sometimes he wears his boat key
around his neck, his years
clenched like fists in his pockets,
because his season is over:
because he stares incessantly onto Eagle Island
where he was born,
where he has always lived in sight of,
where his father taught Admiral Peary to shoot:

Because now the island rises from dawn,
where it has everyday in his eighty-seven years,
woven through in varicose birch,
winding its tongue round his heart
in a skein of ashen silk—

Because sometimes I leave the light on when I go out,
I know that my window illumes the wall opposite my flat,
because at night I can see in from the street
onto my one room life, because at night
I walk up the stairs to the cracked meter
of the wood beneath my feet,
the sky lengthening from the gap beneath my door-

Because I walk his old frequented ways
through the chorus of my days—
because his ocean breathes in my veins.

RIVERINE

Ivan Kerbel

I WAS EIGHT, AND the sky was chocolate brown. I cannot fix the place myself, but I would just as soon let it remain unhinged, floating, so that the mountains and the rain, and the swollen current running through the notch serve as my only guides, not the contours of a map. Through the trees on our picnicking run home, a large stream, darker than the forest itself and sunken in a corridor between vertical fingers of clay bounded by rock, bars our way forward. Ragged clouds like rolling pins appear and tumble down the face of the nearby ridge. My aunt holds a pale hand to her forehead as she gazes at the ridge—a melancholy Eve harried from the doorstep of Eden, the basket of half-eaten cheeses and grapes swinging on her ample forearm.

As we clamber (as I crawl) across the stream along the huge span of a fallen tree, the water below me flushes past in a turgid mass. I peer at its unreflective and muddy surface, the occasional ripple of white froth, and at a black branch rolling end over end downstream, jerking out of the water like the flailing limb of a drowning man, before losing itself behind a boulder. My fingers are cold, clinging to the bark at this moment. It seems as though some crank is loosened from above, a cloud has cracked open, and I am suddenly drenched, and we are all drenched.

I see a fish leap out of the water moments later, a sight which remains with me and is my companion to this day, as are the clouds and birds and sylvan boughs which have held my hand since I was a child, companions more constant than friends. The fish has a tail that swishes once, then twice, cutting the water as its body rises into the air. It turns heavily, one black coal eye catching the forest and stream instantly in its silent grasp, and its mouth opens as if to breathe. The black and silver shape lingers above the surface, and the loudness of the slap as it flops back into the water's vestment, stuns me. I have often returned to this same stream at night, and it always appears the same. A moon path guides my sleepless hours down past the ridge and through the trees to it.

I am in New York City. The light of the haze is soft; the afternoon laziness is entirely within my own skin as I peel cool layer after layer of responsibility and wander about without aim, bum-like across the Prince and Broadway intersection and make my way uptown, at age twenty-three, no less able to gape at an instant of vivacity and solitude, at a pungent smell that scurries up my nostrils as if to escape the light, than when I was a child.

New York City is a fisherman's paradise, a city of streams engorged with traffic and humans and flowing waste where life rushes in to spawn with daylight's first glint off the metal high-rises, where species of officeman, shopper and hustler ride the same narrow channels in Little Italy, the East Village, and the broader causeways of the Upper East Side, where kids on mopeds circle kids on skateboards, and choppers like dragonflies skim low over the teeming city

surface and the prickly spires, all ready to be coaxed onto my line and by the gentle sinews of thought snared and reeled in before my gaze.

Standing on that small island of sidewalk pavement in the middle of Times Square, I look up just as the lights turn green and droves of taxies, smooth-bodied, rush toward me and engulf me in their yellow tumult. I cast and reel, and I am forgotten as I step into the street, the pavement is scorching, and the cool water seeps in over my waders.

I will be, in the future, somewhere at Lake Wanaha's edge again. I will smell the cedar chips by the driveway and see the diffuse sun gilding the tackle racked up to the ceiling inside the caretaker's garage. Breakfasts will be large, as always, and won't conclude till the afternoons when, slowed by hollandaise sauce and bacon, my companions and I will struggle onto the porch facing the lake to drink malt cider, to sink into the wicker chairs, and chase the cloud of drink from our minds with yet more drink. I will be in love with someone; quite possibly I will be in love with everyone. My neighbors out back along the dirt road will dream of someday starting their own ice-cream company, and the paint will peel from wherever it is applied, slowly and steadily, all summer long. We will let the dog in when it wants to be let in, and watch as it chases about the yard in pursuit of no one.

At dusk, I will gaze at the vaguely-defined form at the edge of the pier. She will fade into the water and the forest at the far shore, and I will watch her until I can see her no more. And I will not go out to her, only I will have caught her already, and she will not know it, perhaps ever. Lying awake later, I will hear the creaks of her footsteps on the wood staircase.

In the morning, someone will knock on the screen door, and the wind through the pine needles like a woodwind will guide us down the ridge and through the forest. I will eat an apple as someone searches for a fishing hole upstream and someone else wanders downstream. The sun will warm my hands, and carefully I will lay out my picnic lunch, spreading a bandanna on the rock. I will let the ants climb onto the fabric and trespass over my sliced ham and dates and wheat bread smeared with honey. I will rescue those whose strength fails them when they have wandered too far into the sweet sticky center.

ON ALMOST DROWNING

Benjamin Green

The streambank willows took flight as swallows.
A solitary egret blended into the clear sky.
I don't remember the wind, can't recall anything it said,
least of all a warning I chose not to heed.
However, I spoke, aloud, to myself.
My feet lost their foothold
in the shifting sand and cold water
filled that neoprene glove that was supposed to
protect my body from the cold, the water.
I said, "I'm going to drown.
It looks like I'm going to drown."
That part I remember,
 and how easily I seemed to accept.

And then, having given up, having given up
everything,
a cool rush of light bounced off the river,
and I knew that I would not come back
as something else, as water,
or as willow leaves pooled in an eddy,
and I knew that I would not be released
into something else, as a flashy reflection
of coastal light on a steelhead's flank.

I knew, as my toes felt earth again,
that I would only remain as I am:
as something hard, inert, untransfixed.
And as I angrily trod through
the wet cowshit in the meadow to go home,
I thought how cold I was
and how far from me the world had suddenly slipped.
It was not a good day to die.
I could not go so easily.

I can not.
There is so much work to be done.
Still.

RIO GRANDE CUTTHROAT TROUT *Oncarhyndus clarki virginalis*

BIRTH OF AN ANGLER

Christine Hemp

Since i first picked up a rod and reel a year ago, I dream about fly-fishing almost nightly. I dream of the riffles on the Rio Hondo outside my tower window, the perfect cast, and the tug of a trout on the line; I dream of rivers I've never seen and the feel of water moving 'round my legs. I also have nightmares of landing other creatures: bright green birds with hooks in their beaks, and coyotes; sometimes I start reeling in a submerged beast and when it's almost to the surface I wake with a jerk, my heart flapping.

Predator behavior is new to me. I stop along the highway in September to scoot migrating tarantulas safely to the other side. I hover over injured birds to keep the cats away, and I breathe in and out to calm the wave of heat and sorrow in my arms when I drive past a freshly killed dog. In the mountains of Northern New Mexico, so close to the jaws of nature, I often feel as if my skin is peeled back, everything exposed to the light.

Yet my fishing buddy, James, says that teaching me to fly-fish was like teaching a teenager about sex: I was a quick study. When we practiced the roll cast in his garden, he took a drag on his cigarette, and laughed, "Can't beat that with a stick." My fly-rod has become part of me, its reflex an extension of my limbs. Each delicate flip of the line, each jiggle to dance the hopper upstream, ties me closer to the world of marmots and jays, to a balance I've only begun to comprehend. I am shocked when, every time I feel the rush of a trout on the line and the smatter in the water, an unfamiliar elation washes through my body. I am being carried by a river inside me.

Most of my women friends are married now, on their second child. They call from the east coast and tell me about Jeremy learning the beauty of puzzles, that the little one is teething. I am delighted by this news, and when they ask what's up with me, I tell them I've taken up fly-fishing. There's usually a silence, and a "great, do you go alone?" I tell them yes, and with my fishing buddy, too, sometimes. Then the baby cries and we have to hang up. Today I think of my friends in Boston, look up at the aspens turning on the mountain, and decide to go to the river.

I've been fishing the Rio Hondo for a couple of days now without a strike. I feel cheated, as if it were reminding me again that I'm still a novice. I'm patient, though, watching the fading October sun, minding the shadows, and trying every fly in my small box. After using all the mayflies, caddises, and the last hopper, I wonder what the water is trying to tell me. I've lost a lot of flies, too, because the cottonwoods and red willows hang over the bank. I let them be, knowing the snagged replicas watch me struggle.

I move upstream—slowly—the sun at my back. Then I see a flash, the first in several days, a silver arc appearing and disappearing in the pool under the willows. *Plurp.* He rises to eat the hovering net of bugs. I've never seen a fish rise that high. I feel the rush and cast my last caddis into the pool. It floats, pathetically, downriver.

My hands shake as I tie on a hopper-look-alike, a fly I bought last week, the name forgotten. It's my last fly and I cast near where the fish disappeared. I feel a pull, then nothing. I cast again farther upstream and then everything explodes in a spray of silver and water, or, to quote Elizabeth Bishop, "rainbow rainbow rainbow!" I jerk hard and the trout swings on the line, its body thrashing at the air and the barb in its mouth. It's heavy, bigger than anything I've caught in my short career on the river bank, at least thirteen inches. Gripping my rod, I reach for the swinging line and see just a stump where a fin had once grown.

I remember the tarantulas on the road and picture this fish feasting on mayflies all day. I look at his eyes and wonder why I am now a fisherman. He flips back toward the water and my body tenses while his strong body swings back and forth between the bank and the rushing water. The tail flashes in the afternoon light. No one tells you that fish have eyes. No one tells you that the air is where they finally drown. Yet no one really prepares you for the gratitude and the immense longing which fills your spirit. Why me? I wonder. Why fish? Why now?

I slip and splash ashore, the trout dangling. I manage to get to a dry place on the rocks, trying not to drop my catch into the sand. I bless the fish over and over again in a mantra, partly to calm myself, partly because I'm still not accustomed to the glittery package of life when I finally receive it. I scrounge for some grass, thinking of my Indian friend at the Pueblo who told me his father taught him to wrap his catch in damp ferns. I need a ritual for taking this seasoned trout from his home, for making him drink air.

His mouth gapes, gills quiver. I wet my hand in the water, then pull the hook from his mouth and he *flupps* harder. I wonder what his eyes see now, a woman holding him in an atmosphere as strange as underwater is to me. His scales are thick, a rainbow of distinction. James tells me that killing fish on a rock sends chemicals of fear through their bodies, then eating them is no good; they must die in your creel, he says. So I wrap him in some green grass from the bank, then slip his weight into the back panel pouch of my vest and zip him in. I feel his tail moving against my kidneys. I breathe in and out, in and out, as if to give him my life while he gives me his. In out. In out. The breath of the universe. The breath of

all creatures, human and others, including the trees. Even as I sit to pull my wits together, he wiggles against me. Like the sensations after making love, I feel trembly, spent, and dazed.

I gather up my rod. The sun has gone behind the mountain. I inhale deeply as I walk up through the chamisa, feeling the subsiding life on my back and blessing it again with a sustaining sense of wonder.

Tonight I fry up my big fish, just with butter. He hardly fits in my cast-iron skillet. I watch his eyes turn cloudy white with heat. This morning he was eating the grasshoppers and big flies I found in his belly when I cleaned him. The collection of insects ends up in my sink strainer and I marvel at the evolution of things. Egg in the river, hatched into fly, eaten by fish, caught by me, gutted, and the flies go out with the compost; I eat the fish; more compost, and on and on.

Tonight I dream again, but this time I am pregnant, filled with the fish growing inside me, moving to the sound of water, the river carrying us faster and faster downstream.

ALL IS NOT GOLD

Dana S. Lamb

I WAS BROUGHT UP on dry flies and brown trout. Before I married Edgar I had many a marvelous moment on the Mongaup; learned to float one of Art Flick's stiff-hackled black spiders ever so close to a certain rock on the Brodhead; took a twenty-incher by the culvert on the Beaverkill, and learned how difficult it was to avoid an almost imperceptible but fatal drag in the Wilmington Notch.

Though I took Edgar to the Esopus and the Schoharie over long weekends and even spent a week with him fishing the Battenkill and the Mettowee, somehow he just didn't seem to be able to get the hang of it. He'd done some wet-fly-fishing in Maine for landlocks and brook trout but the technique of the dry fly or of an upstream nymph completely eluded him.

However, he did have the time of his life when Dad took us for a week's salmon fishing on the Miramichi. And although I thought the business of casting endlessly over the side of a canoe for fish I couldn't see was rather dull, he took to it like a duck to water.

When the children came along I put away my tackle, but Edgar found a spot on the Matapedia where he could fish the last week in August and that's where he spent his vacations. Anyone who knew anything about salmon could have told him that that was the worst possible time to fish that river since the fish, six weeks up from salt water, were stale and gravid. I don't consider such fish good to eat but Edgar even made a practice of shipping these soft red salmon home to friends. And although I sought to discourage him he often, if he was feeling flush, sent one home to me. By complicated cookery I usually managed to make the thing edible though I assure you it was never appetizing.

Last August it was so hot in the city that I was delighted to have the opportunity of sending the children out to their grandparents on Long Island and almost wished that I had gone with Edgar to Matapedia. To make the city even more unattractive the garbage collectors chose that inopportune moment for their strike. Naturally I ate out as much as possible, and one particularly hot evening I was delighted, after the Bowers' cocktail party, to have them invite me for dinner at their roof garden overlooking the river. I got home about ten-o'clock and although the air-conditioning was on I realized as soon as I entered the apartment that all was not well. My nose led me to the pantry and there on the dishwasher was the unwanted salmon box, its top thoughtfully loosened by the janitor now retired for the night. Inside, in an advanced stage of decomposition, lay a great red hookbill balefully staring at the ceiling. Clearly prompt and drastic action was in order and I was strictly on my own.

On the shelf above the icebox was Edgar's old suitcase, the one his fraternity brothers had given him when we were married. It didn't look so bad from a distance but inside it was all coming to pieces and I'd been begging him for years

to get rid of it. I put it down on the floor and after I'd gotten the ice out of the salmon sarcophagus I turned it over and the dead fish dropped into the suitcase with a plop. I stuffed some newspapers in on top of him as well as a bathrobe and some old clothes I wanted to throw away. Then I latched and strapped up the bag and staggered out into the hall. It was awkward and heavy as lead but I managed to get out onto the sidewalk where I hoped to hail a taxi. My plan was to drive to the Battery and bribe the driver to help me dump it into the river.

One disadvantage of living in Greenwich Village, however, is that there are few cruising taxicabs, and shady characters are some-times to be encountered in the darker streets. I had on my best bib and tucker, so I felt somewhat nervous on this account and, instead of standing still and waiting for a cab to come by, I struggled as best I could toward the subway. As I neared its entrance the thing I greatly feared came upon me in the form of a tough and evil-looking giant of a man who seemed definitely out of character in offering to help me with my suitcase. Of course I refused his offer but he persisted and following me down the subway steps, as we approached the turnstile, roughly seized my burden and preceded me onto the deserted platform. The doors of a train were just at the point of closing and with a rush he leapt aboard, barring my attempt to follow.

Gone was the thief with my not so precious burden. I

turned and hurried back to the apartment; I built myself a tall, cool drink and scribbled a hasty note to Edgar:

> Darling, your beautiful salmon arrived today. I am so excited. It is almost a pity that it will be all gone when you get home. I hope you hooked a good one today. Devotedly, Kay.

I didn't add, "I did." I thought of the modem-day Bill Sykes excitedly opening the suitcase in the secrecy of his broiling bedroom, and I smiled as I curled comfortably up in bed with a little volume by John Tainter Foote. The air in the apartment once more was cool and sweet.

STARTING OUT

Dana S. Lamb

THE PEEPERS IN the pond are silent and thunder mutters in the April sky. Although the trout are not yet surface feeding and the salmon schools are far at sea, let's load the car before the rain. The starting of a fishing trip is the finest time of all, when all the joys we look for lie ahead; when nothing will go wrong and everything is possible; when hope and happiness ride with us at our side.

A fishing trip is as full of thrills as a plum pudding is of raisins. Some say the supreme moment comes when, from far off, they glimpse their favorite river. Others look forward most to arrival at the camp: the old familiar sights and sounds and smells; the hearty greetings from the dock or doorway; the smell of wood-smoke from the cabin's welcome fires; the merry ring of axe out by the woodpile; the lovely liquid little bell-tones of the wood thrush.

The dedicated dry-fly man may say that tops is when, having found the correct imitation of the natural fly, avoided getting hung up on the back cast and solved the problems of the perfect float, he sees the rise and sets the hook.

The salmon-fisher often times will say there's nothing like the first firm heavy pull that tells him that the battle is joined, though others who journey with him to the Maritimes may cherish most the thought of breathlessly long runs or leaps that stop the angler's heart.

Some seek their satisfaction from an entry in the record book. Others love the rivers better than their fish. Perhaps

they like the gently flowing quiet places where trout lie waiting for the mayfly beside the weaving water weeds, while swallows skim the satin surface of the stream. Some feel exalted by the spray and spume in gorges and by waterfalls in rough wild rivers running hell for leather to the sea.

Some love best the friendships made along the stream. No dairy maids these days perhaps, but brother anglers—nobler than the rest—who now and then confide that "There's a big one by that stone," and say, "You try for him." Or, "Don't you have a nighthawk number eight? Well here, take mine." Or, yet again, "Here, take this sandwich. I've had all I want."

Then others like it best, I think, when they come home and see again the family that they love—their captive audience; the dog who greets them with wild howls of happiness and frantic cart-wheels of delight; the luxury of proper baths, clean clothes, and lemon peel and ice; the hero worship at the party at the country club where the big brought-home salmon or the once-in-a-life-time trout lies grandly, surrounded by water cress from little brook trout streams near home.

But whatever priceless item from the beautiful bundle of a fishing trip especially delights one's heart, the greatest thrill of all is starting out, since therein is the entire treasure of what may be to come. And so, as now the raindrops splash the windshield of our car and lay the dust on little far-off country roads, we feel the freshness and the ecstasy of early morning in the springtime of our lovely ageless little world.

SOUTH FORK KERN GOLDEN TROUT *Oncorhynchus mykiss aguabonita*

WINTER KILL AND OTHER POEMS

Thomas Robert Barnes

It will rain soon.
Brusque as calm fed up is bored with itself
weather breaks by fallen full cups
and we are left to pick through
its shatterings, seepage skittered to gloom.

Just before it and mostly after,
it's the silence we keep
that all of nature pause to inflect
for long after faltering light
its clapped parentheses still ring like an echo

of how we stopped to watch
last reflection of peak upon the lake,
glimmer in two overfilled hands of water ,
barbed nicks of quartz and feldspar,

and in its diorama flickered candle upon mantle.
Where we carved a place to stand upon the ledge
is where we cached the fish we'd caught in snow
enough to sup before we slept

for taking golden trout from this high up
seems kin to stealing coin from the offering cup
and the best we can manage is gratefulness
and be careful not to slip,

slink under the nose
where light fell like a closing door,
its dull blade sharp enough to lop the mountain like a loaf,
flesh of open bread still warm upon the rock,
glowing stamp still warm upon our mind.

And just before we descend, hop scree,
fall in waiting arms deeper shadow of the trees,
scarlet furred manzanita blurry as running mice
and pure as white blood trickled,
car lamps wending the valley far below.

BLOODKNOT

Standing beside church pool it snows to beat the band.
You twist the monofilament back over itself.
Since you are right handed you hold the place
where the lines bend to meet with your left
and begin again the other side
until you've crossed the ends to make the knot.

You've stopped to show me before
in Yellowstone and Tahoe.
You were younger then and
more impatient like our father,
the pressure to learn quickly
unfortunately inverse of the desired effect.

Now forty years later
my eyes are not what they used to be
and I wish for the glasses I forgot to bring
to watch you dab saliva on the string
to lubricate these contorting bodies
as you pull the ends to make them writhe.

It is out of caring, yours, that I believe
I make the effort to want to see
this time how the knot is made.
And even when you'd held the creamy brown trout
up to show me before you let it go
all I could think of was the snow flake you'd pointed out
that stopped to perch where the leaders came together,
the bloodknot touched by a watchful father.

SCALES

Even before the hit
I almost asked,
what color is it of blue?

Under water
a shadow smiles its lack of concern
as it is being eaten by light.

I look past the pliers
that knocked him cold
and the bottom of the boat

freckled with the splatter of his blood.
How could water not miss him,
the company of him

passing through its fingers?
His blue skin shivers
less and less.

This is how a bell
sings to its echo,
a shimmy of dwindled parentheses

and how he gently swims past
what his body
is beginning to forget.

ANGLING THE MEADOW
I too hurry
hungry to be home
but await soft breathing
bells of chickadees
slightly above ski-crunched snow.

Stippled air of their tiny notes
succincts a map of failing light
that if I'd come a different way
down the mountain tonight
might have missed their plucking.

The rule of light is never broken
but I keep adding corollaries of perspective.
shadows umber blue
as acorn masa
palely echo slapped metate.

Turn just once
to see it blush,
my crooked path
tugged like string across
aspenned fingers.

KISS
The sleet that came
To itch the glass

It or me who changed my dream

And led me to your neck

The smile that helped me in
The tucked chin

A moan softer than stripped wind

The welcome rise of trout
To kiss

The underside of waters skin

THE LOST STRIPER

Scott Bowen

THE BIG FISH hit the Deceiver in the swells and raced down the beach. Joe stood in the breakers in his chest waders, the rod high over him like an archer's bow. I listened to the singing of the line running out. I wondered if the fish was able to run down the entire spool. We had never seen a fish do that.

I was sitting on the beach watching the sun come up over the ocean when the fish had hit. I sat with my rod across my legs, nodding with the waves, half asleep, my eyes swollen from the salty air. Then I heard Joe shout. I looked up and saw him whip his rod around in an arc. He reeled once, hard, and then the drag buzzed. He had no line in his basket; the fish had hit at the top of the cast. As I stood I saw a swirl of foam not far away but did not see the fish. Joe's rod turned in his hands and he nearly toppled as he swiveled his body. He put the rod over his head and the line buzzed. Not far out in the slick blue water his fish moved steadily away. This was a big striper.

I watched Joe trot through the rolling breakers, foam washing around his stout legs and splashing up to his armpits. He kept the rod up and watched the reel. I watched him for a few minutes and counted, one-thousand-one, one-thousand-two. When I got to one-thousand-nine and the fish had not stopped running I got up and jogged after Joe because I remembered Joe's predawn remark that his reel did not have as much backing as it should, one of those stupid flaws in your fishing that you idly notice. He had a nice, old Pate reel and it had looked full to me.

Joe left the water and jogged down the wet sand. I saw him go: a stout, pepper-and-gray haired man made ungainly by the thickness of old canvas waders.

It was six-thirty in the morning. Few other anglers were on the beach. The October sun sat round and yellow over the ocean. The sky was hazy around the sun, pale blue above, then it turned indigo over my head and behind me. The ocean was blue-black and roily.

I slogged through the gray Jersey sand, my feet clumsy in the boots. A fisherman running his waders looks like a gooney bird trying to get up speed to take off.

Joe went back out in the water where the waves sloshed up to fringed white ridges; the waves rode under his arms then tipped over in a curl and the foam spread behind him. The fish had turned for deeper water and was running diagonally away from the beach. Maybe this was Joe's lifetime catch.

When I came up beside him in the cold water I shouted, How much line have you got?

Not much, he said.

I looked at his reel. I saw a solid but thin layer of backing. He looked at me with a slightly embarrassed expression.

I've got a spool of braided line in my jacket, I said. Should I tie it on?

Joe said he wanted to back up, as the waves were cresting

at the top of his waders. He steadily reeled line as we walked backward. The breakers weren't rough, just fat, careening belts of water that tipped over at the last second.

I imagined the fish out there: a green, gold, and black torpedo. Friends of mine tell me that trout are the most beautiful fish. They probably are, but I don't think my friends have seen a nice striper flash inside a rising wave in the sun, like a slab of gold and emerald.

I had never tied on more backing before and neither had Joe. This idea was probably illegal, or at least against somebody's book of rules. But we both knew a striper as big as this—one that had shown such power as this one—could easily take an entire spool and then some.

What do you think? I said.

He's going to run again, Joe said, and as he said so the rod nodded and line went out. The fish ran him down to what looked like twenty wraps of backing. Then Joe began to gain line back. The fish was out there; I mean, *out there*. I began to wonder if this was a striper at all, or if a sand shark or a big eel had hit the white-and-green fly.

Joe looked at me. Can you do it? he said.

Yeah, I said.

I got on my knees in the wash of the breakers and blocked the wind with my back. Joe clamped the running line with his fingers and stripped all the backing off the reel, letting it fall on me, and I cut it. I focused on my fingers and worked quickly despite how cold and clumsy my fingers were, and I bound the backing to the braided line in a lumpy surgeon's knot that held when I pulled on it as hard as I could.

I played out the black cloth line from the spool, letting it fly in the air. Joe let it slip through his fingers. I stripped coils and coils off the plastic spool and when I thought I had as much as I dared I cut it and tied it to the spool post in Joe's reel, and then I wound the reel as he tendered the line with his hands. Had anyone seen us, they would have thought us mad. Joe let the line slide through his fingers, the rod taking the stress as the striper mercifully swam slowly as if it was mulling its next move.

The fish ran out more line, well into the new backing, and then it just held down in the water, bulldogging us. Joe tugged back and forth with it for ten minutes, both fighters shaking and shrugging, hanging tough.

As the sun rose Joe reeled in backing. The fish was tiring. Joe fell silent then, and his arms got jerky. That's how he gets when he's got a big fish on: silent, his arms nervous. Big stripers give him a buzz and unsettle him a little, too, the way a good thrill should.

Slowly, as the sun filled the morning sky and the sky itself became a perfect, uniform blue, Joe gained line on the fish. I watched the cirrus clouds smear like icing way high up and watched Joe labor in the breakers as he brought the fish in. He slowly walked back along the sand the way we came.

There's a hole right there, somewhere, he said, pointing just to the left. I want to get past it. It's nice and flat on the other side.

We kept walking. Then we both went back into the water and felt our clumsy feet digging into the flat of water-ridged sand.

The sun was high enough that we were able to see a little into the waves, the ocean changing color as the morning and tide progressed. We saw the fat end of the line but no fish yet in the green-blue water. Our problem now was that the reel was over-filled so the coils bulged and began to catch on the seat housing. Joe stripped line into the basket strapped to his belt where it coiled like cold spaghetti.

I walked a little farther out with our Boga Grip in my hands. I watched the line and saw a golden mote not far away. There it was, the big striper. I waited to see the fish break the surface.

As the line twanged over my shoulder I saw something else out there. I shook my head with cold. Water had run down inside my waders. I couldn't feel my toes. My sides shook with cold and my ears were numb. But I was sure that my vision was not affected: I had seen something very big rise against the surface tension of a slack wave.

Then I saw it, the image we all have in our heads: a shark's dorsal fin. It rose gently out of the water and moved slowly. The tip of the tail fin sliced the water behind.

For a second, I wasn't able to move. This was a big shark. No sand shark either. A bull, maybe, or a dusky. The dorsal fin was very sharp and stout.

Reel in, I yelled to Joe.

I didn't know if he had seen the shark but I heard him curse. I began to back out of the water, the swells rising to the top of my waders. Faster, Joe, I yelled.

I looked back at him. His expression was panicked but I didn't know if that was because of the fight or because he had seen the shark. He bobbed in the waves, rod up, stripping line. As I turned back to the ocean, I saw the whole thing as Joe saw it.

The striper rose to the surface. We saw its broad green back and its bodily glow beneath. It was massive, unbelievable. I heard Joe call out, *Oh, please.*

From the side the shark eased toward the poor striper, taking its time, then it turned with a flinch and speared the tired bass. Its tail fin whipped and powered it on. In the cut-away of a rising wave I saw the whole shark as its broad body bulged out of the wave. I saw the shark's nose, the corner of its mouth, and its big round, black eye. It was a mako.

The shark thrashed and sent up a cascade of foam. Then it disappeared. Joe was still stripping line and cried out curses and undecipherable sounds of protest and anguish. We backed up the beach and stood in silence as Joe pulled in the gory head of a trophy striper.

For a long time we stood looking at it. It was horrible. The striper had been bitten off just behind its gills. The fish's jaws and gills jerked reflexively as if it wasn't yet going to give up. Its blood made maroon puddles on the wet sand.

Joe sat down on the sand and closed his eyes. I didn't say anything, just sighed. There was nothing to say anyway.

We fished all day, not talking, and caught nothing but a few schoolies and snapper blues. The day turned sunny and cold. We decided to go home.

While traveling up the main road I asked Joe to pull over before we came to the bridge over the bay. I told him to park next to a random package store & bait shack, not Betty & Nick's place, no way, because I didn't want people in-the-know to see what I was going to do.

I told Joe I was getting us some ice and sodas for the ride home, and took a small cooler out of the back of the truck and went inside. In the cooler, in a garbage bag, was the head of the striper. Joe had thrown it into the dunes for the foxes, and I had gone in and gotten it back while he was taking a nap.

Joe waited behind the wheel. His face was slack. He stared straight ahead.

Inside the shack a couple thick-necked local men were standing around the counter talking to the heavy-set owner. I went over to them and asked if they had a scale, then I pulled out the striper head. Their eyes widened.

What the hell happened to that? the owner said.

A shark came up into the surf and ate it. Can I weigh it?

The man took the head from me, put some newspaper on the scale pan, and set down the heavy, sandy head. From nose to gills, the striper weighed roughly nine-pounds. The men whistled.

You might have had some kinda record there, one of them said.

I shrugged. I bought several bottles of cherry seltzer, some ice, and walked out, leaving the striper's head on the scale behind me, the three big guys still standing there looking at it.

When I sat on the seat, Joe didn't start the truck. He said, How much did it weigh?

You really want to know?

He looked through the windshield for a moment. He hiccoughed. All right, he said, tell me. But before I got out a single word he said, No, no. No, don't tell me.

I didn't tell him. After ten years, neither one of us has ever said a word.

NO TRESPASSING

James Prosek

THIS SUMMER WASN'T about waiting for my mom to take me to the town pool with all the laughter and sun, diving and splashing, the smells of sun tan lotion and chlorine. As I drew in the kitchen, my dad paced back and forth across the living room like he still expected her to walk through the door.

I took long walks to get out of the house.

One day, on one of those walks, I stopped to listen to the bullfrogs making their *ooouuummm ooouuummm* sounds in the pond. Behind the barn two cows were doing the reverse: *Mmmuuuooo*. Every sound had its own place, and for the first time in a while, I felt I had a place too.

I walked on.

Past the old dairy barn and a big patch of milkweed at the end of our dead-end street, I came to the path that led to the woods and the reservoir. A big sugar maple stood like a guard at the edge of the forest, its trunk posted with a yellow sign with black letters that said: NO TRESPASSING.

I remembered my dad telling me that about a hundred years ago, the water company bought all this land from the people who lived in the Mill River Valley. They tore down the homes and burned the wreckage, and they built a dam that flooded the river to make a reservoir for drinking water. The land around the reservoir, once open farms and fields, slowly became forest. The old dirt road led from our dead-end street into those woods.

I walked beyond the end of the street, down the dirt road, under the shade of the trees, through tall ferns and stands of spicebush and witch hazel. I'd only been down to the reservoir a few times before, with my dad. I always wanted to go down and fish the reservoir alone, but I was too afraid. Kids in town told stories about the ghosts of the people who were forced out by the water company whose houses were torn down when the valley was flooded.

Bird songs echoed under the trees. *A wood thrush.* I came to a place I remembered, where a row of old trees grew along the road. My father had told me the trees—big sugar maples—were planted many years before and marked the front of somebody's property. Nearby he showed me the foundation of an old farmhouse, a pit in the ground lined with stones that looked like pictures of old ruins I'd seen in school textbooks.

I stood in that place, by the row of trees, alone now. I felt alive, my vision seemed sharper. I could imagine a house behind the row of trees, a breeze blowing through the windows, billowing the curtains. The place seemed spooky to me when I was with my dad. Now, I walked on without fear.

Soon I was in a place I didn't recognize, where the dirt road split on the other side of two stone pillars. One road went down to the reservoir. The other went up a hill. I took the higher road.

Farther along I got lost in my footsteps. I was hypnotized

watching my feet fall on the path, until a bird flew so close to my face that I flinched. I looked up and there in front of me was a massive tree with giant limbs, its long roots growing around a mossy ledge like the legs of an octopus.

A few paces from the tree, partly hidden by the leaves, I saw a staircase made of large flat fieldstones. I walked up the stone stairs and straight ahead underneath the massive limbs of the old tree. Light spilled through the leaves onto the ground, where I began to see the outline of a perfect square pit lined with stone, the cellar of an old house, or maybe a barn. A staircase led down into the foundation, and in the center of the square was a huge pile of stones and brick. *This is where the chimney was.* I stood there as a cold breeze off the reservoir lifted the hairs on the back of my neck.

And then I heard the sound of moving water.

I couldn't see any water, but the sound was so close I felt like I was surrounded by it, even standing in it. I walked along the edge of the house foundation and down a hill behind it, in the direction of the sound of the water. I got down on my knees and pushed aside some dead leaves with my hand.

The brook was running underneath me.

Fieldstones, longer than I was tall, made a kind of bridge over the brook. Leaves had piled up on top of the stone bridge, hiding the brook completely from view. I tried to imagine the farmers moving the big stones into place. It would have taken several men, maybe with horses, to move one of those stones.

As I walked farther down, the brook opened up and flowed freely through the woods. Tall green ferns and skunk cabbage grew on the bank. I came to a small waterfall. Deep in the dark pool below it, I saw a flash. *A fish.*

I didn't want to go home. I wanted to stay. I needed to make this my space. I pictured a desk, my lamp, a chair, a bed, my own place, arranged on the leaves that carpeted the floor. I needed supplies.

I arrived home sweating and out of breath. I worked quickly. I feared that if I saw my father, or spent too much time in the house, my vision of the camp would disappear. *Stick to the task.*

I stuffed some matches, crackers, an apple, raisins, a candy bar, a penknife, a flashlight, and a bottle of water in my backpack. I tied my sleeping bag to the backpack with rope and threw in a drawing pad, a pencil, and a hook with some line.

I ran down the stairs toward the living room. My dad wasn't in his reading chair.

I should leave a note.

No.

I put my arms through the straps of my backpack and started back down the street, past the barn and through the woods again. I liked the feeling of weight on my back as I ran.

I took a different route, directly through the woods instead of on the dirt road, in case a warden from the water company was on patrol. I heard sometimes they were out looking for trespassers, but I'd never seen one. I didn't want anyone seeing where I was going anyway. The spot was like a photograph in my mind as I walked. I could reconstruct it perfectly. It didn't surprise me when I suddenly found myself there.

My camp.

I put down my backpack near the stone stairs and found a large flat rock that made a good bench to sit on. I untied my sleeping bag from the pack, took a breath of the cool air coming off the brook, and lay down on the flat rock looking up into the tree branches. The air carried the smell of the spicebush and the rusty smell of water.

I ate my apple, core and seeds and all. I grabbed a hook and some line and headed to the reservoir, past a posted sign on a white pine tree: NO TRESPASSING it read in bold black letters. The sign seemed funny because nobody was watching me except for the birds, whose singing seemed louder and louder.

The water of the reservoir came right up to the trunks of the hemlock and pine trees. Small waves lapped against the stones. The air was warmer here and the pine needles were soft under my feet. I leaned over and saw my broken reflection in the water. I recognized, for the first time, the ghostly image of my mother looking back at me.

Can't I go anywhere without thinking of her?

A small fish broke the surface of the water, disturbing the reflection. Underneath the glare from the sky, I saw more fish. *Sunfish.*

I reached into my backpack for my pencils and paper. I tried to draw the small sunfish. An inchworm fell from a tree above me onto the surface of the water, and immediately one of the fish came to the surface and sucked it into its small mouth. Another inchworm was hanging from its silk thread just above the water, but too far for the fish to grab. One eager fish tried, jumping out of the water, flashing its golden sides and orange belly. I put down my pencil and paper. I wanted to catch one.

I knew sunfish were eager biters. I looked behind me on the bank and saw an anthill. The ants carried small white grubs from the top of what looked like a volcano. I didn't know what the grubs were, but they were big enough to put on a hook. I tried one as bait.

Because it didn't weigh much, I couldn't get the grub out far enough to reach a fish. So I got a stick and tied my line to the end of it. With the stick I could get the line out where the fish were. As soon as the grub touched the water I had a sunfish on the hook.

The fish had blue streaks than ran across its olive cheeks like streams on a map. Its eyes were orange-brown, with halos of green and blue. The sides were rust-colored with dark bands, and its belly was pumpkin orange. I took out the hook and held the fish in my hand for a while.

Maybe I'll keep it. Draw it.

My hand dropped in the water and the fish splashed as it swam out. I leaned back against a rock. I took a deep breath and as I exhaled I noticed the birds had stopped singing. I put down my makeshift fishing rod and sat completely still.

A large bird swooped down from the hemlocks. It landed on a rock right next to me. It was an owl and had tufts of feathers on each side of its head that looked like ears. It seemed so much like a person that I thought it might speak to me. I assumed it would just stay there, but as soon as it landed, it lifted its furry feet off the rock and flew away.

In the first weeks after my mom left, I felt that I wouldn't mind just going to sleep and not waking up. My head was so full of bad thoughts that sleep was the only way out. If I could sleep. I didn't want to draw, or do homework, or move. But now I had trouble remembering those times. I felt different, stronger, and my head was full of things I wanted to do.

What had I been so worried about?

I felt at home in the woods. It was the *only* place where I felt at home. Time didn't mean anything here, nor did money or lack of money, or cars, or parents, or anything. I wanted to shout, *Nothing matters!*

I walked to the old foundation, which was built into a hillside. *If I cover the top with logs, I can make a good shelter over my head.* I set to work choosing long, straight, dead timber, dry and newly fallen, from the forest floor. I lined up the logs to make a roof. I found an old iron bucket, filled it with water, and brought it to my site. I gathered dry grass and made a floor. This was basic stuff I learned on camping trips as a Cub Scout.

When I finished my shelter, I took out a candy bar and walked down to the reservoir to eat it. I watched the sun slip down behind the trees like a piece of melting ice. I was amazed at the idea of watching the sun move. I thought of my father. His voice in my head. "It's not the sun moving that you're witnessing," he'd say. "It's the earth turning."

When were things ever what they seemed to be?

I threw a stick and laughed out loud.

Across the reservoir I heard ducks laughing in a cove.

Whack, hack, ack, ack.

I went back to my camp with a skip in my step, pleased with my shelter. And when I got under the roof, I felt tired. I unrolled my sleeping bag and climbed inside. It was too hot so I unzipped it and lay on top.

I dreamed of flying.

I was walking down the slope of our front lawn, spreading my arms. *Why haven't I done this before?* It was so easy. The breeze lifted my body and I was floating, effortlessly above the tree line. I saw the whole farm below, the pond and the lily pads, the big green fields, the old barn. I flew over the reservoir and saw where the old stonewalls came into the water.

Light as a feather.

But then, suddenly, I was heavy. I lost my confidence, and the more I did, the faster I fell. I steered away from the trees and fell into the blue water of the reservoir.

I woke up startled.

I heard a whistle. I knew that whistle.

I knew that whistle! Two high, bent notes with a straight one in the middle.

Whew—whe, whew.

My father and Uncle John made it up when they were kids in Brazil. They used it to find each other in their neighborhood games, their secret whistle that only they knew.

Whew—whe, whew.

For as long as I could remember that had been our family whistle. My dad taught it to us, and we used it to find each other in the supermarket, in the yard, in a crowd, in the house. It was ours and no one else's. There was no mistaking it. It was my dad. He was looking for me.

My father could whistle very loud. He whistled with two fingers in his mouth. The whistle carried a mile. It sounded close. I heard the sound distinctly, maybe half a dozen times. Then the whistles became more distant and disappeared.

I didn't answer.

I couldn't sleep the rest of the night. I even tried to count the stars. By the time the sun came up I was exhausted. My eyes were burning, and my head felt hot and sore, like someone had been using it as a drum. I wanted my bed: the soft sheets, my pillow, my dresser, my closet, my window. I packed up my sleeping bag and started walking back.

Before I left camp, I took the food I had left and buried it under some rocks near my shelter. I knew some animal would probably dig it up and eat it, but maybe if I came back and needed it, it would be there.

When I get home, I'll draw a map. I'll start a journal like my dad used to keep. Inside the front cover, in a secret compartment, I'll store my map. Even if someone found the map and followed it to my place in the woods, they could never really get there, because the real place wasn't on any map, or in the woods. It was nothing you could see. It was inside me.

PART II

The Great Pool

CROCODILE CENTRAL

Keith Fryer

*I*T JUST HAD to be Tugger, standing there at the entrance to Darwin Airport Terminal, blotting out the sun. "Blue singlet…that'll be me," he'd told me over the phone, but I didn't expect the holes in the singlet or the massive gut threatening to burst through them. Under each armpit, the singlet was stained by a circle of sweat, the gut spilling out over his ancient shorts like a frozen Niagara Falls and his shorts were covered in dried blood and fish scales.

He was a huge redheaded man with a crooked, flattened nose that wandered all over his face and his mouth hung open to draw breath. There was another big man in a blue singlet, also with holes, standing beside him.

I collected my bag from the old carousel and approached them. Tugger was mouthing my name. "Pete? Pete Davidson?" He asked before I could speak.

"Tugger," I responded and shook hands; my hand disappearing into his big callused fist.

"Meet my son, Dan. He'll be comin' with us today," he said, a little awkwardly.

Dan was the spitting image of Tugger except the gut was work-in-progress. Everything Tugger had, Dan had… even the same gap where his front teeth should have been.

They led me out of the building into the searing heat of the Tropics and we climbed into a dirty, old, beat-up truck. As Dan drove, Tugger talked.

"We're got the best barramundi that money can buy. Did you get that fish, Dan?" Tugger asked.

"Yeah. Bought it this morning. Big fella too…it's in the back," said Dan gesturing over his shoulder with his thumb.

"You know, for the photo," Tugger explained to me, "you know…in case you don't catch one."

"So, you don't think I'll catch one then," I said in surprise. "I was told there were barramundi everywhere up here."

"Funny things can happen with fish. Some days there's not a fish in sight and other days they'll jump into the bloody boat," he said.

He was a friend of a friend but, more importantly, he lived on the Daly River where the barramundi bite, and he was a mad keen fisherman, just like me. Sure, he wasn't a licensed tour operator, but I was prepared to cover expenses—a hundred bucks a day…food, boat, bait, tackle, grog and barramundi included.

How good is that?

"Never ever got hurt when I played in these shorts." Tugger said attempting to explain the overpowering smell of fish in the cramped truck, "Never washed 'em. Never will, yeah." He and Dan both absolutely stank of fish. But, then again, who did they have to impress? Not me, that's for sure.

By the time we pulled up at their fishing hut and I changed into my fishing gear, it was five o'clock and coming on to dark.

"We're gonna head up toward a bend near the mouth of the river…'bout two miles. The fishing is best at late afternoon or just on nightfall with the tide going out. Now is perfect. Tide's just turning so everything's just right to catch a few. Rods all ready, yeah?" Tugger asked Dan.

"Ready. We campin' out tonight, Dad?" Dan asked with a smirk, and I wasn't sure why.

I might be a fool sometimes but I knew that camping along any river in the Territory was foolhardy and dangerous.

"Nah, we won't be campin'. We'll get Peter back home tonight. That alright, Pete?"

I nodded, relieved.

"*Lulu* all ready?" Tugger asked.

"She's ready," replied Dan.

"She's a bit old, Pete," Tugger warned. "But we've caught more barramundi out of that boat then flies on a cow pat… let's go."

"Righto," I said with enthusiasm.

We picked up all the gear and headed down the short track to *Lulu* and, as I stepped into the boat, I saw that it really was old…it was bloody ancient. Tugger pushed it off the mud into the water and pointed me towards a flimsy plastic picnic chair beside the battered old outboard engine at the rear of the filthy, glued together, lopsided, ramshackle excuse for an aluminium fishing boat.

Tugger stood hanging onto the center console beside Dan,

who was trying to start the outboard engine, which cranked over and over but wouldn't start. I watched with fast-growing concern as Tugger grabbed a broken bucket and bailed water from the boat before grabbing a screwdriver, stepping past me, ripping the dented cowling off and fiddling with something in the engine.

As the cowling lay there on the floor of the boat, I noticed that not only were there dents but also jagged holes. "Try it now," he commanded.

There was more cranking and it started in a cloud of blue smoke.

"Okay, okay. She's right now," he said as he put the cowling back on. "Keep that throttle up a bit, yeah."

Dan clunked the engine into gear; the boat suddenly jerked forward and big Tugger landed in my lap, crushing me into the chair.

"Whoa, there boy. Hold back," Tugger said without a hint of anger at Dan or apology to me. He got up, staggered forward to the console, grabbed it to steady himself, and another rivet popped out, rattling into the rubbish and water in the bottom of the boat. Tugger made a kick at the rivet, reached into the cool box at his feet, extracted a can of beer, ripped it open, took a mouthful and, through the gap in his teeth, spurted beer over the side of the boat.

"Halfway across the backyard at home. Terrible waste of beer though," he said.

Showing off, Dan hammered the boat into the middle of the river and headed downstream. Dan was a quiet sort of bloke…he really had no choice with Tugger as a father but, then again, I reckon the whole world would defer to Tugger. If Dad threw orders, Dan existed to merely carry them out.

The engine was far too big…too powerful for such a small boat unbalanced as it was by Tugger's massive weight. I watched in disbelief as water started to spurt up through two small holes in the floor. Beads of perspiration—no, it was the sweat of fear— dripped from my nose into the water. The amount of water sloshing around was lapping at my ankles so, by necessity, I reached over, grabbed the bucket, and started bailing.

"Crocs ahead," Dan warned.

I stood up nervously to catch a glimpse of my first crocodile. There on the creek bank was what looked like a log but as we got closer became a crocodile. Seeing one up close like that was a bit of a shock but excitement rose in my belly.

As I stood, Dan jerked the steering wheel left and right, and I was nearly thrown from the boat. They both laughed as I sat down. The joke was on me.

"Are there many crocs along here, Tugger?" I asked.

"Swarmin' with 'em," he replied. "Do not put your hands or feet overboard when we're stopped. Okay? I don't want to lose another guest, yeah."

"So how many guests have you lost?" I asked.

"Sixteen."

I was astonished. "How many?"

"None, mate," he said elbowing Dan in the ribs, "just keepin' you on your toes."

"Hilarious, Tugger," I said.

Something else was gnawing at me.

"So, why did Dan ask if we were camping?"

"We never camp. Crocs would walk a mile across country to eat a juicy tourist like you. They'd pluck you out of the tent and we wouldn't even know you were gone 'til daybreak… unless you screamed like a girl."

It was a bloody set-up. He watched for my reaction. I laughed as expected.

"No, we won't be camping. We just say that to put some fear into our guests. Did we scare you?"

"No, no…I knew…"

"How ya goin' there Dan?" Tugger called out.

"Yeah, I'm okay, Dad. I'll take her up to the Big Bend like we planned."

"Now we get down to business," Tugger said as he squatted down beside me and reached for a fishing rod.

"This here is one of my special barramundi fishing rods. It's got the best reel and new thirty-pound thread line. This is the best money can buy so look after it…have you used this sort of reel before?"

"Yes," I replied, "I've used all of 'em."

"Good. Then we'll have no tangles will we, Pete? This is your rod for tonight and I've got the same. We'll be flickin' the lure into the mangroves and catchin' the biggest and best barramundi you ever saw. We always get big fellas at the Big Bend, yeah. A beer for the first fish, eh Pete?"

Dan blasted *Rattling Lulu* along the river and, while I sat in my wet boots at the stern in command of the bailing bucket and drowning in uncertainty, Tugger stood facing the wind and he burst into song:

I'm a blue baby
Blue Momma
Blue as I can be
I'm a blue baby
I'm square-eyed from TV…yeah.

I started laughing but he turned and gave me a puzzled look. Surely he knew they were the wrong words for that song. It was a love song, for God's sake, and he'd stuffed it up but there wasn't the hint of a smile on his face. Tugger reached down, pulled a couple of beers from the cool box and offered me one. He ripped his open, took a mouthful and spurted beer over the side of the boat. I ripped mine open and took a mouthful without spurting.

I settled back and looked around at the river and its banks as we sped past. There were mangroves and trees along the banks but here and there were mud flats and on every mud flat was a crocodile. None of them was small: most were big and some were very, very big.

"People reckon this is the most dangerous place in the world," Tugger said. "This stretch of the Daly River has more large crocodiles than any river in the world."

I was prepared to believe it.

"Tide's goin' out," Tugger shouted. "They'll all be comin' up onto the banks for the night."

He paused.

"When we stop just come forward a bit…away from the back. Sometimes crocs will jump up and have a go at the engine. The noise excites 'em."

I started to move forward.

"No, no," he said, "you're all right when we're moving."

Dan eased back on the throttle and the boat came to a stop about twenty-feet-out from some thick mangroves at a sweeping bend in the river. I moved forward.

"This is the best spot I know," Tugger offered. "We've always caught heaps here."

We started fishing. I cast just short of the mangroves, careful not to snag the lure, and reeled back towards the boat. Meanwhile, Tugger cast to a spot just to the right of me. Nothing came onto the lures so I cast a little away from my first one and, as soon as the lure hit the water, it was taken. I heaved back on the rod to sink the hook in and played the fighting fish to the side of the boat.

"Hold him. Bring him in now. It's a barra…don't jerk. Get the net. Keep the tip of your rod up. Hold him steady now," Tugger ordered.

Dan netted the fish, swung it into the boat and held it up in front of me. My first barramundi.

"Well, look at that…what a beauty," Tugger declared. "We'll have to call you Barramundi Man…that's what we'll call you. First cast—no—second, wasn't it? Fastest catch I've ever seen."

Tugger and I were both standing there admiring the fish when there was a loud crash at the back of the boat, the boat slewed around and I fell backwards onto the engine. Instinctively, I put my hands out to break the fall and my left hand landed squarely on the head of a crocodile. A crocodile had its jaw locked around the engine. Time stood still. Under my hand, its head felt rough and leathery and the muscles beneath were like steel. Tugger crashed over the back of the boat, onto the crocodile's back and into the water. Horrified, I recoiled, pushing myself away from the crocodile, which then opened its jaws, took a snap at my retreating hand, missed, and then took another grip on the motor.

I fell over backwards.

"Get in, Dad!" Dan shouted.

Dan grabbed Tugger's hand and he clambered back into the boat—I don't know how—while I then stumbled to the absolute front of the boat. Dan grabbed a metal toolbox and banged it down on the head of the croc.

The crocodile loosened its grip on the cowling and slid back into the river.

"Start 'er up," Tugger commanded.

Dan cranked the engine over but it wouldn't fire.

"Come on, start it," I shouted.

"Dad, the carbie, the carbie…," Dan shouted and threw a screwdriver at Tugger.

Tugger tried to rip the cowling off but it wouldn't budge. The attack had mangled it more and it was stuck.

"Give me a hand," Tugger said without a hint of panic. "He always comes back for a second go."

I ordered myself to stay calm and moved past Dan, who forced another screwdriver into my hand. While Tugger tried to pry open one side of the cowling, I jammed my screwdriver under the opposite side and the cowling flew off into the water. I made a grab for it but it slipped from my hands. Through the teeth holes, the metal cowling quickly filled with water and sank. The crocodile had still not reappeared.

Everything was happening in slow motion. There was fiddling with the engine, there was cranking, there were more orders being thrown at Dan and me, there was more smoke and then we blasted out of there. I returned to the front of the boat with my head in my shaking hands.

There was the sound of a cool box opening, beers being ripped open and liquid being spurted overboard through holes in teeth. There was the familiar sound of a bucket bailing water from the boat. There was even the sound of nervous laughter, which increased to a feverish crescendo and a can of beer landing at my feet. I reached down and tried to pull the ring-top but couldn't. I handed it back to Tugger who stabbed the screwdriver twice into the top of the can and, as it spurted froth, I gulped it into my shaking guts. They were in fits of laughter.

"What was that?" I shouted. "Did you bring me here knowing that would happen?"

"Only sometimes…only sometimes at that spot," Tugger said, "He doesn't like the sound of the engine or something, yeah."

"Well, why did you bloody well take me there?"

"Because he hasn't done that for a while…we thought he was gone, didn't we Danny, yeah?"

"Well, you could have warned me, for Christ's sake."

"Yeah, I suppose we could but the last bloke wouldn't come after we told him."

"I had my bloody hands on the head of that crocodile…I think I even touched one of his eyes and…"

"Look, Pete," Dan said, "we're all safe. Dad had a swim, you got to feel a big crocodile and we're headin' back with a barramundi for tea. It's all good."

It was the first full sentence I'd heard from Dan and it made sense.

They laughed, I finally smiled and we all ripped open

another beer. I tried to spurt it overboard and choked so we all laughed and they joined me in shouting obscenities. I was happy to survive the closest call of my life. Tugger burst into song again:

I'm a blue baby
Blue Momma
Blue as I can be
I'm a blue baby
I'm square-eyed from TV…yeah.

I was still shaking uncontrollably and, as we rounded a bend in the river, another rivet popped, the center console crashed over onto the side of the boat and we were thrown sideways as the boat, on full throttle, swerved violently. It was now headed for the mud flats at top speed with Dan underneath the console, helpless.

"Jesus," Tugger shouted.

Lulu sped on towards the bank and I felt it begin to slide across the shallow bottom. The out-of-control engine drove us farther and farther onto the mud flats and we finally came to a halt in six inches of water with the boat leaning over at a forty-five degree angle. The engine was screaming at peak revs and a huge fan of slush sprayed up from the back of the boat. Tugger recovered first and somehow turned the engine off.

"Jesus," Tugger shouted again. I shouted another obscenity and Dan moaned as the weight of the console crushed down on him. Tugger tried to lift it off but couldn't. I stepped over the side of the boat to give myself some leverage and sank, up to my waist, in the mud. There was no bottom. I grabbed the side of the boat to stop myself sinking to China, summoned up enough strength to pull myself back into the boat, gained a foothold and helped Tugger lift the console off Dan who was making gurgling sounds.

"Don't move him. Don't move him," Tugger shouted.

"Where does it hurt?" I asked.

"Here," said Dan pointing at his arse.

Tugger and I looked at each other.

"Ha, ha, Dad…gotcha!" Dan said as he got up gingerly.

"Told ya we shoulda' used bigger rivets."

"I didn't have bigger ones…anyway you drilled 'em," Tugger said.

"Look," Dan said. "I'm not hurt, maybe a bit sore in the chest, but that's all. We gotta get Lulu off this mud flat. We can't stay here all night or we'll be dinner for the crocodiles."

Another positive affirmation from Dan.

I looked around us. Night was falling. The boat was slewed over by the weight of the console and we were open to the crocodiles.

"Yeah…we gotta get outa here, that's for sure," observed Tugger as he opened another beer and offered one to Dan and me. My last beer can was rolling around somewhere in the bottom of the boat with about twenty others.

"You offer me a beer! You offer me a beer!" I raged. "You bring me here in this pathetic excuse for a boat and you offer me a friggin' beer." I paused. "Another bloody rivet popped back at the hut and you saw it and you didn't say a word."

"I didn't see it," Tugger said.

"Yes, you did. I saw you kick it under the console."

"No, I didn't," Tugger said, "I couldn't see it because of all the rubbish."

"Exactly. There's so much rubbish in this bloody boat you can't see nothin'," I shouted.

No response.

"Well. Can we stay here all night? What do we bloody well do? Can we sit here like this? Don't just look at me," I said, trying desperately to calm down.

"If you'd stop shouting, we might be able to reverse out of here and head home," Tugger said.

"Can't," Dan said, "reverse gear died last month… remember, Dad."

Tugger stopped in mid-sentence.

"Okay. Okay," Tugger said. "We can't stay here. The crocs are gonna give us a good licking sometime tonight so we've got to get back to the water…somehow."

Tugger and Dan then started searching around the boat for a volunteer to go over the side.

Their intent was obvious.

The best part of a minute passed.

"All right, all right," I said at last in a voice dripping with contempt.

I moved to the front of the boat where Tugger physically picked me up and lowered me into the mud…a pathetic, whimpering sacrifice to the monsters. The tide was still going out and the mud was slushy and soft; there was no substance to it at all and I sank deeper and deeper.

In panic I shouted, "Tie a rope to me. Quick. Get a rope."

Tugger released me, grabbed the anchor rope and threw it at me. The mud was up to my chin. As he pulled on the rope I reached up and gave the boat a shove but with him pulling and me pushing it was hopeless…I just sank deeper and deeper and the boat didn't move.

They were both at the front of the boat throwing instructions.

"Spread your legs out…like you're wider. So you don't sink," Dan offered.

"Give me a flat board or something," I shouted, "I'm sinkin' here. Give me something to put on the top of the mud. Quick!"

Tugger looked around but found nothing that was flat.

"There's too much weight. Dan…hop out," Tugger ordered. "If we lighten the boat and I stand here at the front it should work."

"No, I'm not getting out, Dad. There's…you know," Dan whispered.

"You'll have to get out," Tugger insisted.

"No, Dad, you get out."

"Dan, someone's got to stay here in case…" Tugger replied.

"In case of what, Dad?" Dan asked.

"To start the boat when you push it back into the river, Dan," Tugger insisted.

"But there's…there's…"

"I don't care, son. Just do it. I'm too big for you to pull out of the mud…you couldn't pull me up."

While they argued I'm sure I heard a slithering and sliding somewhere along the bank and further upstream there was a splash. Dan reluctantly stepped over the side of the boat and Tugger lowered him down beside me. It was nightfall and we were both up to our shoulders in the mud of Crocodile Central. Overcome with fear, I grabbed Dan and tried to climb up him but he pushed me away.

"We've both got to push. We'll get out of here if we both push," he shouted.

"Push," Tugger was calling from, it seemed, a million miles away.

We both reached up and pushed. The boat wouldn't budge.

"Lift the engine Dad, lift the engine," Dan shouted.

Tugger swore at himself and I heard him moving around at the fallen console. There was a whirring sound as the outboard engine raised itself up from the mud. At least the electrics still worked. My hopes lifted. The propeller now offered no resistance to us.

We pushed again and the boat finally moved about two feet backwards.

"Good stuff, boys," Tugger shouted, "come forward now."

I pulled myself forward with help from Dan. Then, as I lay face down in the mud, he used me as a mat and hauled himself over me towards the boat. I was under the bloody mud… completely submerged with Dan's weight pushing me deeper as he slid over me.

As Dan lifted my head up for breath, Tugger was shouting in encouragement, "Like a croc, Dan. Just like a croc. Slither. That's good, boys. Keep going. Keep slitherin'."

I wriggled and pulled myself forward and we sank down into the mud again, legs spread, to push the boat another two feet.

Now it was Dan's turn to be a mat and I forced his head, almost deliberately, farther into the mud as I slid over him. Again and again we stood, pushed, submerged, slid, stood, pushed and slid until the boat was in enough water to float.

It floated away.

I could hear the whirring sound as Tugger lowered the motor and then there was a cranking noise followed by more cranking noises. The noises became progressively more distant as the outgoing tide took the boat slowly downstream.

The hairs on my neck stood up.

"Throw the anchor. Throw us a line," I shouted urgently.

The cranking continued.

"Screwdriver, Dad," Dan shouted at the top of his voice.

It echoed back and forth across the river.

It was pitch black on that moonless night and, soon, we could no longer see the boat. So, there we were…stranded in the middle of Crocodile Central, up to our noses in mud knowing that Tugger couldn't hear us.

The cranking stopped.

Bailing noises started.

At that point, I was ready to die.

The cranking started again but it was a distant taunt…a reminder of my own stupidity.

"He'll be back," Dan said. "Don't worry, he'll be back."

His words were no consolation to me.

In the distance, we heard the engine start. We shouted and hollered and the sight of Tugger, crouched over the collapsed console driving the boat as best he could, with a torch in his big claw, was sweet relief.

We clambered in, levered the console into an upright position, tied it to the other side of the boat with the anchor rope and Dan took us, at half speed, back towards the hut. Tugger and I sat there, him sitting on the rope to keep the console upright and me just holding onto the side of the boat. I was covered in mud from head to toe.

"How about a beer, Pete?" Tugger asked, flashing the light onto the cool box.

I had to do something…anything to deflect the delayed hysteria rising within me so I opened the cool box. The lid was long and flat. I looked at Tugger and he looked back at me.

"Not the cool box lid," he said. "How could I? If I'd given you the lid of the cool box how would I keep your beer cold?"

"What do you mean, keep my bloody beer cold?"

"Well, we don't drink. We're teetotal…Dan and me."

"But you drank beer. What the hell are you talking about?"

"We spurt it out. All you southern blokes turn up here and expect us Northern Territory blokes to be big drinkers.

Well, Dan and me aren't…we spurt it all out. Never drink a drop of it and we never will," he said.

I was stunned.

Confusion and hysteria took a firm hold.

I went off like a cracker.

"Do you know how bloody dangerous you are, Tugger? What about an apology? You bring me here to this hellhole bad place, this bloody boat and the holes spurting—don't you know we're sinking? Christ, I can't believe it," I was fast becoming incoherent, "and you expect me to enjoy this…this boat and this mud. I was in that mud for…up past my head, I was under the friggin' mud and you…you just sat here throwin' orders at me…and Dan. You got out of the water back at the bend. Why didn't you get in the mud with the crocodiles? Oh, no, not you. You had to stay here with your precious top of the box."

In the dark I couldn't really see his reaction and I didn't care. I had to stop him from doing this to the next man.

"And what about the next bloke…you gonna do the same thing to him? Some poor bloke's gonna come here innocent as hell and you're gonna get him killed and you'll tell the cops that it was a bloody accident…well, I've been in court, Tugger, and you can't lie. No, no…although I reckon you could lie, you big heap of bullshit."

"Last bloke went off just like you," Tugger said.

"What last bloke?"

"Last bloke. He lost a new rod and reel over the side. He went in after it."

"What?" I cried. "You chucked a bloke overboard just for some fishing gear."

"No. Didn't chuck him. He jumped over on my recommendation."

Dan was choking with laughter.

"Did he get out?" I yelled. "Just how many men have died here, Tugger?"

"None yet," Tugger said. "But one might soon…from a heart attack."

"Well, do you blame me? Christ, I thought I was going to die."

"But you didn't, did you."

"That's not the point…"

"Yes, it is."

"No, it's not."

"Well, it is. You'll be telling people about this fishing trip for years and your mates will say you're lying…and then you'll get them to call me and ask me what really happened."

"No I won't."

"Yes, you will…and I'll tell them the truth. About how you wrestled the croc off the back of the boat, how you dived into the mud in the pitch black of night with crocs all around us and how you pushed the boat back into the river. That's how brave you were."

"But, but, that's not what happened," I said. "You nearly got me killed."

"No, you saved us. That's what happened," he said.

Dan throttled back on the engine and I realised that we were at the hut.

"Now let's get you blokes cleaned off," Tugger said.

The mud was beginning to dry so I stepped awkwardly out of boat and followed Tugger, resisting the urge to choke him to death, to a chair at the front of the hut. Dan followed and sat down beside me. There was the sound of running water, Tugger put two buckets in front of us and we began to splash water over ourselves. There was a noise near the boat about twenty feet away and I lifted my head. As I did so, a barramundi lure zinged into my bucket.

"Great cast, eh?" Tugger called.

So that's the complete and unabridged story about how

I wrestled the huge croc off the back of the boat with my bare hands and, how I, in the pitch black of night, willingly and without thought for my own well-being, dived into the crocodile-infested mud of Crocodile Central and pushed the disabled and sinking boat back into the river saving all present from certain death.

That's how brave I was. Just call my good mate, Tugger. He'll tell you. And I caught a bloody big barramundi. It was the first cast. How good is that?

THE GRAYLING AND THE BELL CURVE

Elliot L. Richardson

My FIRST DESCENT of a remote wilderness river was the kind of experience one relives many times. The adventure began at Summit Lake, fifty-miles north of Prince George in the heart of British Columbia. A handful of Indians watched us shove our canoes out from the lake's shore. These were the last human beings we saw until two weeks later when, having traveled northward out of Summit Lake by way of the Pack and the Parsnip Rivers into the Peace River, we pulled out at the Gold Bar Ranch just above the Peace River Canyon. Since then a hydropower dam has created a lake submerging the whole lower third of the area we traversed.

During the first several days Dolly Varden and rainbow trout were our only fresh food. But then we encountered a new species of fish—a first for me. This was the Arctic grayling, a species found only in streams flowing into the Arctic Ocean. These are lovely fish: blue-gray with bright yellow spots and a huge fan-like dorsal fin. Cooked over a campfire, they're the tastiest fish I've ever eaten.

I owe one Arctic grayling the most memorable moment in a lifetime of fly-fishing. We had by then reached the Peace River itself, a big river flowing eastward through the Rockies into Lake Athabaska.

Around mid-morning on the eighth or ninth day we beached our canoes at the mouth of a boisterous tributary on the north side of the Peace. Using dry flies, we slowly worked our way up through its rapids and rocks. The sun was bright and the water crystal clear. As to be expected, the fish were wary. Only the best-presented dry-fly had any prospect of attracting either a trout or a grayling.

Such was the state of affairs when, making my way around a bend, I came upon a stunningly beautiful pool. Upstream and to the right was a rock some three-feet-wide. On each side a parentheses of foam curved around a slick of quiet water. "Now there," I thought, "is a place that must hold a fish!" For me the cast to the rock was demandingly long, but for once my leader reached out to its full length and the fly dropped gently into the middle of the slick.

No sooner had the fly settled when a grayling shot out of the water about two-feet to its right. The fish's trajectory through the air described a perfect arc. With its fan-shaped dorsal fin at full stretch, the grayling dropped on the fly. The fish's own descending weight hooked it securely.

Zigzagging back and forth across the pool, jumping, sounding, and shaking its head, the fish put up a gallant fight. When at last I released it, I did so with an overflowing sense of admiration and gratitude.

That experience taken together with an utterly different half-day of fishing in Alaska several years later taught me an important lesson. The memorable feature of the Alaskan episode was that at one stage I hooked a fish on eleven straight casts. And here is the lesson: It is that the enjoyment

of angling is distributed along a bell curve. At the lower end of the curve on the left, you've been flogging the stream for a long time with no results and you're ready to conclude that it holds no fish at all. At the lower end on the right, the fish are so plentiful and easy to catch that no skill is demanded. At the peak of the bell curve, you're not catching many fish, but you feel that your successes are attributable not just to luck but to getting it all together.

That day when the grayling struck was at the peak of the bell curve. Come to think of it, my best days of fishing have all been like that.

ATLANTIC SALMON *Salmo salar*

PANIC ON THE BANKS OF THE GRIMSA

Ed Migdalski

THE GRIMSA IS a prized salmon river in Iceland; it is a river that I love and have fished many times. Never did I dream, however, that I would associate with that beautiful body of water, flowing through pockmarked volcanic rock and intensely green meadowlike formations, the kind of panic and apprehension described below.

The occurrence in Iceland I am referring to did not take place on the river. I was fishing my favorite beat, a handsome stretch of water with snow-capped mountains in the background, when a sixteen-pound (big for the Grimsa) hook-jawed, buck salmon hit the fly and zipped off most of my line backing as I scrambled down river in pursuit. After much give and take between the rod and the salmon, and unnecessary advice from my companion, Foster Bam, the fish was netted by our favorite guide, Sven (Sveinbjorn Blondal). I was so pleased with the way the quarry had taken a fly of my own construction (#10 Hairy Mary), and with the fish's magnificent resistance, that I immediately decided to take this handsome specimen home as a trophy. Consequently, I gave Sven explicit instructions on how to place the fish in the Grimsa Lodge freezer.

The custom at the Grimsa is to fish a half-day at the end of the week on Sunday morning, the day of departure for the Keflavik airport. Fishing until the last moment always creates a problem—time consuming struggling out of waders, peeling off thermo-underwear, removing other paraphernalia, and then dismantling rods and packing duffel packs to be ready when the mini-bus arrives to pick up the anglers.

At the conclusion of our fishing, Sven retrieved my pride and joy from the freezer and delivered it to my room, where I was prepared to incorporate it into my luggage. I found, to my dismay, that the salmon's tail and caudal peduncle, all of about seven-inches, protruded beyond the confines of the bag. Meanwhile, close by my bedroom window in the small parking area, Magnus, the bus driver, was exhorting the guides to start loading the luggage. Time was growing short for departure. To search for a box, tape, and twine to accommodate the salmon was out of the question. I panicked. To settle my nerves I finished the last shot of bourbon from the bottle, sitting like a beacon on the dresser, and made a decision. I pulled off my pants, shoes and socks, placed the salmon in the bath tub, and with pocket knife in hand followed the salmon into the tub. On my knees, with a towel over the ice-cold fish, I frantically began the tough job of sawing off the tail-end of the frozen trophy.

While the fish scales were sprinkling over the bottom of the tub, I finally cut through the salmon skin, meat and bone. Just then I heard Foster, who was standing by the bus, yell to Sven, who was waiting at the loading platform with the other guides to say good-bye. "Where the Hell is Ed," voiced Foster. "He must be goofing off somewhere as usual."

I expected the knock on my door. I shouted, "Come in Sven." He opened the door and exclaimed to the empty room, "How did you know it was me?" I replied, "I'm psychic. I'm in the bathroom. Come in, I need your help." He approached hesitatingly and peeked in as I stood in the tub with the salmon's tail in one hand, the knife in the other and the rest of the fish at my feet. Before I could explain the situation, he stared, gulped and softly said, "Yasus."

After I told Sven not to call Foster for help, I commissioned him to clean up the mess in the tub. I inserted the tail into the long plastic bag with the body of the salmon, rewrapped it all with newspaper and smiled when the bag zipped up without a hitch. Sven carried my rods and other bags to the bus with its impatient passengers. I lugged the last piece, containing the salmon, to the lodge door as fast as I could. Then I slowed down and nonchalantly placed the heavy bag on the platform. As I straightened up I could feel the sweat break out on my forehead.

The salmon arrived home perfectly frozen. In my basement workshop, several months later, I prepared the salmon for molding in plaster. Because of the medicinal benefits of bourbon that Sunday morning in Iceland, I thereupon turned a seemingly acute disaster into a successful and satisfying experiment, producing a plastic mount of a trophy fish showing a distinct vertical wound across its caudal peduncle. I could have repaired the blemish, but I did not do so, because it gives me pleasure when I view that scarred replica of my sixteen-pounder and recall that morning of panic on the banks of the Grimsa.

A TALE OF TALAU

Richard Kenneth Stoll

THE SETTING WAS what made the place memorable. Mount Talau jutted out of a landscape of other table mountains. All mountains were tables in Vava'u. As the local Polynesians told it, Tangaloa, their ancient God, made the mountains that way so that his people could easily live and farm on the tops. The only difference with Talau was that it was made higher than the rest. It was the Tangaloa residence that overlooked the rest of his kingdom.

The islands and peninsulas that guarded the entrance to Vava'u were veritable fortresses. Sheer cliffs jutted out of the ocean on all sides. In days past, not a safe landing or anchorage could be found by invading Polynesian war canoes or European square rigged marauders.

About a mile inside the entrance, the cliffs turned into steep slopes. Talau could be seen looming ahead, a sentinel guarding the narrow passage to one of the most protected deep harbors in the Pacific. What Talau guarded was a refuge. Early Spaniards named it Puerto Refugio: a refuge from hurricanes; a fortress protecting against ancient Polynesian warrior groups that so successfully invaded other parts of Tonga; a safe haven from unbearable rape and pillage by squalid European sailors eight months distant from their homes.

From Talau's summit it was possible to see all approaches to Vava'u. Ancient peoples used Talau as eyes to guard against these perils and to herald welcome visitors. Where

Talau guarded the entrance to one of the most beautiful harbors in the Pacific, Neiafu, the capital city of the Vava'u island group and second largest city in the tiny Kingdom of Tonga, was situated at the innermost extreme of the harbor.

Once inside Talau's protective embrace, rugged landscape gave way to a portrait of abundance. The hills were rich with coconuts, bananas, taro, and idyllic home settings. The waters of the Port of Refuge were calm, glassy, and warm. Dense schools of juvenile mackerel and tuna abounded and fed heavily in the bait rich nursery waters in preparation for their eventual journey to sea. Other than mountain breezes and traditional Polynesian outrigger canoes, fish were all that disturbed the calmness of these waters.

Neiafu itself was a hamlet of new and old. Colonial era gingerbread buildings studded the main street. A new bank building and government office broke the visual repast with a modern touch but were not out of place. The old Catholic church marked the south end of the town; the historical Vava'u Club marked the northern boundary. Both stood out as visible landmarks.

Local Polynesian people calmly lounged under the covered wooden walkway that ran the length of the main street. Others nonchalantly went about their business, seemingly unconcerned about anything in particular. Life moved exceedingly slowly.

On Saturday mornings the old wharf bristled with activity. Polynesian entrepreneurs brought in their fish and produce from neighboring villages for barter to dockside crowds. Fruit and vegetables glittered in the tropical sun. Beautiful selections of mangos, papayas, bananas, pineapples, guavas, taro, and yams could be had for barter or a few pennies. Conversely, market fish were not spectacular, but expensive even in Western terms. Most were small denizens of the deep that took perilously long night hours of bottom fishing from dugout canoes to catch.

Other than weekend shopping events, the only time one could see so many people in one place in Vava'u was during the arrival of the weekly interisland ferry. Then it was evident that Neiafu was inhabited by more than a few dozen people. But after the market or the ferry, people blended into the countryside.

It seems that all island paradises have their certain people who don't really fit. Those in Neiafu were mostly displaced misfits from America, Australia, and World War II Germany. They carried on in unusual ways that broke the monotonous but idyllic pace of Neiafu society. These individuals, with their different and sometimes eccentric ways, became as much a part of the local scene as coconut trees and the ubiquitous Polynesian swine. They were there, but no one paid much attention to them.

I had among my entourage of Vava'u friends three very special castaways. Most evenings they could be found drinking, laughing, and arguing matters of the world and Tonga at the Vava'u Club. Reverend David McClean, Herr Heinz Koester (now IGFA Rep of Tonga), and Professor Steven Anderson were as much a part of Neiafu's character as the old gingerbread houses that lined the streets. Yet, they were as different from each other as mangos and coconuts.

David, locally known as Tee Kanata—Tee was a contraction of Tevita, the local alliteration for David, and Kanata, meaning Canada, his progenitor country—was a fundamentalist minister in his former life. It seemed that he was involuntarily defrocked following an indiscrete liaison with his deacon's wife. Concern for his personal health and wellbeing forced him to accept a teaching job in Neiafu. He soon lost his teaching job because his most liberal attitudes did not set well with the school's traditional British headmaster.

Tee, rarely religious anymore except about his fishing and playing with his seven half Polynesian children, had a slender physique and a magnificently balding head. Every morning Tee donned his dilapidated hat, tied a piece of rope around his waist to keep his pants up, and kissed his golden-skinned wife and seven dirty tykes goodbye before he trundled off to his black coral shop. There he made exquisitely beautiful jewelry from the skeletons of shellfish and coral. He sold some of the pieces to occasional visitors and shipped the rest to tourist locations around Polynesia.

Tee was famous among Vava'u natives for three things: he was a magnificent free diver, a useful skill for collecting the shells and black coral he sold in his shop; he was a most enthusiastic fisherman; and he was a prodigious manufacturer of intestinal gas, which, in turn, affected business in the shop, a consequence that Tee never seemed quite to understand.

Heinz was a German who claimed noble ancestral lineage. He was always impeccably dressed in aloha shirts, the only garment that would fit around his enormous mid section. Heinz had come to Vava'u some fifteen years previous for unknown reasons. Some believed he, along with several other more senior Vava'u Germans, had to escape post-war Nazi prosecutors. Not for one minute did I believe such nonsense about Heinz. But I had doubts about the others.

Heinz was never able to leave Neiafu, although he threatened often to do so. He lived in a Beachcraft that had been crash-landed next to the lagoon over the hill from Neiafu by one Carter Johnson from Tennessee. This caused Carter to stay on and build the Paradise Hotel just beyond the old Catholic church. Carter, a chronic workaholic, couldn't afford to leave, so he built a hotel. But this is the subject of another story. The important parts of the Beachcraft were used to decorate the walls of the hotel bar and dance hall; the fuselage was left for Heinz to live in.

Heinz was not as highly motivated as Carter or Tee. Over

the years he tried just about everything in Vava'u to make a living. Finally Heinz married a local beauty. They settled down in a real house where he put her to work making ice cream—a new invention that sold very well in the sultry heat of Neiafu. This gave him enough money to buy beer at the Vava'u Club and fish hooks from the government store.

Heinz was well known in Vava'u for many reasons, two of which were outstanding. Heinz could drink more beer than any other man, woman, or child in the South Pacific and still be able to stand and talk coherently; and he was an enthusiastic fisherman. In fact, enthusiastic was an extreme understatement.

Steve had the appearance of a desert island castaway, with the nature of a critical philosopher. His sun-leathered face and dusty blonde hair overpowered his slender physique. He was the analyst among the three castaways, playing the role of moderator and critic in all of their mutual conversations.

Steve had immigrated from Australia some ten years previously to build foreign aid-funded rainwater catchment tanks for villagers. He was very good, but he no longer built the rainwater tanks because he out-performed the local companies both in quality and price. The government therefore saw to it that he got no more contracts. So, when the opportunity presented itself, he built everything from houses to fish boats. He was a jack-of-all-trades and was not afraid to admit it.

Steve was married to a very substantial Polynesian matriarch, apparently making her as dominant in the intimate matters of marriage as she was in Steve's other activities. Nonetheless, Steve managed to get her away to the Vava'u Club nearly every day, where he, in turn, dominated discussions between Tee and Heinz, much the same way his wife did at home.

Steve was not a fisherman, except that he was opinionated on the subject and loved to eat fish. He had become an armchair expert listening to the recognized experts in Vava'u, two of whom were Heinz and Tee.

Steve was famous in Vava'u for one outstanding quality. He knew something about everything, which, to the local Polynesian population, was everything about everything. He became the counselor at large for the indigenous locals, as well as an imposed counselor to his club mates. Nevertheless, Steve, like his two friends, was loved by all.

⊢——⊣

I had arrived in Vava'u some three hours earlier via the inter-island bush plane and was feeling quite relieved that the aircraft had managed to make another successful flight. The looks of the old Islander that flew the route from the main island of Tongatapu, nearly 200 miles to the south, did not engender a feeling of confidence in passengers who knew what airplanes were supposed to look like. I had made my way to Carter's Paradise Hotel by hitching a ride on the back of a truck that was in far sorrier condition than the airplane, and I had successfully endured breakneck speeds on roads that were made for bush carts only. I checked into my favorite room overlooking the harbor.

I had come at the request of the Chief Medical Officer in Vava'u who asked me to design new water systems for several small villages far to the south of the main island. I always looked forward to such requests, as they got me away from the hospital on Tongatapu. I had been a public health advisor there for some years and the work was rather droll at times. When I had the opportunity to travel to Vava'u, I had always taken my fishing equipment and made out as how the work would take much longer to accomplish than it actually would. I always personally allowed that no trip to Vava'u should last less than a week, and preferably longer.

After a shower and an hour's rest, I set out for a late afternoon walk to the Vava'u Club. About half a mile down the road I ran into Mosese, the local health inspector, sitting on the veranda of Robyn's restaurant. I asked him if I could borrow his ancient twelve-foot clinker boat that was moored in front of Carter's hotel for an early morning fishing excursion around the harbor. He allowed that I could, but insisted that his younger brother Finau come along. Of course, including his young brother was a ploy to ensure that, if I caught any fish, Mosese would get some or all of them. I understood this motivation, and it was fine with me.

I had no use for fish while living in the hotel anyway. Having completed these negotiations and the downing of some fresh coconut milk, I continued on my way, allowing the local atmosphere to lull me into a sense of timelessness.

The Vava'u Club hung precariously on top of a steep slope that tumbled several hundred feet into the western end of the harbor. It was a stately but tired old building that had seen more dignified days when the elite colonialistic British who built it here early in the century passed through its doors. From its hurricane-flapped windows there was a commanding view of the harbor entrance and Mount Talau. It was a fitting setting for exotic drinks and talk of trade and other matters of this part of the world. Now it was used mostly by locals as a beer joint and snooker room. Still, though, a sense of class remained that went beyond the worn and dirty floors and the smell of beer and cigarettes. As I walked in, I could see Tee and Sitiveni in a heated conversation at a table located at the harbor side of the room. They were seated next to a window and just underneath a stained and torn picture of some British Noble of seventy-five years earlier. They obviously had both been there a while and were well on their way to regretting it the next morning.

"He said he was going to Malinita Island. That's no more than a rock twenty miles out at sea. There's no one to help you out there if something happens," Tee was explaining heatedly. "He said he was going to be back an hour a—, Sir

Richard!" Tee exclaimed, when he glanced up and saw me coming toward the table. "When did you get in?"

"Good to see you mate," added Sitiveni. He stuck out his hand and I took it. "Sit down, I'll go get you a beer." Sitiveni had to fight his way through a crowd of boisterous drunks to reach the bar and order another round.

"I got in on the afternoon plane," I said to Tee while Sitiveni was making his way to the bar. "What's going on? Is there some sort of problem?"

"Yeah, it's Heinzie," answered Tee, a half disgusted-half worried look on his face.

"What about Heinzie?" I asked.

"He's been taking my boat out further and further nearly every day now. Today he said he would be back at three and it's already four," replied Tee. I empathized with Tee, realizing that he knew his boat was not the most seaworthy of craft. Sitiveni had built it several years earlier out of scrap plywood and had used various pieces of whatever he could scrounge out of Tee's yard for structural members. The roof of the small cabin was no more than an old piece of tin that Tee warned passengers not to put anything on, as it would collapse. Sitiveni had been repairing the leaks in the boat ever since. Nevertheless, Tee liked it because, as he always reminded people, "I'm not a maintenance person, so why should I have something I have to worry about? Besides, it's great for jigging out of."

"But not for going to sea in," I had always added to the explanation. But I knew Heinzie and his nearly obsessive ambitions always for a bigger fish, even though he never caught much to speak of. Heinzie went to sea in it.

Sitiveni returned to the table with six beers and explained that this would save one of us the next trip to the overcrowded bar. "I don't know how many times I've told Tee that Heinzie is going to kill himself in that boat if he keeps lending it to him. Besides, there are no fish out at Malinita anyway." Sitiveni was looking at me authoritatively.

After listening to a heated exchange about fish concentrations at Malinita, I found myself absentmindedly looking out the window toward the harbor entrance. I could see a small boat entering the harbor in the evening shadow of Talau. "Hold on, guys," I said, "Isn't that Heinzie?"

"I'll be damned; sure as hell is," said Tee, looking beery-eyed out the window. Tee looked at Sitiveni and relieved the pressure in his colon with a large trumpeting sound. Sitiveni looked disgustedly the other way. Within half an hour Heinzie was at the table with us and eight more beers had been brought. We had all forgotten about the concern for his being late and were anxiously awaiting an account of the trip.

"You should've seen it," Heinzie was saying excitedly in his thick German accent. "I really got a big one. It must've been at least thirty-pounds and, boy, did it fight. I bet I played it for at least half an hour."

"What was it?" asked Sitiveni.

"A big 'Ula. You know, one of those giant trevalle they got around here," answered Heinzie, as he gulped down the majority of a new bottle of beer in one draught. Telling the story obviously made Heinzie thirsty.

"There's no trevalle out at Malinita; they're only on the lee side of this island," Sitiveni pronounced. "It must be something else."

"Where's the fish?" asked Tee. "Let's look at it."

"Well, I hate to tell you guys this, but I couldn't gaff it 'cause the boat was rocking too much and my beer fell over. It got away." Heinzie justified the loss, but attempted to add credence to his story. "You better believe it. There are 'Ula out there. I seen it with my own eyes."

"I'm not going to kill myself going out to Malinita to find out," followed Tee. "Let's all go jigging in Port Morel on Saturday. I got at least fifty *vete* and *mohe'aho* there last week. Filled the whole bucket." Port Morel was a protected little inlet not far outside of the harbor entrance and one of Tee's favorite jigging spots. The *vete* (goatfish) never exceeded six-inches, and a large *mohe'aho* (a small bottom dwelling denizen) rarely broke four inches, but both Tee and his family, including the cat, loved to eat them.

"No thanks, Tee," I replied. "I want to fly-fish coral heads along the shorelines. Maybe I'll go out in the morning and try around the harbor. I've already arranged Mosese's boat."

"Good luck," replied Sitiveni, and he went into a long explanation as to why there were no catchable fish in the harbor, at least nothing over six-inches worth eating.

The conversation deteriorated into things I don't remember, and sometime late that night I managed to find my way to the hotel. Shrouded in the heady sweet tropical smells of night, blooming jasmine and frangipani, I crashed, dead to the world.

⊢⊣

I woke up the next morning with a very clouded head and a start. The sun was beginning to send shafts of light over the mountaintops and there was a head-splitting pounding on the door. "*Lisiate! Lisiate, Ko 'au, Finau. Tau 'alu o taumata'u.*" It was Finau, Mosese's brother, trying to wake me to go fishing. Lisiate was what all the locals called me, which was a transliteration of Richard.

There was nothing sacrosanct about mornings in Vava'u, and even though it was already all over town that I had arrived and was undoubtedly trying to sleep off the excesses of the night before, Finau was determined to get me up one way or another so that he could get some fish. It was no use resisting. Besides, an hour or two on the water might do wonders for my head.

"O.K., Finau, I'm up. You go down and get the boat ready. I'll be down shortly," I hollered back in the Tongan I had managed to learn over the past ten years. I pulled on a pair of shorts, grabbed my rod and fly box, and descended the steep stairway that led down to the waterfront.

The morning was beautiful and a perfect remedy for what I didn't remember of the latter part of the night before. We had decided to run to the end of the harbor and fish down the mile or so of reef that bordered the far shore. We would end up at the harbor entrance, which was an easy shot back across to the hotel. I planned to cast to shore line coral heads as we slowly moved down the shoreline. That way, I could cover the whole area in about an hour and be back for breakfast while there was still some left.

About half-way down the far shore I got a four-pound cora trout, which put up a respectable fight as it tried to dive back into its coral lair. Finau, who hadn't eaten breakfast, couldn't resist cutting off a chunk of fillet for a raw repast. This was a favorite way of taking fresh fish for the local people, which I also found quite satisfying on some occasions, this particular morning not being one of them. I looked the other way as he ate it with relish.

By the time we got to the harbor entrance, the whole side of Talau was ablaze with the light of the new morning sun shining on its spurs. I had intended to go back to the hotel, but the whole sight was so beautiful that I decided to take a quick run across the channel and fish a couple of coral heads bordering the mountain's flanks. Things in town would have to wait if I was a little late.

As we fished the base of Talau, it seemed that even Finau had forgotten about getting fish to take home. It was so enchanting. For me, casting my fly line was a graceful excuse to revel in the mountain and the incredible new day's light. The water was so calm and clear that we could watch coral and fish sixty feet down as if we were looking into an aquarium and it was so quiet that we could hear the fly line settle on the water even with the gentlest of casts.

"Did you hear that, Finau?" I asked as I turned around to look out toward the center of the channel. I could see ripples of water coming toward the boat from further out in the channel, but could not see much else because we were looking directly into the sun.

"*Io. Koe ha 'ia?*" Finau responded affirmatively and questioned what it was in a puzzled tone.

Then we saw it again. About two hundred feet out into the channel, just off the navigation buoy, a great silvery shape porpoised out of the water near where it had obviously done so just seconds before. The morning sun prevented us from seeing much more than the outline of the fish. Finau's eyes were as big as saucers, and mine must have been the same.

"Finau, pull the boat within casting distance of that fish, and be quick and quiet about it!" I excitedly ordered. Finau immediately responded, as I started stripping a few more yards of line off my reel.

I put the first cast fifty or so feet in front of where the fish had jumped and had to force myself to let the line and fly sink a bit. I had just started to retrieve the fly with short, quick strips when there was a heavy yank on the line. Then the line peeled off the reel as the fish headed out the harbor entrance.

The battle that ensued lasted close to an hour. Finau followed the fish like an expert boatman on Florida tarpon flats. The fish never broke water for the entire battle and though I doubted that I would be able to catch it, I still had hopes of getting it at least close enough to get a look at what it might be.

When the fish became too tired to run it sulked close to the bottom. I was sure that my eight pound tippet, with no shock tippet, would not be able to hold much longer, much less get the fish close to the boat. But then, the fish started slowly to ascend from what I assume was protected cover under the bottom of the boat. Finau and I both peered precariously over the side, me with fly-rod in hand and reeling at the same time. The boat tipped dangerously with all our weight on one side. At first we could only see the mint blue-silver color, and then, as the fish got closer, we could see its shape.

"What is it, Finau?," I asked. "It isn't a wahoo or a barracuda."

"*He'ilo*," responded Finau, not knowing either.

The fish stopped directly under the boat and lay there. We could see its tail sticking out from under the lee side, but we had neither gaff nor rope. "What are we going to do now?" I asked Finau. I was sure my line would part any second.

Finau instructed me to sit on the opposite side of the boat. Slowly he bent over the side and with a lightning thrust had his hands around the fish's tail, quickly pulling it up out of the water. Bracing both of his feet on the gunwale, Finau made his final effort, and slid the fish, which looked like it weighed almost as much as he, over the side and into the boat.

Finau immediately threw his body over the fish, whose head was now hanging over one side of the boat and its tail over the other. It was all he could do to keep it from flopping out of the boat or swamping us. I, in turn, with one quick thrust of my knife into the head, dispatched the fish. The prize was ours. It was a Spanish Mackerel of at least eighty pounds. We were exhausted and excited, me with having been able to land the fish, Finau with visions of a great feast for half of the Polynesian residents in Vava'u.

It took us the better part of another hour to get into the harbor, as we had been pulled quite a way out of the channel. A quarter mile before the wharf I pulled up the boat onto a small beach at the bottom of a cliff. Finau's residence was two hundred feet above us and there was a steep stairway that scaled the hill. Finau was up the stairs in a flash to find help to carry his prize home. By the time Finau and the two boys he had cornered were lugging the fish up the stairs, half of the population of Neiafu had already heard the news. There was a Saturday crowd of people waiting at the top of the hill to inspect the prize. I knew the fish would not last long.

⊢—⊣

That evening in the Vava'u Club, I excitedly sketched out the story of my catch to Tee, Heinzie, and Sitiveni. They sat and listened with skeptical interest.

"Impossible," pronounced Heinzie. "There's no way you could do that on your flimsy gear. How can I believe such a story?"

"No Spanish Mackerel in its right mind would come into the harbor," said Sitiveni authoritatively. "Besides, there aren't any in Tonga at all."

"It's easy to check," said Tee. "Show us the fish, Lisiate." Of course there was no fish to show; not a remnant would be left, as even the head was considered a delicacy in Tonga.

"Well," I conceded, "it was a good fish story anyway. What are you going to do Saturday?" I was looking at Tee and Heinzie.

"I think we should go to Malinita," stated Heinzie. "There's that huge 'Ulua out there, biggest fish in Tonga, and I'm going to get it."

"'Ulua, my wife's uncle," declared Sitiveni skeptically.

"No way!" said Tee. "You're going to kill yourself and lose my boat besides. Look," he added excitedly, as he exhausted a great trumpeting blow of gas loud enough to wake up the pigs that slept under the club, "I think we should go to Port Morel. I have a feeling the jigging's going to be great on Saturday. We can get a whole bucket full of *vete* and *mohe'aho* and then have a big feast at my place."

"Yeah," I agreed with pretended excitement. "Sounds like a great idea. Let's do it. You come to the feast, too, Sitiveni. We'll have a great time. Heinzie can bring the beer. Tee's wife is a great cook, you know."

Tee excitedly started telling about his last great fishing trip to Port Morel, while Sitiveni looked on skeptically. Heinzie disappointedly burped beer gas.

I looked out the window and watched the sun set behind Talau. It shot out streaks of light that changed the color of the evening clouds to brilliant blues, purples, and oranges. The exotic smells of night-blooming jasmine and frangipani drifted in the window with the same gentle breeze that blew away the remnants of Tee's gaseous insignia. "It will take about six or eight weeks for the developed photos of the mackerel to get back from Australia," I thought. "But then again, it doesn't really matter. The boys wouldn't believe it anyway."

THE COMPANION

Abu Faruk

WHAT I WILL always remember is the heat. Heat is the one thing you can never escape. Twenty-four hours a day you are uncomfortable—even at night the heat overrides everything. It is impossible to sleep, but if the evening winds roll over the river, you have a reprieve from the discomfort and the mosquitoes, so you pray for the winds. But here is the Nile, one of the greatest rivers in the world, and suffering is part of the adventure. The roots of civilization sprang from the Nile waters, and its allure brought me here.

I looked upon this trip from Alexandria to Aswan as a cleansing. I had just ended a long-term relationship—or rather, she ended it—and I had just finished a grueling prelim examination for my doctorate. Grueling, only because I had gone through the system rapidly, and they wanted me to pay. I paid.

The early morning smells on the Nile are unique: an acrid burnt odor hovers over the land, evidence of the countless dung-fueled fire hearths in the peasant homes along the river. Once you have experienced it, you'll never forget that smell. If you are lucky, there is a faint mist, the *shabura*; you cannot see it, but you can feel it. The disturbing part of the experience is that the more comfort the mist brings you, the hotter the day will be. The locals warned me of this, and they were right.

I had been working on the river for over two weeks,

collecting the Nile's fish and examining their diversity. Two months prior, I was in the Western Desert directing an archeological project; the predominance of fish remains at this remote site prompted me to search for a specialist to analyze the recovered bones. Because there was no authority to call upon, at least none that had been alive in the past fifty years, the task fell on me. If I was to finish my dissertation, then I had to identify the fish bones. To identify the fish, I needed modern examples for comparative analysis. It was a challenge I willingly accepted.

Having grown up on the waters of the Puget Sound, fishing the lakes and streams of Idaho and Washington all my life, I felt at home on the river. Sitting on a boat in the water felt natural to me, although outfitting provisions for the trip was a little different. Back home we adhered to the fisherman's basic food groups: caffeine, sugar, alcohol and salty snacks. Here, alcohol and salty snacks took a back seat to caffeine with plenty of sugar. My fishing partners Ibrahim and Hashem took caffeine consumption to its highest limits, knocking back shot after shot of syrupy tea by the hour. A tall cool one would certainly have made the fishing easier!

We were in search of the *isher bayad*, better known in English as the Nile perch, the largest freshwater fish in the world. These fish easily reach six feet in length and can weigh over two-hundred pounds. I had a modest research stipend, but by Egyptian standards, I was rich and thus we were well

outfitted with bait and tackle. I took my trusty salmon rod with me, which the locals referred to as "the club." It was a stout rod, with a deep-sea salt-water reel. Nothing fancy, but it had brought in its share of salmon and halibut off the coast of Washington.

Yet, with all the gear, the best of bait, and amiable, knowledgeable fishing companions, we had no fish. By the third day, my two compatriots began to mumble the name "Faruk." My Arabic was good enough to understand most conversations, but they knew that if they spoke rapidly and whispered, they could get complicated scenarios by me. What I did pick up was that Faruk was some sort of guru or mystic, and in his company things happened—fish were caught and in great quantities. Finally, after a fifth day of heat and no fish, Ibrahim approached me about Faruk. If we wanted the *isher bayad*, we had to try to bring Faruk on board. My first impression was that this was a scam and how much was it going to cost me to bring another of their buddies on board for a free fishing trip. I countered their request with a monetary limit for supply costs for an additional person. Both Ibrahim and Hisham looked puzzled. Finally, Hisham stepped in and with great reverence said that Faruk would come aboard of his own free will: he could not be coaxed, and he could not be intimidated or bribed. Faruk had no need of money. He chose to go and to do what he wanted and with whom he wanted. If we were lucky and if Faruk approved of us and came aboard, we would certainly be blessed with fish.

My interest was piqued, and seeing that, they explained further. Faruk was a mystical figure to the local fishermen. Egyptian fishermen, like all fishermen, are very superstitious. As we moved to an area of the river where Faruk was known to make occasional appearances, they introduced me to some of the Faruk fishing lore. In the area we were to soon fish, he could appear—any time, anywhere. His presence always was an omen for good fishing. Ibrahim said there was a time when three men were pulling in a two-meter long Nile perch. They had worked it all day and finally were able to bring it along side their small craft. After lashing it to the gunnels, they headed back to shore for a rest. There, somehow, sitting in the forward seat was Faruk. Hisham, not to be outdone, told of a time when late at night they had gone into a military zone to fish, thinking it would be rife with big ones. The area had not been fished in ages because of the army presence. Quietly and secretively, they positioned their small boat in the middle of the river and waited for a strike. Although risking a jail sentence or worse, they stuck it out and caught a beautiful string of *bolti*, many exceeding twenty-five pounds. As they came to shore, they saw movement in the bulrushes that lined the bank; they feared the worse, then out popped Faruk. How he got into a military area under total light surveillance, electronic surveillance, cameras, and a dense minefield, no one knew.

As an anthropologist, I knew that from a purely cultural perspective, I had to meet Faruk. For a day and a half I waited.

On the morning of our seventh day of fishing for the perch, Faruk walked on board. Faruk swaggered around the boat as if he owned it; he was arrogant with the attitude of a gangster. He was important, a boss, and he knew it. He looked us up and down; my companions held their breath, for this was a meeting with local fishing lore, with Nile royalty. I was totally shocked by his presence, and watched him closely. He was nothing like I expected. He was the connoisseur of disgusting, scratching at his privates as nonchalantly as if he were scratching his head. He turned his nose up at fresh fish or meat and dined happily on salvaged road kill we had intended to use for bait. Mouthwash not being big in these parts, I hoped our meeting would not include the customary cheek kisses. I even witnessed him urinate on the leg of a local tradesman we had lured in hopes of acquiring some gas for our stove—it was little surprise to me that no gas was forthcoming. In short, I did not view him as a savior but a social liability and I can honestly say that concerns for the quality of prose prevents discussing the "full milieu" of his habits.

Although I tried to keep my distance, particularly after the gas salesman affair, Faruk latched onto me. Ibrahim and Hisham were overwhelmed with joy that we were found to be acceptable company. I believe they were equally as happy that they were not singled out for special attention, as I was. In fact,

Faruk kept in such proximity to me, they began referring to me by the honorable title Abu Faruk.

We began fishing in earnest with a newfound confidence. Sure enough, within hours "the club" began to dance, and my reel began to sing. I had hooked a big one. I worked feverishly playing the fish, Faruk walking back and forth barking out orders: tip up, tighten the drag. After several hours, a six-foot Nile perch lay alongside the boat. It was true—Faruk had the power. As a reward he was given the cheeks of the fish, which he gobbled up eagerly. Faruk and I spent the next six months together, fishing. I managed to collect enough specimens to ensure completion of my dissertation as well as create a research collection unmatched in the United States.

When the time came for me to leave Egypt, I sat on the boat where I had shared so many adventures with Faruk, saddened by our imminent parting. Faruk, never much for conversation, stared at me with his all-knowing eyes as I contemplated our inevitable parting. We sat for probably an hour. I couldn't leave without him. I rushed to the embassy, to find sheer panic everywhere. I asked a Marine guard what was going on and found there was a crisis in Lebanon, and there was fear it might spread to Egypt. I told him I was trying to get out myself, but needed paperwork done for my companion. He allowed me in a side door and the appropriate paperwork was expeditiously completed and filed.

Next morning, at the airport Faruk and I found that our flight was cancelled, the plane having never left New York. We could, however, hop a plane to, where else, Beirut, with a connection to Athens, then Rome, and finally the United States. We decided to take it, and thirty-six hours later arrived in the United States. Incidents on the plane were many, including Faruk's independent attempts to gain special access to the mystery chicken dish served on board the flight, as well as an uncanny attempt to visit the city of Beirut under siege.

Faruk and I spent the next seven years together fishing. He was the best companion I ever had. And he *was* a mystic. Whenever he was on board, fishing was always spectacular. He had an innate sense of timing and territory, always knowing when and where to signal me to begin fishing. One would think that traveling to a new county, he would have been intimidated or even shy; this was never the case. I took him fishing everywhere. He was always sure of foot, even in roughest of waters. I never had to worry about him. He never wandered too far from the boat in unfamiliar areas or too close to unfamiliar people who might be prejudiced against his background. His complex nature clearly came through on our long fishing trips far from home. And, when I moved to Illinois to take a position at the university, he followed me. He was as the Nile fishermen say the *efreet*—the spirit, the one with knowledge.

What was most amazing about Faruk was that he was a

cat, and I didn't even like cats. He was one of kind, more like a dog in his loyalty and ability to travel and nearly human in his ability to communicate. He was the greatest fishing partner I ever had and my closest friend. Faruk finally succumbed to a congenital defect in one of his circulatory valves, but sometimes, I can still feel his presence and can still hear him barking out orders from the bow of the boat.

RAINBOW TROUT *Oncorhynchus mykiss mykiss*

AN EARLY WINTER

Daniel Stranahan

SOMEWHERE IN WESTERN Kamchatka, early in that Eastern dawn, while it was still dark and long before the stove in our yurt would be lit, and with a tent flap outside snapping violently in the wind where, through the scratched portal above my cot, I could see in the dim moonlight the dark clouds race furiously by, I lay awake, taking stock, and having badly to piss. I tried for sometime to fall back asleep, but the wind shook the yurt wildly. And while it was not raining evenly, every so often a gust of it would slash hard against the canvas walls, until finally, I found myself standing outside, fumbling in the blustery, cold, the riven, and utterly typical, Kamchatkan predawn. And alas, whilst I stood there waiting, I had this epiphany: the Vikings, and their goddamned treble hooks, were winning.

A week in camp, and I had felt the pull of probably nine steelhead, and still had handled none. It was a poor ratio. On this trip, the failure to bring a fish to hand was not only a failure to one's pride, but to science itself. We were here, after all, fishing for science—for the conservation of the species. These Russian *mykiss* were among the last of the great runs on earth. Our duty as sports was solemn and simple: go forth and fish for steelhead on the fly; collect scale samples and other life data; and return them peacefully to their diluvian cosmos.

At the end of each day, a group of scientists awaited us in camp and took our envelopes containing the scales and other data and entered them all into a larger data base which, in turn, recorded the life histories of several generations of these profound fish. I, however, had collected no scales. I had taped neither girth nor length, nor had I inserted a single tag. Svetlyana, the chief scientist, whose decades of ill-funded research might credibly place her among those who cared most about the fate of these fish, and who was like a den mother to the expedition, had clearly begun to regard me as her problem-runt. And like the runt, forever trying to do better, I resolved on that morning to do better. As the sky went from black to purple and the air warmed just a little bit, I let my relief carry generally into the wind—somewhere, I hoped, in the direction of the Viking's tent.

The Vikings were two brothers, Tom and John Erik, and their father Bjørnør—the three Norwegians with whom I had fallen in on this trip. They were a boisterous, big brood who embraced each other with a continuous and tempestuous bombast of shouted, loving abuse. It was an effort in which the sons were clearly outmatched by their father, and they had to team up daily just to stay even. They could all, admirably I thought, insult each other in evenly contemptuous salvoes of both Norwegian and English. And when the rude consonants of the Anglo-Saxon ran out, there were always harder and ruder ones to be pressed from the Norwegian. They were accomplished Atlantic salmon fishermen—a blood sport you might think from them—in native Norway. And with their stout tube-flies and razor-sharp trebles, their catch rate rollicked on.

We had all arrived five days ago in Petropavlosk, I from Anchorage, and they from Oslo. On our arrival at the airport, we were loaded into a van which took us for awhile through the town's dusty streets. What stand out now are the multiple, cantilevered concrete block houses, crowned with their thorny antennae. These aerials were different, and oddly, reflected for me some symbolism of a Soviet-Orientalism. We drove past groves of white birch trees stained to one side by diesel soot; past an old Soviet munitions yard housing gutted tanks and stripped out Migs; and then, for a long while down a dirt road which took us into the woods somewhere until we turned into a thicker wood where, hidden amongst the trees, was our hotel. It was also concrete, though less Sovietly so. A long, two-story cantilevered block—the bottom half painted a woodsy green, the top an old flaking cream.

I was given a room with Nick, who I had met on the flight in from Anchorage. There were two narrow wooden beds, each about the width of an average man's shoulders, whose mattresses sagged almost to the floor, so that when lying in them one was tightly ensconced, a bit too much like a coffin. There were thin slips of fabric covering the windows, and a taller slip hanging as the entrance to the tiny bathroom. It was like a student's garret, but in the woods. Nick pushed his bag under one of the beds, and sat down in a small chair by the window. He watched the breeze blow the light slip of fabric for a moment and then got up again.

"I'm going outside," he said, and left.

It was mid October, and mild enough still to enjoy the breeze through the window. The air was finally fresh out here, scented of birch and pine. I settled in on the narrow bed, and opened my book, a thick anthology of Turgenyev, and read for a few moments about snipe and old hunting dogs, then lay the book down on my chest and went to sleep. I sleep better with an open book on my chest, the older and heavier the better. I don't know why. The words put there so many years before are a comfort, their weight a warmth upon my heart.

That evening we assembled in the main room of the hotel. The room was not very large, and served as the dining room, bar and lobby. The front desk was in the hallway opposite the front door, where an old babushka sat with a rotary phone and notebook, both perched atop an old steel ice-cream cooler. It was the Sunday turnover day, with incoming and outgoing sports. Before long, the small room was a crush of fishermen. Some were on their way home, and others like me, on their way, the next day, out to the camps. There were others too, an Anglo-Italian group who were here on a climbing expedition, and various Russians also here to climb, and a group of petro-geologists whom I recognized from my flight.

I took a seat at an empty table and was soon joined by

Steve. A young man in his thirties, in very dirty khakis and a crumpled, blue dress shirt. He looked as though he'd gotten horribly lost last casual-Friday. He cradled a bottle of vodka in the crook of one arm.

"You look as excited as the rest of them," he said, sitting down and pouring himself a glass of vodka at the same time. He looked for awhile at the jostle of fishermen around us. Truthfully, I was excited. And, unsure of his approach.

"Are you fishing or climbing?" I asked.

"God, neither," he said.

"Why are you here then?" I asked.

"I am searching for my father," he said. "You haven't seen him?"

He laughed. "I was stood-up in Anchorage. I signed us on for three weeks. It's his birthday, or it was last week. I don't think he ever left L.A."

"Have you been to the camps?" It was still the beginning of my journey, and my mind, like my body, could move in only one direction.

"Yes. Out and then back again," he said. "They recognize me on the helicopters now. The helicopters are shit, by the way. Prepare to die."

"Anyway, I'm waiting for a seat to clear back to Anchorage." He smiled, and then poured me some of his vodka, and pushed it across the table.

"I'm waiting for your seat to clear," he said.

"I'll be needing mine. Thanks," I said. "They only fly once a week."

"Yes, I know that. And they're pretty full too, for Eastern-fucking-nowhere."

He seethed again at the crowded room. "I wish one of you would just have a bad fall out there, and give me my seat home."

"You don't fish?

"No," said Steve.

"Your dad?"

"I thought it'd be special if we learned together." This last was a sneer.

"Good luck," I said. "I'll be back in two weeks." He got up and went away.

The young, blond girl who had checked us in now tended the bar. She was transformed in an old, red tube dress, her face heavy with pancake. Gradually, there were other girls. They arrived on the arms of big, Russian bearish looking men in leather coats. A group of them stood around in the hallway, before the old babushka took them down into the rooms. In waves they came and went, some were quite young.

Slowly, the room got drunk. The food, which was pushed away after a few bites anyway, was quickly replaced with vodka. The din grew louder, and some of the night-time girls began to mix with the sports. I saw the petroleum geologist sit a girl on his lap while she fed him drags from a cigarette.

Along the length of the back wall there was a gloomy bar that loomed heavily over the room. Arranged on the shelves behind it were dozens of brands of Russian vodka. These were all national brands, and they came in smaller sizes, half-liters, to allow, I suppose, for a more personal, a more reflective alcoholism. The bottles were strangely packaged, some wrapped in cheap foil like last minute gifts, and others capped in fantastical plastic spires, like the onion domes of St. Basil's. Behind the shelves and the bottles was a large mirror, patinaed and stained with smoke, and tinted a garish bronze, so that this big byzantium of booze was reflected back upon the room in a turgid, lurid glow.

Before long the group zeroed in on an expensive looking brand in a brown bottle, and soon these were everywhere; pushed together in small clusters at the center of each table, double fisted in the hands of charging, heroic fishermen. As outgoing fishermen comingled with the incoming, and stories of big steelhead were confirmed, as we realized that we had come to the right place, that this outpost in the East was not just a confusion, then the din fairly roared and the excitement grew.

The room soon swayed, and a person getting up too quickly at one end was likely, at the other, to send another flying. Such was the state of things. And the tawdry bar, smoke-stained and overwrought, looked over us all. I half expected to see the commiserative visage of some Eastern

Icon, beclasped and worrying the room over—a Constantine or Vladimir, peering out from its patinaed glow.

I awoke around midnight, dried-out and unable to sleep. Outside my room's balcony, in a little courtyard under the trees, was a rustic thermal pool, built from cedar; it steamed under the stars and the boughs of the birch trees. A fresh breeze blew in through the window where the moon was bright, and I sneaked down to the pool in my towel, slipped into the hot water, and soaked for awhile in the bright night. I listened to the sounds of the Russian woods, of the familiar made foreign, and to a faint, human sound—a girl upstairs with her trick.

The helicopters flew fine, and that is all one should know. They flew us fine through a high snowy gap in the mountains and out over the flattened drainages of Western Kamchatka. In about three hours we arrived at the camp, which was set on a steep highbank, above a channel of the Utkholok River. Laid out in a square, the camp had on its east side the highbank and river for a boundary. To its north was the kitchen-dining tent, a walled outfitters tent with a wood floor; the store tent, a blue yurt; and a little beyond on the fringe and out of the wind was the outhouse, whose main amenity was a squishy foam seat that held ones warmth well. Parked to the side of the outhouse was a Soviet-era armored personnel carrier, a full track, covered partially in blue tarp and snow. On a make-shift rack, set next to the half-track, chunks of caribou meat were hung out to dry.

The east and south boundaries of the camp were formed into a smart backwards "L" of large four-man expedition yurts. They were orange and sprouted from the tundra like great fungi. These were set up over loose two-by-eight lumber, were tall enough just to stand in, and had cots upon which we slept high off the floor.

The centerpiece of each yurt was a rusty firebox made of thin steel with a stove-pipe rising out of the roof. On the end of each box was welded a perforated cylinder that looked like a large-caliber flash-suppressor, and through this the Russians would jet a stream of kerosene onto the wood inside and so stoke the little tinderbox that its sides would quickly glow red. An old soup can slid over the perforated end and allowed you to carburete the blaze. But usually, no matter the amount of tinkering, the box just glowed red anyway, and it was easier to moderate your own body temperature than that of the stove. At nighttime, when we sat and talked, told jokes and drank our vodka, our confabulations included a lot of dressing and undressing as one might remove a sweater here, in mid-sentence, or add a second layer there, listening to a reply.

The steel fire-boxes did not last the night, but before long you were warm in your sleeping bag and deep adrift in sleep until morning. Then, just before dawn, one of the camp staff would sneak into the yurt, and before you had time to wake fully and register the plastic crinkle of the kerosene bottle (they did not trust the sports with the fuel), the rusty box would glow red again. Often I shook my eyes awake just upon noticing the fleeting black boot of the firestarter as he slipped back out the door.

By breakfast we stank of kerosene, yet mornings in the dining tent were leisurely. We'd eat and then drink coffee for an hour and wait for the sun to warm up Kamchatka, if it would. On some mornings we'd play poker. One morning I came into the tent and found Bjørnør there teaching the Russians to play. The Russians spoke no English, did not play poker. So, he dealt the cards. And, arranged their hands for them. And, managed their bets for them. And then, invariably, he took the pot from them. As a guest in a Russian camp, whose staff were primarily veterans of the Soviet-Afghanistan war, and who were now the demobbed and forgotten minions of a bankrupt Russian military, this game began to feel a little dangerous. So, I sat down for a few hands and made sure to lose them all. He smiled at this.

"Going to keep the peace are you, eh?"

If you let Bjørnør smile at you, you were his, plain and simple. And very soon into the trip I was his, and the guides were his, and the Russians, this camp was his. The first night in camp our American director tried to explain to him that the dining tent was non-smoking. Bjørnør just smiled at him

and shook his head and lit his cigarette anyway. And that was that. The tent was pro-smoking again, which endeared us to the staff.

Bjørnør was about six-foot-six, and his sons not too far behind him. The three of them were at the end of a year spent travelling the world as a family. The mother had come around as far as Oslo, and there the boys had left her for their Kamchatka expedition. There was a third brother, a little brother, a golden child. Taller than his father. And he had died a year ago. He died in a fall; a random, stupid thing. And in the year since, the family had stuck together.

I learned this thing about Vikings: that their history, the narrative of their culture and race, is really predicated upon the aggressive introduction. So with these three there was little time for friendship before the social pillage began. They slandered me, I slandered them back, and so was brought into their fold. They told jokes and old stories from their previous travels. These never let up. When Tom started in on a joke the old man's eyes would begin to twinkle—he knew all the jokes, I realized, but was not trusted to get them right. And as he followed the narrative his eyes would squint and his mouth form into a puckish grin, his head would quickly nod, hurrying the punchline, though he never gave it away. Clearly, he loved more to let his sons tell them and they told them well, keeping most of us in laughs for two weeks. The jokes and tales kept coming, from one meal to the next. A joke was often the last thing I heard before drifting to sleep, and then again the first thing I heard before fully waking. I heard one as Tom and I passed each other on the path to the outhouse; another while shaving at the outdoor sink. Many were told above the whine of the jetdrives, their punchlines shouted between the boats as we sped back to camp from the river. After dinner, when the tables were cleared and the bottles swept away, still they came, one after another, cracking on. And in the midst of the laughter, often I would catch the old man's face, which, in this continuous telling, would look upon his sons with an urgent love.

On the morning of my rueful epiphany, facing outward into the dark expanse beyond the camp, the sky went from black to purple and gradually to blue. The camps create a false boundary, one that diverts the gaze, keeps one's focus in. When I had to get up at night, I walked behind the Yurt and faced out. The Yurts faced in, onto the camp. Behind them, was without. To face without one faced Kamchatka and was made small, the hugeness of the land pressing in on you. To face within, one faced the camp. Any camp. It was essential therefore to look outward, to look away from the locus of the camp, in order that you look at Kamchatka. Although, that is a conceit—Kamchatka, rather, looked at you.

That morning I fished downstream with Ed. We went far downriver to within a few miles of the river's confluence with the Sea of Okhotsk. The runs here were named things

like Next to Last and Last. It was the end of the line for a river fisherman. Close enough to the see that your fly could get swept upstream by a change in the tides. The barometer had dropped, and off the Okhotsk there blew a cold wind. With the air temperature in the low thirties neither of us wanted to measure the water temp. The water was cold, we both agreed, and tried not to pay too much attention to the shelf ice forming at the river's edges.

Earlier that week I had fished with Ed and he, at my invitation, fished behind me, taking three fish from runs through which I had just swung my fly. I was new to spey casting, and it was good for me to watch him work through a run. Ed—Ed Ward—is well regarded as one of the sport's young masters. And with him fishing upstream of me I found the audible rhythms of his casting were like a metronome to which I could adjust my own play: anchor, sweep around and cast; anchor, sweep around and cast. He worked the two-hander low and close to the belly, his fists doing a sort of dance there and then. "Aim for the treetops," he would say, before throwing the line straight and beautiful, with a tight, unfurling wedge that clove the sky in two. With a deft mend, the big, winter fly was swum through the current. And three times that day I watched the line pull tight; and watched Ed set the hook home, as he was rewarded with that sound, the heavy head-shake of a steelhead as it first comes to the surface.

A note about that sound. Sit a group of steelhead anglers

together and they will share with you the minutiae of their sport. What stands out for each about their fish will often be different. Some are in it for the jumps, others for the reel screaming runs, and many more say they are all about the grab—that moment when the steelhead takes the fly into its mouth and turns, when the hook is set and the line goes tight. Others are happy simply to watch their flies swim in the water. One friend of mine wants only to catch a fish, and then sit on the bank and drink wine, and turn the water over to his friends. But what I love are the sounds of the sport. And in particular, that sound: when a steelhead is first hooked and it thrashes its head at the surface before it runs and spools you senseless, or takes flight and cartwheels into memory, or whatever. That sound, a counter-point to the river's own notes, to the quiet reverie of a day spent on the water, is when, suddenly, the river is cleaved open and in that heavy displacement of water I am awakened into the present. Of this, the present, Blaise Pascal wrote, it "is never our end. The past and the present are our means, the future alone our end. Thus we never actually live, but hope to live." When I read this I knew that it was true. And, I also knew that as with the present, so would I always be lost to that sound.

The fish Ed brought to hand that day shone brightly in a rare sun, we taped them and took the scales and tagged them. Then we admired them, they never left the water but one, a thirty-seven by twenty-two-inch doe, which Ed hoisted

briefly for a quick picture. Now, three days later I was ready to catch a fish, and Ed, discretely I think, asked if I didn't mind if he went off to take some pictures of the landscape. I didn't mind, and he had shown me much and now the only thing I lacked was the absence of an audience. Something Ed, the good instructor, seemed to know.

It had snowed a little and the shelf-ice creaked at the river's edge. On the opposite bank I watched a red fox weave through the tall grass, her tail bobbing in and out of the dense clusters of blades. The tail stopped suddenly once, going rigid, and I could see back in the grass from within a dark mask her eyes blinking as she carefully looked upon me. I stripped line from my reel and let it hang down in the current below me. The run was flat, with a good flow, but marked mainly by subtle wrinkles on its surface. These might indicate a slot, or a salmon redd, or a log sweeping out from the tundra bank opposite. I cast and worked down, getting a feel for the run's volume, adjusting the angle of my swing, mending, checking the flies pace—giving it swim, as I had come to think of it. I thought some about the fox. People talk of spirit animals…it is a flaky talk, but still. My toes began to numb.

When I looked around again, I saw that I had worked down to the tailout. The run dumped off into a narrow little riffle, but here in the slick tailout there were mostly more wrinkles. Sometimes the wrinkle was pronounced, like a boil, a salmon redd usually, or a rootwad held under the surface. And, other times it was hardly noticeable. A wrinkle, literally. A wink in the surface of the river's flow, put there mysteriously, where there was no branch, or current-seam or gravel shelf to explain it. A phenomenon of the water itself: its own language-pattern, like the smoke from a cigarette, but of the water. Of the water, the mountains, the sea—and of the compulsion of their own mysterious will.

I cast to the wrinkle for no better reason than its mystery, aiming for the treetops, which were backlit nicely by a gray sky. The line straightened out much like Ed had shown me, though not as far, nor either as predictably fine, yet it found its target. I flipped a mend into the line, swimming it through, down into the wrinkle were I slowed it with another mend and there it stopped, before the current caught it again, swinging it out to the middle of the river—a mystery after all—where it stopped again, hard.

Did I tell you it was cold? It was, and in that cold a muted stillness reigned. The sky to the west was of a deepest gray, a beautiful, silent gray—all thunder and quiet. And Kamchatka was suddenly large and empty. Cold and mute and stilled, and I alone in it. But for that sound—of the river's opening up, of a flashing boil upon its surface, a bright shining buck, and of the present come breaking into life.

His wrist was double mine and with a twenty-one inch girth I held him deep in the icy water where his gillplates glowed rosily, refracting and pulsing while the river rushed over. We did the science, my hands went numb. Ed steadied him and took some scales. Then we taped him.

"…by thirty-six," Ed said. "A nice fish."

"The nicest ever," I said.

We sent him on his way, then I went to the boat and rested, while Ed took a few more pictures of the river, and soon the sky began to darken. Ed returned and started up the boat and I climbed in.

"You know," I said, "we never tagged him."

Ed stood up, smiling, and pointed the bow upstream, "I know."

That night we drank the Norwegian's Aqua Vit, then the beer and then the rest of the vodka. The Russians collected at the other table, laughed and played cards, and smiled among themselves. Tom and John told the remainder of their jokes, and when they had done, Tom disappeared into our yurt for a few minutes and came back with more. I asked him where he had gone, "My Palm," he said, and held up a PDA. "More jokes." Bjørnør looked fondly on his sons. These would be the last moments of autumn, the last hours of the fall run. We had all had enough. We were all happy. Outside the wind blew. It howled outside the dining tent, howled when I went out to the tundra beyond the camp, and howled some more as we got into our bags and went to sleep. The next day the snow coated the ground in winter. And we were done.

NIOKOLO KOBA

Aaron Alter

A FAMILIAR CLOUD OF dust, risen from the road to chase our remodeled Toyota pickup, settled on us as we rocked to a halt. The taste of eight months of rain which hadn't fallen on southwestern Senegal was fresh in our mouths. Behind us tire tracks led a path over cracked, brown savannah.

The dilapidated Niokolo Koba National Park guard station, with no signs of human life, fit in perfectly. This was a place that, after months of drought, seemed to have been left to the animals. The black plastic of the seat which seemed to peel away from us was the last result of the hot, dry, cracked landscape. Following our guide, knees aching after hours in our safari-mobile, we slowly wound our way through leafless trees. Overcome by the mid-day heat, a large warthog did little more than grunt to acknowledge our presence.

At the end of the forest our small trail seemed to disappear into the heavy air in front of us. The Gambia River, which I had to convince myself wasn't a mirage, filled the valley below. This was wild Africa, a place that, despite enormous population and developmental pressure, remained almost untouched.

After spotting a large troop of baboons socializing on exposed river rocks, a small herd of Roan antelope drinking cautiously in the distance, and the hippos silently holding their dominance in the depths, the majority of the group returned for siesta at the guard station. It had been a long day, and riding over the unpaved roads was tiring. Personally, the river had suddenly provided me with a boost of energy. I ran back to the pickup to grab my travel rod, tackle box, and enough sunscreen to safely protect an entire village. This was it, one of the few places left on earth that I was sure bred fish of a mythical caliber.

I tried to picture where the fish had to be holding. Riffles, exposed branches of fallen trees, a huge boulder, all the makings of what seemed like the Mecca of fishing holes. Then I saw him.

Squatting on the top of an exposed rock, intently watching the twitches of his fishing line, was the oldest man I had ever seen outside of a nursing home. A small dugout canoe rocked in the water next to him. Here I was, in what had to be the finest fishing hole I'd see in a lifetime and all I could do was watch. With an old spool of monofilament wrapped around a rectangular chunk of wood, a meticulously sharpened hook and chunks of meat I watched him systematically pull out catfish, each time carefully avoiding the larger but apparently less appealing fish which waited near the surface.

He knew I was watching him; careful glances studied the way I reacted to his performance. The fisherman inside of me wanted to believe that we were one in the same, two people from completely different lives connected by the river, the fish, the memories and the dreams which such a place grew. He had seen my eyes light up each time one of the big fish which waited at the surface surged towards his hook. He had

noticed the way I studied the river; knew the images which filled my head each time my attention stopped at a spot that was sure to hold a legend of a fish.

After catching what I assumed was a day's worth of catfish, he quietly gathered up all his gear and sat down. For several minutes he just watched the river, and smiled. Seemingly pleased, he used his little boat to return to dry land, shook my hand, and disappeared back towards the guard post. I had never been more ready to fish.

After putting the four-piece rod together and threading the dark green super-braid through the guides I reached an important stage in any fisherman's day: what would catch the big one? Fishing in a place that had only ever been fished by an old man with a wad of meat, my options seemed endless.

Looking through my tackle box, my eyes jumped from poppers, to in-line spinners, to huge jigs, to all forms of plastics, buzz baits, spoons, and then on a familiar red and white pattern. If there was one lure which had proven itself versatile enough to catch fish, and often the big fish, anywhere, this was it. The biggest Daredevil my local fishing shop had to offer.

Assuming that the handshake had meant that I was welcome to use his dugout canoe, I put all my equipment in the bottom of the boat, pushed it out a little, jumped in, and was off. I had watched large fish chase the old man's meat once it hit the water in the shallows. The only logical decision

I could make, as a result, was to find the deeper water, where the parents of these shallow-water youngsters were waiting.

I paddled confidently. It wasn't long before I was out past the old man's perch, passing in to slower moving, deeper water. Eventually, I stopped paddling, letting the canoe drift towards the bank. An over-confident cast later and I had to paddle in to recover the daredevil from a tree. Cursing myself for misplacing even one cast in this ideal location, I was determined to make it my last.

Untangled, regrouped and ready to go. I decided to move farther up stream to where there was a big rock in the middle of the river, away from any additional snags. On a mission, I was careful even with my paddling. I worked hard to make each stroke silent, not wanting to scare any big fish away.

Gliding towards the rock, I watched intently. Directly in front of me, something swirled beneath the water with enough force to create little waves that lapped against my boat. Any experienced fisherman knows this feeling, when you are finally in the perfect place at the perfect time and the perfect fish shows itself.

Unfortunately, after its head emerged from the water and it loudly shot the water out of its nostrils, I realized that my perfect fish was actually a five-thousand-pound female hippo that I had, so cautiously, sneaked up upon. Now, to be fair, my mind did not completely shut down with shock. Three images crossed my mind: a photo from a National

Geographic special which showed a hole in a man's leg which they referred to as "large enough to hold a beer bottle," the result of having been attacked by a notoriously aggressive male hippo; a fancy graph which ranked hippos in the top three most deadly animals in all of Africa; and beautiful, large fish waiting to be caught back in the shallows.

It took a minute for the big lady to even notice my boat as it drifted towards her. When she did, she let out a noise so loud that it caused a normally very agile baboon to fall out of the palm tree next to me in to the river. The baboon, clearly shocked, swam spastically back to land, where it yelped its way up the bank. It isn't often that jealousy works its way back down the evolutionary ladder.

The hippo dove back under the water. My boat, still moving fairly quickly after my careful paddling, floated right over him. Seizing the moment, I grabbed the paddle and started making frantic stokes. Sometimes things have to get worse before they can get better, and directly off to my left a baby hippo rose to the surface. For a moment I just agreed that this had to be my time, that being put in between a mother hippo and her baby was just my way out. It took a loud splash, announcing the resurfacing of the mother, to knock me out of my self-pitying stream of conscience.

Remembering that what I was paddling away from was several thousand pounds heavier than what had just surfaced next to me, I quickly convinced myself that nothing additional had happened, and continued my retreat.

Behind me, it sounded like a car was racing through the water as loud splashing seemed to chase me towards the shallows. I didn't turn around to check, but unless my senses were truly skewed, the hippo was not far behind.

I doubt that anyone has ever paddled like that before, but I will never question it. The next thing I remember is the sound of gravel against wood as my dugout canoe hit the banks. I quickly jumped on to dry land and ran to the edge of the steep valley. When I finally turned around, the entire scene was as peaceful as ever. In the depths a baby hippo rolled, just under the surface.

I slowly walked back towards the little boat, constantly scanning for any sign of my new, personal demon. Once there, I collected all my fishing supplies and started the walk back to the guard station.

Playing the whole thing back through my head, it was hard to comprehend what had just happened. Was I dead? No, that didn't seem likely. Maybe I had just learned a lesson, that even fishing can be potentially deadly.

When I got back, all of my friends were asleep. I searched eagerly from body to body, trying to find someone awake enough to listen to my story. Eventually I caught eyes with the old man. He was sitting, frying his catfish over a homemade charcoal grill. He smiled at me, walked over and handed me his rectangular chunk of wood, a freshly wrapped piece of meat and a knife. Pointing towards the river, he made a little gesture that I now know as the universal motion for "shallow" and patted me on the back.

SCRATCHING THE SURFACE, IN BORNEO

Peter Fong

THE GOOD SHIP *Jellyfish* is a narrow fiberglass hull amply powered by a ninety-horse Mariner. Its home port is Kota Kinabalu, a city of 200,000 Malaysians on the island of Borneo. The gunwales sport a single functional rodholder, and the deck behind the console is awash with empty pop cans and cigarette packs. There are six of us aboard. Paisal, Basiri, and their two cousins are the locals. None has yet to outlive his teens. Larry and I are the tourists. Although we have just met, thrown together by an international conference of educators, I can tell by his duct-taped collection of rod cases that we have at least one noble trait in common.

I tote a few pounds of tackle wherever I go, and typically much more than that. Since this week on Borneo is not a dedicated fishing expedition, I have brought only five outfits: nine-weight fly, six-, twelve-, and fifteen-pound spinning, and thirty-pound conventional. I feel comfortable with this range of gear, knowing I can target everything from big mullet to small marlin. Not entirely secure, but comfortable.

To begin the afternoon, we run north of the city's concrete office blocks and into the mouth of a turbid river lined with mangroves. But the tide is wrong there, so we motor back into the South China Sea and tie up to a barnacle-encrusted freighter swinging on a permanent mooring. When that fails to produce, we anchor over an inshore patch reef. At any one time at least three of us are fishing, and we have utilized all the available technology—everything from handlines and sardines to high-density sinktips and Clouser minnows.

Though he does not own the *Jellyfish*, Paisal enjoys the role of captain. He chain-smokes, makes sporadic calls on his cellphone, accepts when I offer to share the roast duck purchased from a stall with the winning name of Big Old Brother Fast Food. We talk a little about his uncle (a commercial tuna fisherman), about the weather, about the pleasures of fishing and the perils of making a living in a global economy. Then it is time to return to the jetty, where my wife and children have promised to meet me.

I stow the fly gear and rig the twelve-pound spinning rod with a magnum Rapala. Trolling back towards the concrete towers, their windows gleaming under the hard sun, I feel a slight bump, as if the lure has snared a shred of weed. When I sweep the rod tip back, a few yards of line slip from the drag. I lean on it again, and there is the slight but unmistakable throb of a fish. I pump and reel briskly, curious to learn what the sea has offered. All of us peer over the side to mark the flash of blue and silver, fringed with bright gold. A small yellowfin tuna.

I toss the lure back in the water and ask Paisal to take another turn in the bay. The next fish is a real scorcher. After a few minutes, the spool begins to look dangerously empty, so Paisal gives chase with the boat. A long battle begins. The fish makes a brace of deep runs, and we all think tuna. Then there are several stiff headshakes, and the line rises towards the surface. The gleaming flank is long and trim, almost white in the depths. Mackerel perhaps. Then the head looms into view—barracuda. And a big one at that.

There is no gaff, of course. Everyone leans toward the water, and I caution Paisal not to touch the line. Together, the two smaller boys manage to boat the fish, one grabbing the short wire leader, the other latching on to the thick wrist at the base of the barracuda's tail. Their movements are swift and competent, and I am mightily impressed. We all laugh and celebrate and admire the fish. I don't have a tape, so I measure the brute with a length of shock tippet. (Later, back in the hotel room, the coil of mono will stretch to fifty-one inches.)

Now it's Larry's turn. I hand him the rod with the magic lure, while Paisal swings the *Jellyfish* in a wide arc. Before we can find another taker, however, a wooden-hulled water taxi cuts close across our stern. The drag whines; Larry curses. The boys listen attentively to this unfamiliar English phrasing, then the line parts.

People find themselves on Borneo—the world's third largest island—for any number of reasons. Most have no choice in the matter; they are simply born here. Others are attracted by wild tales of orangutans and headhunters, virgin jungles and unspoiled reefs. Unlike these adventurers, I merely followed my wife. (And towed our kids.) To tell the truth, Sarah is the international educator, while I make awkward attempts at an international education.

Back at the jetty, in the long shadow of the Hyatt Hotel, Sarah fends off the touts hawking island excursions and snorkeling trips. Though persistent, they are not entirely irksome. A few hours earlier, Paisal was one of them. He'd offered to take me fishing for one-hundred ringgit, about twenty-five U.S. dollars, so how could I refuse?

We show off our fish, and the boys ask us to wait while they clean the catch. For a moment, I'm tempted by the prospect of yellowtail sashimi, but Sarah and I already have plans for dinner: steamed clams, chili prawns, conch with ginger. I tell Paisal to keep the fish. The boys grin broadly, then I reserve their boat for the next afternoon too.

My son Dave takes Larry's place in the *Jellyfish*. He is in the second grade, and likes to fish, but a short chop provides even more fun. He stands holding the bow rail, laughing uproariously as the hull hammers through each wave. We spy a free-jumping marlin, but can't establish contact. After a fruitless hour of trolling, then a brief stint with a live trevally under a balloon, Paisal and Basiri invite us to their village.

The Kampung is a conglomeration of stilt huts stretching far out into a sheltered bay from an island named Gaya. The entire community hovers above the water, linked by rickety walkways and weathered boards, complete with shops and a mosque. Every household has at least one working boat, and

the resident cats and chickens might pass their whole lives without ever touching topsoil.

Basiri, the elder brother, introduces us to his wife, his two grandmothers, his uncle. Yesterday's barracuda, he tells me, has fed all of these people and more. I admire the rooms, furnished with neatly made beds and bare wooden tables. As we talk, he gently guides his two-year-old son back from the edge of the boards. I ask if the toddler has ever fallen into the water. Basiri shakes his head. Not yet.

I read a lot of fishing magazines, most of them word for word, even the classifieds. I'm tempted of course by the ads that promise "Sailfish on a Fly" or "Tarpon Guaranteed." But then again, if the fish were actually guaranteed, would I really want to go? In our recent travels through Asia, I have sometimes declared victory just by wetting a line, whether I find fish or not.

More and more these days, my pleasure lies in the confrontation of limits. I used to love fly-fishing because it seemed like the most elegant and effective means of catching trout. I still love it, but now I appreciate the frequent opportunities for humility, tempered by the occasional moments of transcendence. (Which also explains my passion for duck hunting—but that's another story.)

For our final day on the water, Paisal recommends that we try Pulau Tiga. That is the island where his uncle goes to make big catches, but it's thirty-miles away, too long a run for the *Jellyfish*. Tiga also is the island where the first episodes of Survivor were filmed, but Sarah and I don't let that stop us. We buy a road map, rent a car, and set out for Kuala Penyuh, the hamlet nearest to Tiga. As it turns out, driving in Borneo is an absorbing experience. There's the predictable assortment of vehicles—nimble sports cars, sluggish passenger vans, and suicidal motorbikes—along with the acknowledged king of the jungle: the fully loaded logging truck. The highway surface vacillates from dirt to gravel to asphalt, in various stages of disrepair. During the frequent blinding downpours, water fills the potholes to the brim, creating the illusion of a level pavement. And if you require any further distraction, you can keep one eye on the fickle parade of bicyclists, pedestrians, cats, dogs, goats, and water buffalo.

Nevertheless, we arrive intact at the harbor, and I make my first inquiries for a charter at a Chinese grocery. The proprietor sends me to the Shell station. The manager there hazards a few phone calls, without success. I walk out to the jetty, where a fiberglass center console outfitted with twin Honda outboards rocks alongside a rusted trawler. There are two men on the trawler, swinging from hammocks, and a group of local twenty-somethings standing on the pier, wearing T-shirts that proclaim "I Survived Pulau Tiga." I ask about the skiff, but nobody seems to know its owner.

I try the hardware store next, and am directed to another Chinese grocer, who walks me to an open passageway

between two stilt houses, shielded from the sun by a blue plastic tarp. A bald man sits shirtless in the shade. When he smiles in greeting, I can see both of his teeth.

"You want fishing?" he says. "I give you your choice." He waves a hand towards two plank hulls, each about twenty-five-feet-long. Both feature a large insulated fish-box just aft of amidships, backed by a tiny cabin scarcely roomy enough for a short man to sit cross-legged inside. I can see no evidence of inboard engines, and the transoms are bare.

Three-hundred ringgit, the man says. About seventy-five dollars.

I am artlessly skeptical.

We do everything for you, he continues. Got everything you want. Then he leads me into a storeroom. It is chock-full of outboards, American and Japanese, some vintage, some new.

I choose a newer-looking Evinrude and, remembering Paisal and the *Jellyfish*, suggest that one-hundred ringgit might be more fair. He does not respond.

"O.K.," I say, "Two-hundred." But the bald guy can read me like an open checkbook.

When we clear the harbor channel, I drop a small jethead back in the propwash. At full throttle, our hull speed feels like twelve knots. That's about right for this lure, which bubbles enticingly, but it looks lonely back there. Without rodholders, however, I don't dare another flat line, and I haven't packed any teasers. During the short run to Tiga, the only look we get is from a black-naped tern, who makes a half-dozen earnest stabs at the lure before veering to the north.

Although we've named our daughter Marina, she loves the beach far more than the water. She and Sarah disembark at the dock serving Tiga's lonely-looking guest house. No one emerges to greet them. The two are equipped with masks and snorkels, a bottle of spring water, a takeout carton of chicken rice, and a warm can of Guinness. Dave and I promise to pick them up in a few hours, then the boatman backs into the sea.

The waters near Tiga are clear and green, deepening to blue as we cross the reef. I try to convince the boatman to troll parallel to the reef line, but fail to make myself understood. With no apparent instinct for fish-catching, he steers the craft in lazy loops and arcs. I snap on a deep-diving plug, hoping for grouper, then brace my back against the cabin, gripping the rod in one hand. The bottom wavers from sand to grass to coral, while the sky gleams with fierce white clouds. Dave reclines on the fish-box, shades his eyes with a book. I scan the surface for signs of life. Nothing.

When my right arm tires from the constant throb of the lure, I switch to the left, and use the right to eat and drink. First the water, then the chicken rice. At a moment when the plastic fork is poised in mid-air, something raps pointedly on the plug. I lean forward, upending the carton of food, and give the lure a fetching sequence of twitches. That does the trick. I set the hook several times, then once more for luck.

The fish responds by ripping off nearly 200 yards of line. The scream of the drag wakes the boatman, who looks amazed at this new turn of events. After that initial burst, the fight is routine. It's a narrow-barred Spanish mackerel, what the locals call *tenggiri*, about fifteen-pounds. Again there is no gaff, so I hand the rod to Dave, move to the transom, and swing the fish aboard.

The boatman looks even more surprised now, and listens attentively as I ask him to circle the area several times, as these mackerel often travel in schools. But the other *tenggiri*, if they are there, remain indifferent to the lure.

Later, the chef at our hotel will serve this fish grilled over a fire of coconut husks, along with a local specialty: stingray wrapped in banana leaves. Even without knowing this beforehand, I am happy.

Sarah and Marina are sitting on the dock when we return, swinging their legs in the sun, pleased with the afternoon. The resort manager sits with them, chatting amiably. Pulau Tiga has no guests at present, but he expects forty Korean tourists for a beachside barbecue later that day. One night only, he says, shaking his head. They come, they eat barbecue, they go. Very hard work.

Back on the main island, we finish unloading our gear just as a real fisherman arrives. Using handlines and dead bait, he has filled his fish-box with amberjack and grouper and huge rosy-colored snappers, each as long as my arm. He has *tenggiri* too, stacked like cordwood on the dock, and a fine pair of giant trevally.

The bald man watches as I admire the fish, inspecting the unfamiliar species, hefting the largest ones in my wistful hands. "Next time," he says, "I tell the boatman take you there."

PART III

Whatever Rises

THE ART OF FLY-FISHING AND THE AESTHETICS OF SOLITUDE

Ron McFarland

Fly-fishing may be properly defined as a method of angling which assures the angler that he or she will be granted ample aesthetic distance. So it is that nearly all paintings and photographs showing fly-fishers in action depict them as solitary figures, and if the artwork happens to be a close-up, it will show them happy in their solitude.

The most important corollary to this theorem is what serious fly casters know as The Ratio of Ineptitude. This holds, simply, that one's solitude, and therefore one's satisfaction, is inversely proportional to one's skill as a caster of flies. A highly skilled fly-fisher will be almost certainly doomed to company at approximately rod-length if the said angler is so foolishly proud as to show off his or her talents. It is axiomatic that he or she will be promptly flanked by other anglers, often the very crudest of bait-fishers.

The wisest anglers with the fly, therefore, know when to take a little heat off the old fast-ball so to speak. The best recourse of the savvy fly-caster, upon seeing other anglers in the vicinity, is to lash the air wildly, as if attempting simultaneously to cast an enormous distance, swat a mosquito, and wipe sweat from his or her fevered and quite possibly pathological brow. An optimal tactic, not recommended to the amateur, is to alternate very skillful casts with unpredictably random tosses, throws, hurls, pitches, flings, and flops. The experience for the onlooker should be akin to that of a batter facing a pitcher who can throw fast-balls, curves, sliders, change-ups, and (most important) knuckle-balls in an apparently unpremeditated combination. Wary bait-tossers will head for calmer and safer waters.

In the hands of a skillful angler, the fly-rod can be a lethal weapon. No one has kept accurate statistics on the number of bait-throwers blinded in one eye by a Caddis tied on a #12 hook, but the figure is probably staggering. Every year for the past ten seasons in the Pacific Northwest an average of 9.7 bait-hurlers are known to have been strangled by fly-line, a statistic fish-and-wildlife officers are understandably eager to keep from the public. The practice of a modicum of common sense on the part of bait-throwers (I include spin-casters in this crew) could save dozens of lives nationwide: Simply give the fly-fisher an ample berth. Best advice? If you see a fly-fisher on the stream, go to another body of water altogether, preferably a reservoir.

But as I have suggested, intelligent fly-casters are well able to take care of themselves. Just last week, for example, I was fishing a favorite run on a favorite stream (anonymity in such matters is always advisable) when I heard a trail-bike putter up behind me. A less savant fly-angler might have despaired. My old pal Jim would most likely have muttered a round of profanities, packed up his reel, and skedaddled. But not me.

"How you doin'?"

"Caught a few small ones."

Please observe here the absolute veracity of the fly-fisher. The fact is I had also caught two or three impressive rainbows and a cutthroat that brought tears of gratitude to my eyes, but I had indeed caught "a few small ones" as well.

"Mind if I join you?"

My blood chilled. Truly, are any words more aggravating to any angler? Of course, I minded! But the fly-fisher, man or woman, is the highest evolved sub-species of the type piscator. We are civil to a fault.

"It's a free river."

Here, I confess, I mis-spoke. At such a moment every word is important, each nuance of diction, every loop of syntax. Here are some recommended options: "It's not my river." "Yeah, I guess so" (followed by a deep sigh). "If you must" (followed by appropriate profanity, solo voice). "Yes, I mind!" (followed by loud and erratic obscenities).

"How long you been here?"

"I dunno, a few hours."

Nothing at this point in the dialogue is problematic. Only the rankest amateur would have said something like, "I just got here." You might as well pack up your gear and resign the hole. I suggested, with pretended solicitude, that these trout were not susceptible to bait or spinners, but it was a forlorn hope.

"You can't beat meat!" the bait-chunking interloper

hollered as he let out his line with a resounding splash. I've seen surf-fishers use less lead.

To make matters worse, the guy turned out to be a talker, quite loquacious in fact, a blabbermouth of the old school. He was from California, predictably, and he was here on vacation with the wife and the rug-rats. Two chunky lads of the pre-teen variety promptly rattled up, as if on cue, on their own trail bikes. I was relieved to see they had no fishing gear, but then I noticed they were wearing swimming trunks. My heart sank.

"The wife's back at the old Winnebago," the bait-flinger announced. He ran a computer business of some sort out of his home, so he never had to go in to the office; in fact, he had his lap-top right there in the Winnebago. The wife was a nurse, he said, and this was her vacation. She had wanted to go up to San Francisco (they lived near L.A.), but he had just laughed at the notion, he said, and pointed out to her that the trout fishing there in the Bay was pretty poor.

"Whatcha usin' for bait?" one of the boys bellowed.

"Flies," I said quietly.

"Like grasshoppers and stuff?" the other one brayed.

"Like Humpies and Cahills," I said, almost whispering as I thought of Isaac Walton's admonition at the end of *The Compleat Angler*: "Study to be quiet."

"Huh?"

"Them's artificial flies," the father announced, obviously proud of his lore. His line dangled listlessly a few feet from the bank, and I could see the gnarl of worms being picked at by two or three fingerling trout. "You boys should watch him. It's a real art."

Now of course I had to agree with the guy on that score. Fly-fishing is an art in several ways. There's the art of the fly itself, which should be right up there with painting and sculpture, and there's the performance art of the cast which, properly executed, is as exact and graceful as classic ballet. Of course there's the drama of the catch, and there is, finally, an art beyond the sum of its parts, call it the inner music of fly-fishing.

But being alert, as I obviously am, to the Ratio of Ineptitude, I performed no work of artistic merit in the next several minutes. Instead, I whipped and twirled and looped and flopped, and with a snap that sounded like the crack of a .22, I popped off the Adams that had been serving me so well. In all candor, I must admit I had not intended quite so impressive a proof of the old corollary. The man looked up kind of goggle-eyed and the two boys fidgeted nervously. Think of an actor flubbing the "To be, or not to be" speech, the prima ballerina falling flat on her face in the middle of "Swan Lake."

Pretending it was business as usual, I scrambled across the slippery rocks, nearly toppling into the stream in the process, in order to tie on a new length of tippet and a fresh fly. My fingers were shaking, whether from anger or frustration I cannot say. Finding no other Adams, even after sending a Ginger Quill and a Coachman into the water as I searched (retrieved both), I decided on a Gray Wulff, but for some reason the hackle was lodged in the eye of the hook, and no matter how I tried, I could not manage to thread the leader. I shifted to a Light Cahill, threaded the leader, started to cinch up the blood-knot, and then remembered I needed to attach some fresh tippet, as the tapered portion was now broken off at about the twelve-pound test level and could not have been more than twenty-inches in length.

I fumbled with the clippers. The afternoon heat was intense, and mosquitoes were beginning to find my range. Behind me the rug-rats were arguing loudly and their father was yelling at them to shut up because fish never bite when you're noisy. I attached the fresh tippet, deftly tied on the fly, and clipped the end of the tippet and the tippet itself in one clean snip. Salty sweat washed into my eyes and my hands trembled with consternation as I reattached the fly and plotted my next move: a whip-cracking, eye-threatening, bait-fisher-strangulating maneuver for which I could only regret the lack of a good video camera.

Picture those scenes from the film of Norman Maclean's *A River Runs Through It*. Imagine the exact opposite. Or try to recall an appropriate Disney cartoon involving either Donald Duck or Goofy. Popular art, that's what I had in mind.

And I carried it off brilliantly. A virtuoso performance. I all but strangulated myself in the process, and I did manage to stumble chest-deep into the head of the rifle I was trying to fish, but I emerged wet and proud. All to no avail. These onlookers were no more conscious of an artless cast than they were of their own imminent jeopardy.

"Ain't that nice?" the Californian said after I inadvertently dropped a fly about how and where it should have been. A rainbow flashed past the fly, but did not ingest. "It's a real art," he repeated, as if he actually believed what he was saying.

I gave up. I slapped another mosquito, reeled in, and headed for the car.

"You have a good afternoon," the father sang out as his boys scrambled down the bank. "Don't you boys be jumpin' in there now!"

Too late. The pair entered the stream with a resounding, trout-scattering splash.

At that moment, the dramatic elements of the art came back to me, the importance of ritual, the litany that applies to all angling universally when the sweet, still-point of solitude has been painfully and ruinously disrupted, so as I pulled away, I called out, "Good luck!" I believe I actually meant it. The man said "thanks," not without a touch of sarcasm, and I graciously repeated, "Good luck!" I felt something for the poor guy that could almost have been called compassion.

While it is true that the foregoing episode recounts an unfortunate failure of the corollary of the Ratio of Ineptitude, I would hasten to point out that this was an extreme event and that it was also a rare exception to the rule. An adept fly-angler can achieve remarkable feats under most circumstances in order to assure his or her solitude. Speaking for myself, I can say that I have become so skilled at alternating artful and inept casts that some of my best friends and fellow anglers have been known to express some doubt as to my seriousness, and indeed even my talent, as an artist.

SEA MONSTERS

Susan Borden

As a child growing up in Iowa, I was fascinated by the idea of aquatic monsters. I would scan the shelves of the city library, which smelled strongly of smoke after the fire, searching for books about the Loch Ness monster, the beast of Lake Champlain, and assorted mysterious swimmers in the open ocean. Then I would pore over the eyewitness accounts ("it had a head like a horse, and a whitish mane straggled over its long neck"), the sketches, and the grainy black and white photographs, most of which showed little more than gently undulating shapes in the water. I was utterly convinced that the accounts were all true, that deep in rivers, lakes, and seas there lived a variety of sleek, agile water monsters. I imagined them paddling with diamond-shaped flippers, preying on silvery fish, darting their small, keen, heads in underwater caverns, and I was content.

"It could happen," I explained to my ever-patient mother. "There was this fish, a coelacanth, it's called, and the scientists thought it had been extinct for millions of years, but they found some alive! It's a living fossil, and the Loch Ness monster could be like that. A left-over plesiosaur! Loch Ness used to be open to the sea, and it could've stayed and lived there even after the land came up. It's a really deep lake, and there are lots of fish and the water's dark…." My mother listened. She wanted the monster to be real too, for my sake.

I dreamed once about a water monster, one of those extra

vivid dreams that you remember all your life. In reality, the yard behind our house tended to become a slough in the spring, with pools of standing water suitable for wading if I wore my mother's rubber boots. In the dream I saw the yard submerged, not just in small pools, but in a flat spreading lake. As I watched, the grey lake began to roil and the monster surfaced. I can still see it in my mind's eye—coils rising, wearing a tapestry of black scales that winked in the sunlight, turning to let the water pour off. Its head was not like a horse's; it was like a dragon's, large and furious. For one thrilling moment, the glittering eyes looked into mine, and then the monster exhaled vapor and crashed into the lake once more. I recall clearly the buoyant swell of joy I felt in the dream, knowing that a monster lived in my own backyard lake. I could watch for it and surely catch sight of it again and again. It would live in the lake and never be captured-no, never that. This is the only dream that I remember from my childhood.

About this time, my brother happened across an ancient beige and yellow fishing pole in the basement, the small hoops that guided the line now brown with rust. He used it to play with the cat. I used it to fish in the backyard slough. Wearing my mother's white rubber boots, which buttoned at the side with a figure-eight piece of elastic, like a child's rain boots, I cautiously strode through the standing water. The drowned grass swirled lightly before me, and bits of sediment blossomed in the murky water with each step I took. Carefully drawing the pole back and to the side, I released the sticky lever on the reel and let the aged fishing line fly. There was no hook at the end of it—just two split-shot weights and a faded gold clip, on which lures could be attached. I was not allowed a hook or lures, but the clip looked promising somehow. Knowing full well that there was nothing to catch in the skim of rainwater, I fished nonetheless, hopefully, misguidedly, still carrying visions of sea monsters behind my eyes.

Within weeks the pools would draw in upon themselves, grow shallow, and disappear, leaving behind fetid mud and then mats of tangled, yellowish grass, which we children had to rake up. Not so much as a tadpole survived. There had never been any tadpoles to die.

The notion of sea monsters subsided as I grew older. The early morning fishing jaunts of high school, which usually yielded only a small whiskered catfish or two, trailed off after my friends went off to college, I stayed home, unwillingly. Then a slashing blow fell. My mother died suddenly of something from which she should not have died. She was fifty-seven and I was twenty. I kept my head down, oppressed by the same streets and the hot, green fields of corn that banded the city and flowed over the countryside. I felt unable to escape from the shrinking pool of my own circumstances. Eventually, I rallied feebly enough to send away for information about study abroad programs. Gingerly, fearful of failure and disappointment, I reached out for something new.

That first trip to England for a summer school course brought me around and shook me out of my lethargy. The next summer I went to Great Britain again, eager for reassurance that the world was big, that I could travel, that I could change. England introduced me to the sea and Scotland to deep lakes, which seemed like the sea temporarily captured. The ragged, rocky shorelines under solemn skies intrigued me more than any tropical beach; these waterscapes possessed the rasp of real life. Their roughness matched my mood, and, paradoxically, made me happy. On my third trip to Great Britain, I tentatively planned a journey to Loch Ness. It had always been one of my goals in life to see it, yet I feared my first glimpse. Would it be ringed with deluxe condos? Would wrappers from Wimpy's hamburgers drift on its surface? Would I be forced to give up my long delight in sea monsters after all?

I have a photo of myself from that trip to Loch Ness, aged twenty-seven, taken by one of my traveling companions. The grey-blue loch ripples in the foreground and smoothes to pewter near the horizon. Clouds sail in a white sky , dropping shadows on the heathery hills. The grass is high and full of tussocks and small flowers that look like daisies, but aren't. I sit on a low stone wall, my head and upper body outlined against the loch. I am wearing the scarlet argyle sweater that I'd found lying on a London street several weeks before, blue jeans, leather sneakers scuffed in the grass. The

wind has tousled my hair, which is still brown and golden, and I have a broad, genuine smile on my face. No silhouette of a graceful serpent's head and neck appears behind me, yet I remember how glad and lightsome I felt, being at Loch Ness after so many years of longing. This is my favorite photograph of myself I keep it on the desk where I write, hoping it will give me inspiration.

Nowadays I live in Minnesota. Is it a coincidence that I moved to the land of 10,000 lakes? During the years when I struggled through graduate school and then a series of pitiful part-time jobs, I promised myself that after I finally landed a good job and saved some money, I would buy a canoe. On the same day that I started that "good job," I had my first date with Pete, who would become my husband several years later. He had a canoe! On our second date we paddled White Bear Lake on a serene day in September, and we spent many hours and afternoons afterwards, paddling and fishing. I loved gliding over the cool translucent water, watching the tiny sunfish flash through glades of underwater plants and fire away from the prow of the canoe. The fish moved every which way, up, down, sideways, and diagonally, navigating many planes while I was stuck mostly in one. And when we reached the deeper water and Pete let the anchor rope slide between his fingers, I put down my paddle and peered into the lake. The shafts of slanting sunlight couldn't probe far here, and I felt both frustrated and intrigued that I could not see into the depths. Anything could be down there!

I had not fished since high school, so I had years of catching up to do. We fished every summer weekend, and some weekday evenings, too, talking quietly, eating sandwiches while the canoe rocked, guarding the red and white bobbers zealously. And when my bobber jigged coyly, paused, and then dove under the water's surface, I was ready with a sharp pull and the breathless phrase, "Got one." I reeled madly, the line zinging and throwing out stray sparkles, the rod arcing enticingly. The weight of a fish on the line, even a small fish, delighted me. Up through tiers of lake water I drew the fish; it jerked and swam madly to the side, but could not escape the hook and line. When I pulled it up into the air and saw it spinning on the line, its fins flipping helplessly and its gold and black eye staring, I felt a gust of guilt and wanted only to return it to the water. Wetting my hand to avoid disturbing its coating of protective slime, I gingerly grasped the cool, struggling body, and, as gently as I could, removed the hook from its pouting mouth and opened my hand at the water's surface. The fish flapped back into the lake, drilling downward and out of sight. Gone for good. Exhilarated, guilt-free, and once again eager. I strung another half-worm on the hook and flung the line out into the dusk as far as I could.

One evening, late, the bobber disappeared decisively with no preliminary dancing; it had been floating passively on the surface, and then it was gone, with seemingly no action in between. The taut line sprang straight down, as if I had hooked the lake itself. I heard Pete's excited commentary, but couldn't listen; I set my feet more firmly in the bottom of the sandy canoe and began to turn the reel's handle, fumbling at first and then finding a smoother rhythm. The weight on the line, the powerful pull emanating from the water, the slight list of the canoe in the direction of whatever swam below— these things filled me with anticipation and fear.

Then the connection snapped. The weight vanished along with the sense that I had something alive attached to my rod, and my line floated in the slight breeze. Crestfallen, I examined its shorn end. Only the bobber remained; hook, worm, and sinkers had vanished. "It was probably a northern," Pete said. "They'll bite right through the line unless you have a steel leader tied on." I sat slumped in the prow, my grey life jacket pushing up around my ears. "Here," he leaned forward with his smallest tackle box in his hand. "We have plenty more hooks and sinkers." I flipped open the box and caught a whiff of the familiar scent of worms, metal, plastic, and lake water. And then I straightened my back, clipped off the end of the fishing line with the scissors from my Swiss Army knife, selected a hook, and tied it on.

The surface of the lake was calm, opaque, mysterious. I imagined snouts nuzzling through green fronds, flat eyes peering though layers of water, currents flowing over agile bodies, and the last light filtering down to touch rowing fins and glittering scales. Anything could be down there, I believe.

MR. PINKY
GONE FISHIN'

Taylor Kitchings

MY BROTHER AND I loved Mr. Pinky across the street. Our grandparents were dead before we knew them and Mr. Pinky was our most important elderly kind person. I didn't know till he died that he never had any grandchild of his own, his only daughter, Lindy Rae, weird and fruitless, lost to New York years ago.

Mr. Pinky in his seventies wore a style that was more than his pin-striped suit, brown or light gray, bought from McRae's at a good price, or his chocolate suede and corduroy fedora, or the Old Gold that hung from his lip when he read the paper on his front porch, the only place Miz Madora allowed him to smoke. He had a way with a paper match that came with the ownership of certainties about the world; a gentleman's assurance that had seen four wars and the Great Depression. I loved him, and I envy him now that I'm older and don't have two convictions to rub together. Thomas Pinkerton Neely, retired businessman, knew things.

Mr. Pinky knew that you go to the Baptist church on Sunday morning and Sunday night and Wednesday night for prayer meeting, regardless of personal preference or theological fine points. He listened politely that day, slouched in the frayed green and white checkered lawn chair on the dam at Elwood's Lake, fishing pole in one hand, vodka and Sprite in the other, as I nudged forth my poor opinion of organized religion.

"Who says all that God and Heaven stuff is real?" I asked.

I paid special attention to my cork, sorry to have said so much in front of Mr. Pinky, the habitual Baptist. He peered out at the far sheen of the lake and spit stray bits of tobacco from the Old Gold. Then he squinted at me and allowed that "nobody really knows," like he was surprised I hadn't realized this before.

Mr. Pinky knew about fishing. He taught me to stick a bream hook under a cricket's chin and run it down his gullet and bait two at a time if they were small, and how to get maximum distance on an underhanded cast. When something stripped my hook without pulling much, he knew it was probably a turtle and the only thing to do was move a little further down the dam. He always made sure we had our fishing caps on and our arms and legs covered up against thorn bushes, mosquito bites and too much sun. According to him, you wore your sleeves rolled down. To roll them up without a good reason was to declare yourself prissy.

Having won and lost fortunes in cars, appliances and insurance, Mr. Pinky knew that money was right up there with church. He didn't easily give over the price of a pack of Juicy Fruit. Caruso and me had to buy our own cane poles, cricket canisters, tackle and drinks. Mr. Pinky brought along his vodka to mix with Sprite, a source of unease between him and Miz Madora, who, as a choir member and former president of the WMU, objected to alcohol, any time, anywhere. He drank vodka because it had the least

detectable odor and Miz Madora's sinus problems usually protected him from trouble, but not every time. When the fishing wasn't good he might have more than a couple, but he never became, as he put it, "greedy." Not until that afternoon at Elwood's Lake.

Fishin' and the Ole Miss Rebels—those were our two favorite things with Mr. Pinky. He taught us about the glory days of Johnny Vaught, Charlie Conerly, Jake Gibbs, Archie Manning, and how to care deeply whether the Rebels won or lost. He took me and Caruso to games at Veteran's Memorial Stadium, back when the Rebels played in Jackson two or three times a year. He even drove us down to Baton Rouge once.

Just about whenever the Rebels played on TV, me and Caruso watched it at Mr. Pinky's. Miz Madora would make us lemonade and popcorn and sometimes chocolate chess pie, and we'd sit as close to the screen as she'd permit. Mr. Pinky sat behind us in his big recliner, grumbling to the coach or the quarterback or the referee the whole time. Sometimes he'd fire off a bad word and Miz Madora would say, "Pinky! You ought to be ashamed." If the Rebels scored a touchdown, he gave a holler that could scare a person and jumped out of his big leather chair like it was on fire. Miz Madora would holler, "Pinky! Get back in yo chayuh!," but it tickled her to see him get so excited.

The team Mr. Pinky most wanted to beat was the Alabama Crimson Tide, maybe because he could remember when Ole

Miss regularly whipped them the way they whipped us now. The team I most wanted to beat was LSU, because people in Baton Rouge spat at me and threw oranges when I cheered for my team. If we couldn't watch the game on TV, we'd take a radio to the lake and listen while we fished.

Mr. Elwood ran a cattle farm near Clinton, just past Kickapoo Road. He and Mr. Pinky had gone to Central High School together when it was still a high school, and Mr. Elwood lent his old friend unlimited fishing privileges. Every time we'd drive up, here came Mr. Elwood jogging around the corner of his dingy old white house, grinning and waving, reporting on the condition of the road, and reminding us not to leave the gates open. He was pessimistic about the weather, but happy about everything else, in spite of always having to replenish feed, replace salt licks, mow and bail, mend fences, doctor sick calves, and herd complaining bessies into chutes so he could staple their ears and squirt medicine down their throats. He kept chickens, too, and raised a fair crop of corn. It never tired him much that I could tell.

What I remember about weather and fishin' with Mr. Pinky was that it was raining, or had just rained, or was just about to rain. Caruso and me never talked above a whisper about the next day's trip, so the clouds couldn't hear us. This particular day it had been drizzling off and on since sunup. We got out to the lake around twelve-thirty, trying to get a hook in the water before the Rebels kicked it off at one o'clock.

Mr. Elwood was breathless, bulging out of his overalls in all directions. He leaned into the front window of the car, grinning at us. His breath smelled like mothballs and Red Man.

"How you boys doin'?" he said.

"Fine," we said together.

"Phew, it's muggy, ain't it?"

"Sure is."

The drizzle had turned to a fine mist now, but it wasn't helping the heat any, just made your back feel greasy.

"I can't remember when it was this hot in October," said Mr. Elwood.

Everybody in Mississippi forgets from one fall to the next that it can get real hot in late October. They lie around in their shorts and act put out, like it hadn't always been this way; like they haven't worn shorts at Christmas.

"Y'all ain't thinkin' of catchin' any fish today is ya?" he said.

"We was thinkin' pretty hard about it," said Mr. Pinky.

"I tell you what, this rain ain't done with us yet. But y'all go on, you want to, if you can make it through the mud."

I wasn't worried. We were riding in Mr. Pinky's '79 Monarch, and had never been stuck before.

"I brought my raincoat," Mr. Pinky said, lifting his arms from the steering wheel as if to prove it. His left sleeve caught and he frowned at the door. He opened it and gathered in the tail of his coat.

"Reckon that ain't the first time you've had your tail in a crack," grinned Mr Elwood.

In the rear view mirror I saw Mr. Pinky purse his lips at Mr. Elwood, like he didn't think that kind of humor was appropriate around us boys. Hell, I was goin' on thirteen and Caruso already had his license.

"How's Lelia doin'?" Mr. Pinky always asked about Mrs. Elwood and it seemed to make Mr. Elwood just the slightest bit uneasy.

"She's fine. Just fine. Y'all don't forget to close them gates back, hear?"

We bumped and jostled our way up and down the hills that led to the lake. The cattle grazed along the slopes on both sides of us, every one of them facing east. Mr. Elwood owned mostly Herefords, a handful of Black Anguses, and one supremely large Charlay. Some of them were standing in the watering pond, trying to keep cool. Now and then a big old bessie would eye us as we drove by, chewing at her own good pace, just mildly interested.

Sitting behind Mr. Pinky, I watched the wrinkles on his neck like the designs on a drying mud bank and the wisps of hair swirling over the tips of his ears. I steadied the bundle of cane poles that jutted out the window by my head, minding the hooks that they didn't come unstuck from the bottom of the poles and snag me in all the bouncing. I wrapped my other arm around the tackle box and two canisters of crickets and held a bucket full of minnows between my feet. Mr. Pinky's equipment was in the trunk, except for the six pack of Sprite on the floorboard and a bottle of Taaka on the front seat.

Caruso rode shotgun. Older brother privileges. He was shorter than me, lean as a cardboard cutout and very cool, with his black bangs flopping when he jumped out to tend the gates. Mr. Elwood had been right about the road being muddy. On the last rise before the lake we lost traction and started spinning. Mr. Pinky gunned it several times, but the Monarch just kept whining and spinning.

"What's supposed to happen now?" I asked.

"Shut up, knucklehead," said Caruso. "I can go back and get some boards for them tires, Mr. Pinky."

"Y'all just hold on a minute," said Mr. Pinky.

He stared at the accelerator like he was giving it the strength to free us. When he floored her again, we spun, lurched, swerved and jerked over the top of that hill, cut a sharp right and bounced down to the south end of the dam as gentle as you please.

"Heeyah!" yelled Caruso.

"Now we can do some fishin'," said Mr. Pinky, slinging it into park and stoking an Old Gold. I felt damn well taken care of at that moment and sorry for the rest of the world that could not share this fishing afternoon with Mr. Pinky and his gentleman's assurance in the ways of stuck tires and lighting cigarettes.

We unloaded everything in two trips. Caruso carried a carton of night crawlers to the other end of the dam, looking for a bream bed by a couple of fallen cedars trunks. Mr. Pinky and I sat together on the near side, next to an overturned johnboat that had never been fished in, far as I could tell. I dug in my heels on the short slope, protected from mud by the weeds. Mr. Pinky sat in his green-and-white checked lawn chair. He liked to put a minnow on a bass hook and get it way out in the water. He'd cast and cast until it was out far enough, and if I ever reminded him that we could be sitting in that johnboat and dropping our hooks wherever we wanted, he just grunted, like that wouldn't be fair to the fish somehow.

Further down the bank, a plump water moccasin watched us from the end of an old log, like he dared us to top the fishing he'd seen. Later he got bored, dropped into the water and curled away. I had my eye on a big stick if he showed up again. Mr. Pinky said not to worry about him.

I got me some nibbles right off, but after I pulled up a bare hook a few times I figured it was just a turtle and moved further down. Then I didn't get any more nibbles. Mr. Pinky wasn't having any luck either, but he seemed more than okay about it, especially once he could turn on the radio and listen to the Rebels.

Pretty soon the mist turned back into drizzle, which turned into a hard and steady rain.

"Hey Caruso!" I hollered. "You doin' any good?"

"No!" he shouted and made a big shrug.

"Hush!" said Mr. Pinky, adding some more vodka to his can of Sprite. "Y'all gonna scare away the fish."

There wasn't a self-respecting bream in the state that would bite in the middle of the day with it pouring like that, but was important to act like we didn't know it. I held a Styrofoam lid over my head and listened to the game, as the Rebels went down fourteen points in the first quarter against an AA team from Arkansas.

"Goddamn son-of-a-bitch pansy-ass Rebels," muttered Mr. Pinky.

It was understood that I couldn't hear him when he talked like that.

By halftime the rain eased up again, but the Rebels still hadn't scored, Caruso had worked his way across the dam back to us and still not caught anything, and we still hadn't eaten lunch. Even though fishing was one of our favorite things to do with Mr. Pinky, I was ready to call it a day.

"Mr. Pinky," I said, "did you ever think it's a mean thing we're doing to all these crickets and minnows, sticking 'em on hooks and drowning 'em for no reason?"

"It's the way we were given to obtain food, son. You can't question God on such matters."

"Still. You would have expected God to come up with a kinder way."

"God isn't likely to be what you'd expect."

"How we supposed to know anything about Him then?"

"You could try gettin' your mama to take you boys to church for one thing."

"I been to church. Didn't like it."

"Why not?"

"It was a bad show. It didn't seem real." That's when I came out with: "Who says all that God and Heaven stuff is real?"

I couldn't believe I had doubted God in front of Mr. Pinky. Caruso glared at me. I studied my cork. When I looked up again, Mr. Pinky was squinting hard across the lake. Then he squinted at me.

"Son, nobody really knows," he said, popping the tiny shreds of Old Gold between his lips.

We sat.

"I think I might have seen him though," Mr. Pinky said.

"God?"

"Once when I was driving past Hernando on I-55 and a flight of blackbirds shot out of a stand of young pines and fanned up and out all above the highway. And once when the Alabama football team ran on the field at Veteran's Memorial Stadium. That was the year they spotted us twenty-one points and went on to win by about a thousand. But I didn't know they were gonna win when I watched 'em run onto the field. It had nothing to do with that, nothing to

do with football. I hate that it was the Crimson Tide looked like God to me that day, but I can't help it."

"They say the Bear used to control rain at practice," said Caruso.

"I've heard that," smiled Mr. Pinky. "But the Bear wasn't around when this happened. Maybe it was him up there sending me a message, I don't know. I tend to think it was their visitor uniforms."

"Our uniforms look a heck of a lot better than the Tide's," I said.

"I know, son, but theirs are so plain, just about all white, and suddenly there was sixty of 'em running onto the field right together, seventy, eighty of 'em. That's God: the whole same thing, over and over again."

"You don't think it means God favors 'Bama?" I asked.

"Shoot no, knucklehead," said Caruso. "God favors the whole SEC."

When even Mr. Pinky was tired from not catching anything, we left our poles in the water and unwrapped Miz Madora's homemade pimento cheese sandwiches and garden tomatoes. Caruso and me drank warmish Sprites out of the can. Mr. Pinky added some more vodka to his. I was balling up my wax paper to throw into the paper sack we'd set aside for garbage, when Mr. Pinky's pole scooted out of the crook of his chair and snaked off the dam. It was moving fast.

"Look there!" I shouted.

Mr. Pinky dropped his can.

"Hey! Hey!" he shouted.

"Caruso! Get the boat!" I shouted.

Caruso was already turning over the johnboat and dragging it into the water.

"I can't find no paddle!" he screamed. "You gotta help me!"

I helped him shove it down the bank and into the water, our feet sliding in the mud. When we looked again, Mr. Pinky's pole was dancing into the middle of the lake.

"Some kind of monster on that line," I said.

"Y'all get 'eem now!" hollered Mr. Pinky. "Y'all get 'eem!"

"Get in the dang boat!" yelled Caruso. "You gotta help me!"

He had already pulled ten-feet away from the bank.

"I'm wet enough!"

"You get in the dang boat!"

We made the best speed we could, slumped over fore and aft, arms for paddles. When we passed the log where I'd seen that moccasin, I just paddled faster. I wasn't worried about getting bit, or wet, or anything else. All I saw was how far we had to go to catch up with that pole, still sailing, and all I heard was the lake water splashing as our arms swiveled through it and Mr. Pinky shouted somewhere in the distance.

Every time we were almost close enough to stretch out and grab the pole, it would glide a little further away. When we finally caught up to it, we were on the other side of the lake

and the thick end of the pole was tilting up out of the water, like hook, line, sinker and shaft was all about to dive to the bottom.

"She's goin' under, Caruso!" I shouted. "What kinda creature is that?"

"Ain't nothing but a big old cat."

Caruso leaned out as far out as he could. When I stood up to help the boat lurched, and he waved me back to my seat. Mr. Pinky looked tiny back on the dam, waving his arms over his head and shouting.

"Here goes," Caruso said, leaning out, trying to grab the line. Soon as he took hold of it, it went taut and zipped through his hand.

"Son-of-a-bitch!" he shouted and turned around to show me a bloody stripe across his palm.

We had to paddle some more to catch up to it again. Even a few feet was hard with arm paddles and mine was about worn out. This time he put both hands on the pole and wrestled and tugged with it till you would have thought that line was nailed to the bottom.

I was about ready to leave that pole to whatever wanted it so bad when my brother jerked up the fattest, slimiest, ugliest catfish I'd ever seen in my life. That thing looked like it had been swimming around since the world was new. And it shone with a prize luster.

"That's a fifteen-pounder," I said.

"Twenty." Caruso was grinnin' like he'd won the Louisiana lottery.

He held it high for Mr. Pinky, who leaned out with his hand over his brow, then started jumping up and down on the dam, whooping so loud I was afraid he was gonna scare Mr. Elwood's cows. It was raining pretty hard now and a long paddle back, specially when we were keeping one foot each on one of the biggest catfish in Hinds County.

"How about that, boys? Took it clean out of my chair and all the way to the other end of the lake! I don't 'spect Elwood's even gonna believe this."

"He'll believe it when he sees the fish," said Caruso.

"Maybe now he'll buy some paddles," I said, rubbing my hands on my jeans.

"Mighty fine, mighty fine. Fine a catch as I ever saw in my life," said Mr. Pinky, holding it up to the sky. "All right, boys. Now y'all get you one."

The rain turned to drizzle again, then back to rain and finally quit. We stayed until the Rebels barely pulled it out against a sorry team, but we didn't get another nibble. When we slipped that big cat into the ice chest, Mr. Pinky hovered over it and stared as proud as if he'd made it himself. Then his head got wobbly, and he caught himself with one leg just before he fell over.

I had never seen him like that. I told myself it was the heat, even though I counted four empty Sprite cans in the grass and one empty fifth of vodka. I didn't want to hear the groans he made when he slumped behind the steering wheel or see the deep drowsiness that had settled over his face when I wasn't looking. Hell, I knew he was at least seventy-five-years-old. Mr. Pinky was supposed to be old. It went along with his knowing things. He was supposed to be old, but permanent. He wasn't supposed to wobble.

He drove us back okay, stopping to brag to Mr. Elwood, who declared it the biggest fish to ever come out of his lake. Mr. Pinky was fighting that vodka for all he was worth, frowning something fierce behind the wheel, doing no more than twenty all the way home. He kept asking us whether he ought to mount it or eat it. He said he hated to lose sight of so fine a catch by putting in his stomach. If he took it to the taxidermist he could admire it on the wall for years and years. He talked real slow, like he was trying to prove he could talk. We were hoping Miz Madora would let him in the house.

We got out of the Monarch and said thank you and goodbye and carried our poles across the street. Mr. Pinky grinned wide and touched his fedora in a broad salute. "Go Rebels!" I shouted over my shoulder, which ought to have been a fine thing to say, but rang stupid somehow.

I pulled Caruso's sleeve and we watched Mr. Pinky dip three times trying to pick up the ice chest before he finally locked on it.

"You should have helped him with that," Caruso said.

"He wouldn't let me," I told him.

"I sure hope Miz Madora can't smell the vodka."

"I hope Miz Madora ain't even home."

"Well there's the dang Buick right there in the driveway, brainiac."

Mr. Pinky stopped at the bottom porch step, set down the cooler, straightened his back and adjusted his fedora. Then he flicked a match, took a powerful drag from an Old Gold, stomped it out, dragged the cooler up the steps, and slid it inside. We could hear Miz Madora even after the front door closed: "A man of yo' years, with yo' standing in the community, slinking into the house drunk as a skunk…two young boys in the car…shameful, just shameful, dangerous and shameful." Bless her heart, good woman that she was, she knew how to fuss.

I could just see him nodding patiently like everything she said was true and she had every right to be upset, holding back that grin, waiting for when she had to stop to take a breath. Then he'd throw back the lid and say, "I'm sorry, darlin'. You're right. But look here at what I have in the cooler."

Later, when me and Caruso were throwing a softball, we heard hammering from across the street and knew he was getting that catfish ready for skinning. He had decided to eat it.

That was the last time we went to Mr. Elwood's lake or any lake with Mr. Pinky. Seems like it wasn't but a few weeks later he had the stroke, and not much after that they asked Caruso and me to be pall bearers, and we unpinned the flowers on our coat collars and laid them on the coffin before they lowered him into the ground.

If he was right about Heaven, I expect they have fishin'. That's the next time I'm going.

THE FISH GARDEN

John Struloeff

THE DRIZZLE WAS steady, a clinging mist like perspiration on my hands and face, feeding from the surf that struck the rocks. It was December, and I had come to fish. I was half a mile along the South Jetty, carrying my pole and tackle in one hand, staying my balance on the rocks with my free hand. The jetty stretched in a narrow line of cold gray boulders a mile or more between the Pacific and the churning mouth of the Columbia River. Every few seconds a wave would roll along the Pacific side and burst into a spray high above my head before continuing on. The wind was strong, carrying a thickening mist, grating like ice across my face. I stood, shaking, peering over the rocks to the Columbia. The water there was gray and choppy, without the roll of the ocean. Faint in the mist were the dark mountains of Astoria. On both sides the water stretched unbelievable distances. I looked back to the line of jetty rocks curving to the beachhead where waves rolled like mighty hills.

There was a large level rock, and I sat, wiping my hand across my forehead under my hood. The chill was incredible. The wind fluttered my jacket and drove a shiver into my chest and arms. I leaned back, feeling the flat, cool surface of granite through my jacket. My pole was already rigged, something I'd done in the car as the wind rushed the windows and the sky began to light. The pyramid weight swung beneath the curve of the pole, and I slipped the treble-hook from the large base-eye to feed the curling worms onto the barbs. The worms were thick and meaty, slimy from the dense mud beneath my wife's rhododendrons along the front of our house, and for a moment I could smell the soil of my home over the kelp and salt of the ocean.

A wave burst into a white fountain, smattering drops around me. A fine mist covered my face, and I swung the pole behind me, feeling the weight pull until it settled, and then I whipped it forward. The line whizzed fifty or sixty feet in a smooth arc. The waves thundered on the rocks and the wind blew—enough so I couldn't hear my rig hit the water.

The line released a few coils silently before I set the reel and eased it tight. One more wave crashed, jerking the line, and then it was snug. I leaned back, resting the pole against my leg, keeping pressure on the line. I hadn't fished in years, and it felt strange doing it alone. My father had raised me fishing, but I had married and had stopped, trying to make a home among the trees in the mountains with my wife. I squeezed the cork handle tightly, sensing from it the years of fishing that still lingered in my grip.

The water was gray-green and held that tinge of steel that shows it's frigid. The line pulled taut, then slackened. They say every fifth wave on average will reach its potential, rise up into a cap enough to roll over, and between is just a slow and steady rise and fall. It's not like you can count five in a row, and every fifth is a riser. It's more random. That's the nature of the sea. Sometimes, after a great while, you might face a

tremendous wall that seems to push from the ocean's floor. If you're around the ocean long enough, it will come—waves like mountains.

The tip of the pole began to pull toward the water. Not a jerk like a trout or perch. Just a pressure. My heart started up, and I leaned forward. The tip stayed its position, curved as if pointing a long thin finger at whatever was playing my hook. The pull was hard, steady. I held my breath, tightening my grip, then gave a hard yank, standing up to reel the line. The tip didn't move, but the pole bowed heavily, and I knew I had snagged something big—a monster or a rock or submerged drift log.

"Christ Almighty," I said, sitting back. I kept pressure on the line.

A wave struck and sprayed towards me, tickling my hand and putting a salty mist on my lip. The wind whipped, carrying stinging beads of water, pushing my hood across my eye as I gave the pole little jerks.

Dipping my head away from the wind, I yanked. The tip didn't move. I gripped tightly with both hands and pulled as hard as I could. The pole arched until I thought it would break, shaking when my muscles met their limits.

I sank back against the cool rock. There's an art to keeping your lines free of snags, one my father had mastered in silence. He was a much better fisherman than I—something that was disappointing, but he had earned it with decades of his life. I sighed and let the line slacken so I could cut it. My scaling knife was sharp, finely honed surgical steel, as it should be, and the line separated with a little sound. Quickly the ocean absorbed the hazy white coil.

Out at sea a ship called with an echoey bass. Visibility was worse, less than a mile into the gray gloom. It struck me again how vast the ocean was—even with the fog, I could sense its magnitude. My brother had flown to Dutch Harbor the week before to go long-lining off the Aleutians, a few thousand miles straight out from where I sat, something he did every year after Christmas until early March. The job was dangerous, with high, frigid seas that dwarfed the waves along the jetty. I imagined him leaning low over the side into a mist, gripping the next three-yard leader and pulling the great orange bulk of a halibut over the side, straightening his back tight before the slippery weight thudded on the deck and slid to another man who guided it onto a conveyor, breathing through the frozen hairs of his beard as the winch coiled the longline up another three yards, having to lean to grip the next leader. I've seen his pictures. Workers like Titans in a rolling, frozen sea.

It took some time to rig another leader with a pyramid weight and treble-hook. All the knots—one for the weight, one for the top of the leader pin, one loop for the hook-leader, one for the eye of the hook—were driving me crazy. My fingers were so numb they seared with pain, and every few seconds I held my fingertips to my mouth and breathed slowly across them just to feel the skin burn a moment before going numb again. I finished my father's six-coiled fisher's knot on the eye of the hook, tightening the knot with my teeth. The worms were motionless, and I fed them easily onto the barbs.

I guided the tip of the pole behind me, readying my arms for the quick unleashing motion I had to use to get good distance from the rocks. The weight steadied, and I let fly. Again, a clear, smooth arc twenty yards out and a soundless entry.

I set the reel and sat back.

The rocks vibrated with the steady boom of waves, and the line pulled snug, easing and tightening slightly with the rise and fall of the waves. I watched the motion of the water—how the surface would reflect the pale gray of the sky and then sway to expose a deep green beneath. I had no idea how deep the water was beneath my feet. I tried to glimpse the depths when I could, when the reflection was gone, but it did no good. It was all blackness. So I watched the water drip from the thin ice-crusts on the rocks, holding the pole tightly to my leg, waiting for that downward pull.

There was an old sailor's song I tried to remember. I relaxed against the cool rock and hummed the notes. Before long the words came, and I sang, "Farewell and adieu to you fair

Spanish ladies….Farewell and adieu to you ladies of Spain." I laughed and coughed onto my chest.

An old crabber had sung it once when he and my father and I had gone out of Garibaldi. My father had said the old man was my grandfather's step-brother, but I have only seen him once. He and my father had that quiet way of years spent together, and we all worked silently, laying the rings out part-full of corncobs and dead carp snagged from the man's irrigation ditch. We'd lay anchor for a time and then pull it and circle slowly back through the fog, following the plastic milk jugs that were his markers. It was cold and choppy, the type of sea any crabber would call home. We'd hook a ring-line and pull it up, and he'd hum a few phrases and come in with those words, his voice rough. Farewell and adieu….

A shock went through the pole. The tip started downward, and I sat forward.

Then the tip dropped, the line whizzing from the reel. "Holy Christ," I said. I had the drag set tight, something I'd learned from fishing salmon—it should slow the line, but it kept pulling. Not hard like a salmon or steelhead—determined, heavy like a sturgeon. I tightened the drag as far as it would go and grabbed my scaling-knife in case I had to cut the line.

The reel slowed to a stop. After a moment the line went slack, then eased tight and moved from my right across to my left in a long slow circle, keeping the line snug.

"What's this?" I said. I was beginning the fisher's monologue: talking to his catch, a forced calm in his voice like he's talking down a gunman or a child on the verge of dropping an ancient vase. I stood and felt out a footing on the rocks, excitement and calm mixing my blood. It's a glorious feeling.

The resistance kept up with little tremors. I reeled slowly. You keep it steady, they won't feel it.

After some time, maybe ten minutes of play, I still had no idea what was on the line. That was one of the excitements I remembered from fishing the jetty with my father—the absolute mystery, the feeling of something unknown but strong and alive guiding your line. In the rivers and streams there's finite variety—in the ocean, it's up to God.

Then it surfaced.

It rose slowly to just a few inches from the surface, enough so I could see a long black shadow, perhaps three-and-a-half feet long. The head was huge and round, oversized for the body as a tadpole's is. It rode the swell of a wave in front of me, bumping a rock. I stepped down to a smaller rock so my boots were close to the next wave's rise, reeling until a yard of line was between the tip of the pole and its mouth. It was a fish, certainly, inky, black and amorphous in the water. Its front fins flapped slowly, its direction steady, body looking heavy and strong, resting.

A wave crashed, sending a bitter mist across my face and slopping water up my thighs. I set my feet and leaned back to heave my weight against the fish's, trying to hoist it out of the water. The head broke the surface, large as a bowling ball, and I could make out nubs, what should have been eyes—bulbous, black, reflecting the sky with a glossy sheen. It seemed to stare at me though there were no eyes.

I leaned back further, and the mouth emerged, gaping wide with a sheer black depth, so wide my own head could have fit within. The hook was embedded in the thick flesh of its upper lip, and with the new pressure the body was about halfway out of the water. The pole bowed so sharply I thought it'd snap if I lifted it any further—a good hundred pounds. I eased the fish back into the water, and it opened its mouth once, its gills expanding.

My breath clouded in front of me, and I looked down the long stretch of rocks to the shore. "Christ," I said, then turned back to face the fish I had just caught.

⊢—⊣

Halfway back to shore, my hand cramped, so I found a flat rock and eased myself down. My shoulder hurt from leading the fish. It had been amazingly patient, even puffing its gills and flicking its tail to help.

"Farewell and adieu to you big bug-eyed bastard," I sang softly. I supposed then it still wasn't finished. I hadn't won yet. Not when the fish was still in the water.

"Alrighty," I said, conceding that much, and switched the pole to my other hand to flex my fingers. I lay the back of my hand against my cheek: cold as the sea.

When I was a few hundred yards from shore, the pain was agonizing, and I stopped to switch hands, flex, stretch my back and shoulders. The fish seemed to get impatient, moving in little circles, stopping to face away from the shore and flutter its front fins.

Then, with a rush of the tail, it made a run. The line whirred from the reel, and I dropped the tackle box onto the rocks. The box hit with a crack, and my hand cramped. I held with just my left hand, flexing my right as best I could, watching the reel spin. I breathed onto my hand and stuffed it in my pocket, flexing my fingers. I couldn't reel, so I watched the line draw further and further. It stopped weaving in the water and was on a straight line towards the deep. I felt a dread watching the line go.

After a time, it began to hesitate, then slow—and as the line thinned on the reel and I could see the white plastic of the spool, it stopped. I slid my left hand up to grasp the line firmly against the pole. My heart pounded and shook my hands. The fish was tired—a second run is deathly exhausting.

I reeled quickly, holding the handle against my palm instead of up high between the knuckles of my thumb and first two fingers. I reeled until my hand cramped with a sudden and terrible burn. I pulled the line tight against the pole with my left hand and put my right in my pocket. I did this until the pain stopped at a sustained ache, and I was able to keep reeling. The black liquid body rose, its head surfacing for just a moment.

I started, as if it were lunging at me, but its body was limp and went with the sway of the water. I stretched the pole to the side and pulled in some of the slack line to twist a loop-knot behind the second eye on the pole to keep the fish from making another run.

I sat back, exhausted. The waves rolled with the wind, shooting up like geysers. What was I doing? All the pain and numbness, the damage I was doing my tendons and muscles, and the cracking skin on my hands that would take days to begin feeling normal. Maybe for native whalers centuries ago, but for me?

I had a refrigerator full of food. A wife who was surely sitting on the couch in the warmth of central heating, sipping hot coffee, reading a book under a lamp while the wind blew outside through crackling firs and alders and across the frozen ground of our new land. A house with electricity and a new roof. A car and a job and parents and family and a savings account, a computer.

As I stood over the sand, I looked back along the jetty to where I had hooked the fish. My back ached, and I stretched, breathing hard. It had taken at least an hour. Exhilaration filled my body, and I whooped at the gray clouds. I felt I had done something very great. I had conquered. I imagined my brother working on his boat in the sweeping winds and high seas. We were a family of fishermen.

I hopped down onto the soft sand, and the wind nearly vanished, the roar easing to a breeze. A wave receded, and the black gleaming dome of the fish's head became exposed as the water eddied around and past it, leaving a line of thick yellowish foam where the water had reached furthest. The fish's gills widened the back of the head, then retracted. When the next wave began to peak, the fish was fully exposed on the sand. It was a huge fish, somewhat flattened now that it was out of the water, so that the first part of the belly behind the head was now wider than the head. The gills worked once, slowly. The way the nubs were arranged, on the top of the head and towards the front, bulbous and glistening, the fish seemed to stare, its large, soft mouth open.

The wave curled into a crash, and as the foam tumbled forward and started its long reach across the sand, I dug my heels in and pulled the fish away from the water so it couldn't turn back to the sea. I stopped at the water mark from the last high tide, where the foam dried in a white flaky line, small sticks strewn densely far down the beach.

The wind picked up, and the fish began collecting a thin coating, its inky skin losing its sheen and turning a mottled dark green. I stooped and looked closely. Its lower lip pulsed, the gills still.

"I guess you're about done," I said, reaching out and touching a smooth patch of skin between the nubs. It was sticky, springy like gelatin. When I pulled my finger back, it had a grimy coating of sand that I wiped off on my pant leg. I watched the nubs to see if they moved or opened into eyes, but they didn't. They were black and motionless. I looked at the fish for a time, and as I hoisted it into my arms, I remembered how difficult it is holding your kill in your hands.

⊢—⊣

The fish took up the whole back seat of my car. It slid like a snake out of my hands and fell onto the seat, making the car rock. As I lay my tackle box on the front seat, I saw a large crack in its corner and some of my lures and all of my weights were gone. With a sigh, I took the driver's seat and shut the door. A warmth moved across my body, and there was a hum in the quiet where my ears had lost the constant rush of wind and roar of waves. The wind belted the passenger side windows, but it seemed distant, a memory. My dashboard clock blinked the time: 9:37 A M. I lay my head back and closed my eyes, listening to my breathing for a time before reaching for my keys.

The car warmed with the vents wide open. Something smelled thick and fetid, like from the bottom of a mud flat. I thought it was the worms, the dank way worms and earth will smell when mixed. Then I heard a long, draining gurgle and knew it was my friend on the back seat. I leaned forward to look into the rearview mirror, and I caught the black tip of a dorsal fin. Who knew where that thing had spent its years? Anywhere the seas connect, anywhere in the great open.

The grass rolled in dark green and gold waves as I followed the beachhead out of the parking lot and onto the main exit-road of the park. Ahead were the dark slopes of the Coastal Mountains, and I soon passed the boat towns of Hammond and Warrenton, curving through the streets and climbing arched bridges above gillnet boats idling in the haze of exhaust and fog. I took a left onto Highway 101 and spanned the Youngs Bay bridge to Astoria, the jetty far across the bay where the river, bay, and ocean all mix waters. Here the mist thinned, and the mountains loomed across the river. The tops of the mountains could not be seen for the mist and clouds. Everywhere the world was wet and dark.

⊢—⊣

My parents' house was a faded burgundy ranch-style. It stood in a clearing walled with firs and maples, all darkened with winter's coloring. The house was fronted by thick rhododendrons as high as the eaves, much larger than my wife's. Father was surprised to see me. He opened the door in his robe and looked at me. His eyes were large and wide in his reading glasses. I hadn't seen him in weeks, not since my brother had left for Alaska. He seemed to have thinned some again, and his hair was a little disheveled, as if he'd been napping.

"Well, hello," he said, stepping back. "Come on in."

I had my hands deep in my pants pockets, and I tilted

my head toward the car. "I caught something out at the jetty. Thought you might want to see." I was nervous for him to see the fish, and my voice shook a little.

"Oh?" he said, his face relaxing into a smile.

"Mom around?" I asked, looking behind him to the darkened living room. The pictures on the walls glittered with flashes from the television. In high school she would take pictures of my brother and me with our catches, sending copies to relatives along with our school pictures.

"In the restroom," he said. His voice was hoarse and quiet.

I turned and walked slowly back toward the car. He stepped out and closed the door. His slippers skated across the cement behind me.

"I used the treble-hooks you gave me for Christmas," I told him as I opened the door.

He stood beside me and stooped forward, giving me an expressionless look before peering into the dark cab.

"Good God," he said, adjusting his glasses up his nose. "What in the hell did you catch?" He looked at me with a strange, startled expression.

"I have no idea," I said. The fish had slid across the seat, its wide head mashed against the armrest on the far door. It looked utterly grotesque now to me, and my face grew warm with embarrassment.

He held the tail fin in his hand. The fin had collapsed together like an old Japanese fan and pointed straight back.

He spread it wide and looked at it for a moment, then gripped the tail firmly and slid the whole body toward him.

"What is this thing?" he asked in a whisper, the way he used to do to his wood when he was working out a bad groove. "A bullhead?" He smacked the fish's back, and it wobbled. "Jesus Christ."

He leaned back, pushing his hands into the front pockets of his robe. He looked at the fish, then spit on the gravel. "You going to eat that thing?"

"I don't know."

He nodded and sniffed once. I could see in his withdrawn expression that he didn't understand why I had kept a fish I couldn't identify.

The front door opened, and my mother stepped out onto the stoop and put her glasses on. "Oh, hi," she said, smiling. "I thought that was your car."

I smiled for her and nodded. "Caught a fish out at the jetty—just showing Dad."

She closed the door softly and hurried to where we were standing. She put an arm around me, hugging me tight for a second, then stepped forward to look into the car. "Wow," she said. "That's some fish. Never seen one of those before. Kind of like the bullheads I used to catch when I was a kid."

Father cleared his throat. "You ever catch a bullhead that size before?"

Mom laughed. "Oh—well—"

Father spit again, then looked up into the fir trees at the edge of his property.

I suddenly recalled how long the fish had been out of water. I moved toward the driver's door. "Geez, I should get going. Got to get it put away if I'm going to do anything with it."

My mother shut the car door. Then she snapped her fingers. "Oh! I should get my camera."

I looked at the black mound in the back seat, and it gave me an odd, sick feeling in my stomach. "That's okay." I opened the door and sat down.

Father moved closer, his hands still in his pockets.

"Thanks for stopping by," Mother said. "That's quite the fish." She laughed as if we'd been sharing a story about high seas adventure.

I shut the door and rolled the window down. "Well, I should get this thing put away." I started the car.

My father leaned his head toward the fish. "You planning on eating that?" He still didn't understand. And by then, neither did I.

"I don't know," I said.

I backed away. My mother waved, smiling wide and putting her arm around Father who stood with his hands in his pockets as I drove beneath the dripping maples and onto the slick, dark road.

—⊢——⊣—

I pulled around the side of the house and into the grass. My wife came to the kitchen window wearing her glasses, and when she saw me she smiled and waved, then hurried to the sliding glass door and opened it. She was wearing a gray sweatshirt and jeans. She had never known me to fish.

"Catch anything?"

"Not really," I said.

I opened the back door, grabbed the fish by the tail, and heaved it out. It hit the ground with a squishy thump.

"My God," she said from behind me. I turned, and she was walking up slowly, her arms crossed over her stomach, her hands holding her elbows.

I dropped the fish's tail, and the rest of the body flopped into the grass.

"You caught that?" She moved her head slowly back and forth. "That is the biggest fish I've ever seen." She looked up to me, her eyes bright.

I put my arm around her, smiling for her like I had my mother. But it wasn't right. The fish wasn't right.

She smiled wide and hugged me close. "You're my fisherman."

She was beautiful to me then, with her awe of me she sometimes shows, her tenderness. But those feelings only saddened me because I knew she didn't know what it was to be a fisherman amongst the men in my family. The fish was just a dead thing to her.

We stood for a time and stared at it. Its mouth was open, fat lips grayish black, limp. The breeze picked up, cold and moist like at the ocean. She shivered against my side and pulled away, crossing her arms tightly against her chest. Then she leaned up and kissed my cheek softly before going inside, a tender smile still on her lips.

On the wind I could smell the ancient dankness of the fish, and then I knew where it belonged—a place where I'd seen my father bury hundreds of carcasses.

With a groan, my shoulders aching, I grabbed the fish's tail and began dragging the body to the soft soil of our garden.

AT HOME IN THE MIDWEST

Robert Tisdale

Night arrives on time, no sudden
unknown interiors, no vacancies
they have not discussed and put by for.

To be at home in the Midwest
is to know it all from here to horizon,
to inhabit with caution a dream of peace

through the sky fail, to grapple
life from concrete abstractions
—yield per acre, percentage of moisture.

And for satisfaction, to cast or troll
for the mystery, the unnecessary,
when the lure, the shining, gaudy

spoon of metal brings up from the deeps
something hitherto unpossessed
—wet, silent, vicious, alien,
and finally, demonstrably there.

FEAR AND LOATHING...IN ALCOVA, WYOMING

Cale Van Velkinburgh

We are somewhere around Laramie, nowhere near the twenty-second parallel, when I notice the trailer lights are out.

"Holy Christ!" I scream, easing my SUV with trailer and boat in tow onto the median of Highway 287, stretching a long straight distance between our last stop in Fort Collins, Colorado and the next stop in Alcova, Wyoming. "It's nothing." I tell the two drunken fools to my right, "Just forgot to plug the trailer lights back in. Fixed in a jiffy." But I return to tell them that the past forty miles of flying asphalt has disintegrated the female end of the six-way electrical plug dangling beneath the hitch. An impotent collection of wires is all that remains: various blues, blacks; greens and reds, shining copper tips ground to slick finish.

What can we do? Return to Fort Collins, wait until a Super Wal-Mart opens and buy a new plug? This will limit our fishing trip to one long day of driving and only one short day of fishing. *No, absolutely not! I begged for these three days off. Should we press on?* This highway is polluted with state patrol and sheriffs hoping to catch drunken cowboys driving back in their duallies to Laramie from the Sundance bar in Fort Collins. Will we make it? I'm sober. But my cohorts are not. *What if the cop searches the car? What can he find?* Four cases of beer, three pairs of leaky waders, a film canister half full of pot, five fly-rods, a prescription bottle of muscle relaxers, twenty-three fly boxes of various dries, nymphs, streamers,

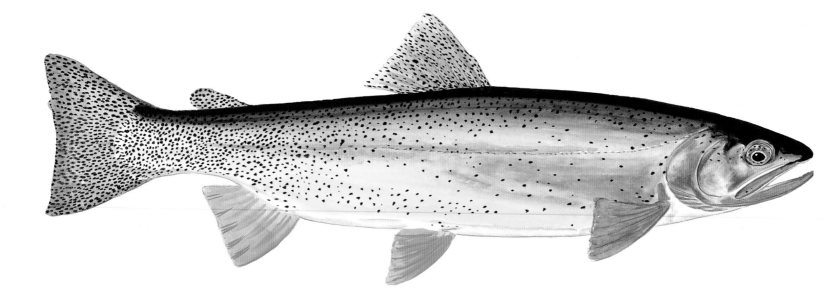

SNAKE RIVER FINESPOTTED CUTTHROAT TROUT *Oncorhynchus clarki behnkei*

tippets, leaders and a puppy dog. *No, nothing wrong here officer. Please don't trouble yourself with us. But those damn Colorado plates, forest green and as big as billboards in this state.* In Wyoming they hate greenies and our greenie status was against us since the border. But there's no turning around now, no way, a midnight run to Laramie is our only choice. Thirty more miles, no trailer lights, an SUV with a purple cataraft behind it and gigantic greenie plates off the back. Its going to be close.

Awaking early the next morning in a cheap Laramie hotel room, with damp shag carpet that reeks of cat piss, we wander outside to attach the new plug to the trailer, purchased at the local Super Wal-Mart upon our late arrival. A nasty cold front arrived making the small wires almost impossible to handle in the negative twenty-degree pre-morning air. Justin looks over the wires, frost hanging from his young but graying hair, and performs a jerry-rigged miracle. Three cups of crap-flavored highway coffee with some moldy convenience store turnovers and we are back on the road. Fully legal and capable of everything expected from an out of state angler. Warm in the car, Justin asleep with his dog in the back, I suspect its only getting warmer outside as the sun leaps up like a magnificent fiery trout, out of the icy waters of night and into my fisherman's view. I have navigated this stretch to Alcova some umpteen times before, laden with the oddest of angling mishaps and conflicts. Sipping my coffee, looking for the day's first pill,

onwards through the Wyoming wasteland and set to make the river by eight.

⊢——⊣

The Alcova trip is nothing more than stories ushered forth from fishing buddies and pictures of goddamn gigantic rainbow trout. For us, Alcova is not a town near great fishing but a destination for pure angling gluttony; a campsite along the water where we push all vices, along with fishing, to total detrimental excess.

The centerpiece to these angling adventures is the Sunset Bar and Grill, conveniently located across from the turn off to the boat ramp. Two run down trailer homes peek from behind the bar's rustic roof, and behind those, a lone, barren Wyoming hill. The bar displays several beer signs outside, fading from exposure to the severe winds of the area and the relentless Western sun. A blaze orange sign stretches across the front welcoming hunters into her depths to enjoy ice-cold Bud Lights. Yes, a place where even the most trigger-happy redneck could feel momentary peace from the onslaught of liberal punks who seem to be invading their West.

They knew our faces at the Sunset, for one fateful evening some months earlier Pat and I arrived with our roommate, a Catholic raft guide from Utah with no fishing experience to speak of. The two Pats (both large, rough, ex-football types with a passion for beer and whiskey) and I sauntered into the bar on a rainy September 14, 2001. Because of the timing, we were in no mood for anything remotely disagreeable to our dispositions, whatever those may be at the moment.

Rain flowed from the dark sky, extinguishing any hopes of setting up camp, so we decided to wait it out in the Sunset. There were only two women in the bar, both working behind it. One, a weathered blonde, tall and slender with a rasp in her voice; who with the right kind of eyes might almost encourage your lust and the other a young brunette, full of piss, vinegar, and a baby.

"Wyoming is in a terrible state, it has the highest teenage pregnancy rate in the country," said the very young and very pregnant girl. We laughed a little too loud.

"I partied with .38 Special," the blonde bartender interrupted, "They're baaad!" she said with a sassy smile. Pat the angler had just put on a song by that very band and feeling whiskey confident cut loose with the blonde bartender. We all cheered and laughed together. But eventually as all good bar scenes must, it ended abruptly with my declaration that the bar was indeed a racist bar and they should fix themselves up to not be such assholes. I had noticed that one of the many autographed dollars bills that adorned the ceiling said "KKK forever."

"Perhaps you would be so kind to remove that," I told the pregnant girl.

"Yeah, a little unnecessary given the times, don't you think?" Pat the Utah born river rat chimed.

"I can't. It is not my bar."

"Well, then…whose goddamn bar is it?"

"It's my mother's and I can't remove it. Only she can. It's her bar!" Seems logical, I thought. But I wasn't backing down quite yet. I ordered our fourth round of Admiral Nelson shots.

"Well damnit. I am the customer, and that is offensive. You need to remove it, or I will be removing it." I spoke, the whiskey burning the words from my mouth into absolute conviction.

She returned from serving two shots to customers at the drive up liquor window and warned that she would call the sheriff if I did anything of the sort. Pat from Utah erupted in obscenities and an enormous shouting match began. Pat the angler looked around nervously, after all, he had much more to lose. He knew many of the local guides by name, and had once guided in the area. He knew what might happen if the wrong person walked in that door and what kind of hell would ensue. The sweat on his brow, the shots at the drive up window, and the drunken political tempers that were flaring created a crescendo of indicators that reinforced the nagging feeling in my gut: that even though we were fishermen in a fishing destination, we were as foreign to this state as French fashion. I began to travel Wyoming with sensitive ears and eyes, loathing my own greenie status.

Shuttle arranged, coffee warming the guts, we arrive at the ramp in full form.

"Pass me the schnapps!"

"Pass me the grass!"

"What are you tying on?"

"How much weight you going with?"

"Let's smoke that after we get the boat in the water."

"Alright, on three."

"I think my waders are leaking."

"One!"

"Where's the dog?"

"Two!"

"Let's just smoke this here, no one's behind us."

"Three! Push!"

"Damn, I can't feel my toes."

"You remember to leave the keys in the hitch?"

"Damn, I can't feel my fingers either. Let me row first."

"Grab the dog. Pass me the schnapps too."

When arranging the shuttle at the gas station they had told us not a single boat had gone down in two weeks. We smiled wholeheartedly at this, thinking of nothing but magnificent five-pound beast in the depths of this tail water, which had been free from all angling pressure for weeks. Furthermore, the cold front upon us set records for the year, maintaining a steady fifteen below. Certainly no purists, no pretenders, no guffawing local guides with attitudes would show up to frown upon our angling-ethic maladies and shenanigans. Free to freeze and hoot and drink and curse as if this river were our own home water.

Unparalleled confidence surging through our veins, our lips tugging at the bottles, sips of schnapps running down our chins and freezing to our beards, this is a fishing adventure! And on any angling adventure the foremost rule is pure Horatio Alger: you earn your fish. We earned ours the night before on that high plains highway. Driving an illegal vehicle with greenie plates through the heart of this wild Wyoming country. My fingers already stiff on the oars, my mind reeling from the mild drugs and the heavy boozing that had begun, I smile with every current of peppermint burn that rolls between my lips, stinging my tongue. I think of fish that have no purpose today other than engaging in a tug-o-war with a couple of greenies.

We had broken all of the boat ramp's rules, we were drunk and stoned by nine AM, had taken our own sweet-ass time putting the boat in the water, we swore loudly and aggressively, looking each other in the eyes, and even went so far as to rig nymph rigs while standing smack in the middle of the ramp. But there were no witnesses to our boat ramp faux pas, and we pushed off without any delay but our own. It should be smooth but cold floating from here.

⊢——⊣

The scene at any boat ramp is always a circus, anglers who

manage themselves well on the river, and perhaps at home as well, somehow become bumbling morons at the boat ramp. Some decide to rig their rods while their boat, trailer and vehicle block any passage for other anglers patiently waiting their turn to stall the process. At Alcova, the problem is compounded for the fool or fools when they have greenie license plates and behave like tourists. The growing combative presence in their rear is chalk full of true Wyoming grit. They consider boat ramps sacred places. Places where business must be tended to, and grab-ass is highly frowned upon. Kind words are hardly ever exchanged here.

Pat and I were well versed in the tacit rules of the Alcova boat ramp. Be quick, no dillydallying with dogs, equipment, oars, and straps. Things here ran like some obsessed, redneck Third-Reich. Don't pause for the slug of whiskey, keep all paraphernalia hidden until the first bend of the river, put your boat in the water, get out of the ramp, and look no one in the eyes. Make it a quick in and out job.

Pat and I were already known greenie culprits at this ramp.

On all our trips, weather permitting, we chose to camp next to the outhouse at the prep area across from the ramp instead of the designated campground. This saved us from camping fees and gave us an edge in the early morning rush since we could park our boat in position to wake up, drink heavily before the locals arrived, and back straight down the ramp, drop the boat, and straight out.

Though on some mornings the locals arrived early to see our vehicle fresh with frost or morning dew, us in brightly colored Marmot sleeping bags, beer cans lining our pillows, passed out in *their* boat preparation area. They tried to be nice, but failed from pure shock. I think they wanted us out, and afraid we may grow wily or return in greater greenie numbers if approached by legal uniformed means, they devised more tactful strategies.

One early October night, Pat, Ogey (we nicknamed him Ogey after a character in our favorite movie, *Slapshot*, because of his all-around skuzzy appearance: fiery red beard and matching afro) and myself sat around our boat next to the outhouse finishing a bottle of cost-conscious wine, laughing about the day of fishing behind us. This was Ogey's first trip to Alcova. He, too, was an experienced angler, a guide on the Gunnison and a greenie at that. The fishing had been spectacular, but we managed to stay on the loose end of things and missed many catch-able opportunities. The first bottle of Beam was done by nine AM, and two more bottles of wine followed thereafter. At noon, I could no longer stand in the bow of my own raft, so I took the oars and promptly passed out, letting the ghost boat drift onto private land. A voice shook me out of my drooling, and I lifted my head off the oar handles in time to hear threats from the only guide who had been there his whole sorry life. The three of us tried to remain calm and serious in the face of this angry professional but completely lost it when he told us what embarrassments we were. Ogey slurred something profane, and I admired how effortlessly he followed our example and heeded Pat's fishing philosophy: "Fishing is a party and not to be treated otherwise."

While reminiscing on the day's debauchery and working on another case of beer, a crazed set of headlights came charging down the road, and before hitting us at our illegal camp site, turned down the ramp towards the wine-dark river below.

"Who the hell was that?" Ogey said from behind his red Norsemen's beard, lantern light revealing wide eyes beneath his pinkish-red Afro. The headlights came back up the ramp with such speed that when the decrepit old van decided to stop next to us, it skidded through the gravel a good ten feet before stopping just shy of the beer cooler. I dove to save the cooler. "Ohh fuck, were in for it now," Ogey said. We jumped to attention as a Johnny Red leapt from the duct-tape driver's seat.

"Hey boys!" he yelled through the quiet night. "You fishing 'morrow? Should be good! Helluva boat you got there, mind if I look at it?" His worn jeans appeared cleaner than his face, his beard looked worse than stained shag carpet, and a black cap that said in yellow letters CAT was perched high on the back of his head, sloping forward to a creased bill which covered his forehead down to his eyebrows.

"Sure," I squeaked nervously, "Have a look."

He passed by, shaking our hands quickly, grabbing a beer from the cooler, and began to rub a wrinkled hand holding a lit cigarette over the rubber tubes of my boat.

"You guys smoke?" he asked while pulling a lighter from his pocket.

"Yeah." Pat said, thankful for the common ground.

"No, I mean are you boys right-handed or left-handed?" This question drew glances from all three of us.

"Uh...um, right handed?" Pat replied cautiously.

"I'm a lefty." Ogey spoke up.

"No," the Johnny Red said, frustration slipping into his voice, his head shaking. "I mean do you smoke cigs or grass?" Ogey erupted in a cowardly confession.

"Sure as shit!" he said.

So we reluctantly piled into the back of his van, just hoping to get on his good side and avoid any further unpleasantries. An hour later rolling out on a cloud, laughing and hugging, we passed the wine bottle around with insistence, trying to behave like good hosts.

Our evening almost felt natural until, in an eager act of show and tell, he pulled a 9mm pistol from a duffle bag.

"Holy shit!" Ogey blurted. When I turned to scowl at him, Ogey was gone. My eyes adjusted a bit and I saw him peering from the far side of the boat, refusing to come out. Pat and I shot looks back and forth, wanting to appear comfortable in front of this strange man. We tried to humor this Johhny

Red, and compliment this fine piece of shooting machinery but grew nervous when he took out his prized and illegal extended clip, slid it in with a metallic click, and pulled the slide to load one round into the chamber.

We're done for now God, thanks! We've pushed it too far, and the locals want our demise. Pat had gone speechless and I was sure Ogey was halfway back to Casper.

And for ten terrifying minutes he waved that gun around, loaded with the safety off. Neither Pat nor myself in any condition to respond to this unforeseeable terror, standing petrified, only our eyes moving and following that gun ready to duck. He grabbed one more beer, shoved the loaded weapon down the front of his pants, and without saying a word to us hopped into his van which had been running the entire hour of his stay and drove off, spraying rocks and gravel with each turn and each weave he made.

Justin's rod bends with the first pig, a twenty-something-incher. "Let me take a picture!" I holler from the oars. "Okay, just hurry, she's cold. So are my fingers," he says in his comically squeaky voice. Justin stands there before us, very unlike Paul MacLean, anchored to frozen wading boots as his face huddles back beneath a cloak of North Face, Patagonia, and Orvis apparel. The trout's bright red lateral line sticks out against his gray complexion and the dismal sky behind him.

"Quit breathing for a second, your breath is blocking your face. There!"

Pat lands the next fish almost immediately, noticeably larger and again picture worthy. That was to be the last picture of the day. Not because of the fishing, but because of the effort it took to pull one's gloves off, pick the fish from its icy home, pose, and return the fish to water and the hands to gloves before the muscles in either froze solid.

For the next five hours we drink and we catch, and we catch and we drink. We only tie on flies when bare hooks with shreds of thread and material meet our eyes. The temperatures keep falling, making the knots nearly impossible to tie, but the fishing remains consistent. The schnapps are the next thing to go, but the Beam tastes even better, and our blustering songs shouted at random periodically interrupt the long spells of fishermen's quiet.

Justin's dog climbs out of his duffle bag cavern lined with layers of wool and fleece. The miniscule black lab whines a bit, we laugh back and point as the dog circles on the front platform next to Justin's frozen feet, then pisses in steaming relief. With another whimper, the puppy is back into his cover, occasionally peeking out with a wet nose. Three miles out from the take out at Lusby's we round a long slow bend, Justin roll casting off another large rainbow, when the reality of the cold weather hits.

"Hey," I whisper from oars, "is that…?"

"Ice?" Pat says.

"Yeah. But…it looks like it's…damnit!" I stop rowing, letting the cataraft drift silently until it bumps into the leading edge of a frozen river. From where I sit the river looks like a vast ice flat; a Wyoming winter wasteland that, as far as I can tell, extends to the takeout miles away. They've finally done it! My mind shrieks. *The locals, seeing our lack of response to past warnings have gone all the way, and frozen the goddamn river! Oh God!*

"What now, boys?" I ask.

"Pass me the Beam."

"Should we hike it?"

"No! God no, we'll get shot. Its private land, and you know how these people treat greenies! Furthermore, what the hell we gonna do when we get to the car? Drive back, get permission to pull our boat off on their property cause we're idiots and the river we drove three-hundred miles to float has frozen across."

"Dude," came a squeak from the stern, "get me over to the bank, I'll hop out and take a look." I pull on the oars and back row from the ice and onto the bank, which really isn't a bank but just more ice. Justin lumbers out and suggests we push the boat along the solid ice bank. But for how long, how far? There is hardly room to pull the raft out here, and around the corner this bank disintegrates into impassible cliffs along the shore.

An argument ensues about the realities of us becoming sled dogs in waders.

"Hey, I can see the river coming out the other side," Pat interrupts, "see it there, it comes back out about a hundred yards or so, maybe we can just break through using the oars." Justin rounds the corner of the bank, weary of landowners, and confirms that the river fully opens up a little ways down. Pat and I row out to the middle, but the boat gets spun around and I find myself hanging off the stern breaking the ice with one oar while Pat poles us forward with the other from the bow. Our heads begin singing whiskey tunes, our bodies numb with laughter about the stories we will tell.

However, the ice soon becomes too thick to break with the oar, so in one magnificent move I leap onto the ice holding firm the frozen metal foot bar attached to the stern. With my weight primarily on the foot bar, I gently bounce on the ice until it cracks with a chilling cold POP, and then heave my butt over the foot bar, clearing the ice with my frozen boots as Pat poles us forward. He starts up with some made up sailor's tune about fools with fly-rods breaking ice on frozen waters. Then the ice breaks a little too quick, and my skinny ass misses the metal foot bar. In I go.

I manage a hold on the foot bar, which keeps me from going completely under, but the metal is crusted over with slick ice and my fingers slip repeatedly. The sudden chill of the water squirting down my waders is like fingers clutching at my throat, where I holler help in this bad dream yet nobody hears the screams but me. Pat sings merrily, laughing at his own creative lyrics, pushing the boat right on top of me. The current sucks my legs completely under the ice, then begins to pull at my waist. Justin sees my plight, I am sure of that, and he jumps and points from the bank, but his voice falls short of the boat. The water roiling about my chest is an inch from the top of my waders, my grip slips a little, and I know that when the icy Wyoming water begins to fill my waders it will pull me off this boat like a para-sail, sucking me somewhere under the ice. I can't hear anything but rushing river and that obscene singing from the front of the boat, then more laughter, until I finally break the curse and manage a pathetic "help."

"What?" Pat pauses his song, "Dude, Justin's freaking out on the bank, what's he…CALE!" he says with a laugh, and in a bound heaves me from the river, laughing as I collapse onto the deck and watch the water freeze instantly to the outside of my neoprene waders.

I couldn't stop shivering that night, sitting in a hotel hot tub. *They had won. No warnings of ice, no mention of it. Sure, come fishing, its great right now, not a soul out here, the river will be yours. Tailwaters weren't supposed to freeze, not there, not so close to the dam. But they had willed it so.* I sat and shivered as bubbles popped from the chlorine water all around us. We debated about the next day. It was supposed to warm up some. We had, after all, driven many miles and caught more fish than any bunch of loose cannons deserves. I believe they were expecting us to give up, call it a loss, head home to the security of Birkenstocks, Democrats, dreadlocks and greenies. *No,* I thought as sensation tingled in my feet, *damned if we'll be run out like this!*

HOOKED CLANDESTINELY

Jimmy Hodges

"JIMMY! WE ALWAYS go to the Pork-Puller! Let's go somewhere nice for a change!" That was my wife, Mona, and she was in charge. And so, on that particular night in late July, when it was just too drippy humid to cook even a BLT sandwich, and there was no milk in the fridge for cereal, I knew I wouldn't get to enjoy the Extra Saucy Pork-Puller Combo. I also knew what this meant: nice clothes.

I begrudgingly pulled off my old hospital scrubs (the best for hot weather) and T-shirt. "Jimmy! You can't walk naked around the house! The neighbors will see!" she crowed as she stuck her head around the door frame to catch me in the nude.

I did a few floppy jumping jacks to show her I still had a little spark in me, then sauntered off to the bedroom where she would surely be putting on her black and pink dress.

Sure enough, she was squeezing her torso into that odd polka-dot tube, which I thought made her look like a hog at a discotheque, but which I always swore was beautiful. It would be a night on the town for the Hodges.

At six o'clock or so, our old beater putted just over the big hill and started our journey toward town and food without BBQ sauce. The other restaurant we'd gone to in the last thirty years was Lettuce Souprise You. After a few minutes drive, I could see it down the end of the long straight-away by the river and began the long slow-down process. The brakes didn't work very well, so about a half mile in advance I'd start lightly tugging on the faithful e-brake.

We were at a near stop when I saw a big piece of plywood nailed across the door frame. "FLOODED!" it read in sloppy spray paint, and I wondered how they could be exuberant enough to include the exclamation point. With the brake taken off, our old car glided slowly and silently past the scene. We peered out to see a fire truck parked on one side with its pump apparently inside, spouting water out the dining room window. The owner's two kids happily splashed in their swimsuits. Those Lettuce people were odd ones.

We hadn't been beyond the medium-nice restaurant in a long time, probably ten years. It was nice to have a change of scenery. The river wound closer to the road here, and the elm trees cast long shadows that we drove in and out of.

We continued on in silence for a good ten miles before I spotted an old log cabin I'd long forgotten stuck out on an oxbow bend of the river. It had a new sign painted on the roof in big block letters. It read "Clamdestiny," with neon Miller signs lighting up either side. It looked like my kind of place.

The head waiter had rubber boots on, and he smelled vaguely of fish. In fact, the whole place had a decidedly fishy aroma. Not the gross dock dead fish smell, but rather that aroma that pervaded my grandfather's house after he returned from noodling catfish. At the bar, there was a single hollowed-eyed man muttering something about midges. As Mona walked by, he grabbed her pink arm. "Too

wily!" he whispered, and then returned to rocking back and worth. There was a strange air to the whole establishment.

The rubber-booted waiter sat us down in the middle of the only table in the restaurant, one long and crowded enough for a medieval hunting feast. We found our way to two seats across from each other, smack in the middle. A couple next to us were loudly arguing about something.

"You want the usual?" The waiter asked. "Two," I responded, without bothering to point out that I'd never been here before.

"So what's the usual?" I asked the man next to me. His mouth was full, and he jabbed a fork in the direction of his wife.

"The usual, huh? You'll find out. But let me tell you a story about a Usual. A Usual, size #10, just pretty much a little tuft of rabbit on a hook. Cahills were coming off, looked like snow over the river. Browns were hammering the Usual. But I spotted one who stood out from the rest—a lunker with shoulders the size of my thigh. Just finning there, I watched him not taking, just waiting for a perfect Cahill to pop off."

She talked at an amazing clip, while still managing to stuff food into her mouth during pauses. As she continued, her husband began to behave strangely. He intensely analyzed the ceiling, while opening and shutting his mouth. Bizarre. I turned my attention back to the woman, as she started to wave her knife back and forth in the air in a casting motion and threw herself into an even louder, higher pitch to capture my wandering attention.

"Threw a long loop, had to double haul it just to get my line out there—but it landed sweet, just as soft as a feather it settled onto the surface. Just watched it float down toward him. He spotted it a long way off and I knew right away he'd come up."

The man's fork clattered onto the hardwood floor. He pulled his open palms up to his neck and started gently flapping them back and forth. His eyes rolled up toward the ceiling. Something out of the usual was going on here. His wife continued.

"So he comes up real slow, you know, just to torture me, slowly looking it over." I looked over at the man. He delicately tilted his head to one side. She continued. "I could see his huge maw open, just enough, and just sip that sucker down."

The man definitely was looking like a fish now. He opened his mouth, displaying a half-chewed usual and finning his hands in crazy excitement for one second. And then his wife set the hook. With a quick upward pull of her hands, she sent him into a frenzy. One finger hooked into the flesh of his cheek, he bolted up, spilling his beer all over me splattering food throughout the restaurant.

"As soon as he was hooked, he ran!" The wife shouted. But she didn't need to explain. The man tore across the restaurant, in short shuffled steps, wagging his butt furiously like a pulsing tail.

"Man, did he ever took off. Had me into the backing in

seconds!" She shouted over the din of pounding feet and fishlike gasps. "So I had to palm the reel and stop him!"

The man started straining against the imaginary line. Even a non-fisherman like me knew what was coming next. It started as a wiggle in his feet, that built to a wag at his butt, to a full thrash in his torso, and then he was up! Head shaking, desperately leaping, trying to shake the curved finger from his cheek. But he was hooked, and hooked well. The battle would be over soon.

The woman panted in excitement as she finished the story. "I knew I had him beat after that ferocious jump, so it was just a dogfight. I worked him in slow against the current." The man, laid out flat now, flopped across the floor in a pathetic version of the worm. His one hand waved slowly as he turned on his side, and then flopped onto his back. His wife reached down and pried the finger from his mouth, setting it kindly back down to start flapping again. She stroked his heaving side, and pushed him back and forth in the imaginary current. He gasped his mouth as the gills started to process oxygen once more. Finally, she gave him a pat, he stood up, returned to his seat, picked up his silverware, and started to gather his food off of the table.

"Good thing you're a catch-and-release fisherman," I offered in the ensuing silence.

"Yep," she responded, and returned to her dinner.

"He's quite a catch," I retorted.

"Sure is."

"The biggest fish in a little pond."

"That's my husband."

With my wit exhausted, I happily returned to the Usual. And that's how the Pork-Puller lost my faithful business.

GITTIN' MYSELF
A GARFISH

Mark Spitzer

STILL, IT'S FRUSTRATING not to git a garfish. Something there is in me that's just gotta git one. My bruised fishing ego is at stake.

That's why I found myself taking my friend Kevin to the levee again. The day before, we were out there catching minnows to feed my pet catfish when we stumbled across a gar spawning spot. The water was high and they were rolling in the grass in the afternoon heat. I had to git me one!

So I waded out with my minnow net and began stalking garfish. They let me get pretty close and I could see them pretty clearly; they were a couple feet long with oblong black spots, swimming in pairs. Must've been fifty or sixty of them.

I'd get as close as I could, but then they'd shoot off. I'd plunge in my net, and miss every time. Until I snuck up on a stump, where I could see a couple on the other side, rolling in the weeds. The smart one saw me and shot off, but the dumb one stayed behind. That garfish was a sitting duck.

I positioned the net right above its head, and went for it. *Splashhh!* The garfish shot straight into it. I pulled the net up on the stump and the gar came with it, splashing like crazy. I had it. It was mine. Finally, a garfish!

But then it flopped out of the net and started slapping around on the stump. I dove for it, slipped, and fell into the muck, allowing the garfish to slap back into the bayou.

So that's why we were heading back. This time, though, I

was armed with a brand new net from Wal-Mart which I had reinforced and extended with a mop handle.

"*Lepisosteus spatula*," I told Kevin as I drove, "is known by many other names: gar pike, gator gar, diamond-fish, devil-fish, jackfish, garjack, bony pike, billy gar, et cetera."

Kevin didn't seem to be very impressed with my bevy of gar-knowledge. He lit up a cig while I continued: "Garfish have lung-like organs that breathe air. This allows them to lie in muddy creekbeds waiting for the rains. Or gulp air on the surface of low-oxygen ponds."

I was an encyclopedia of fascinating gar-facts:

"The roe of garfish is toxic to humans. Indians made arrowheads from their scales. There's a saying in the Carolinas which goes 'as common as gar-broth.'"

"What do they eat?" Kevin asked, blowing out a plume of smoke.

"Nutria rats," I told him, "ducks, bugs, herons, fish. Some have allegedly eaten soap, as well as giant turkeys, small dogs, and decoys."

"What about humans?"

"There's never been a verified account," I answered, totally prepared for this question, "but there have been reports of gar maulings. The most famous is from 1932, in Mandeville, Louisiana, at the height of American gar-paranoia. A certain Dr. Paine reported that he had patched up a nine-year-old girl who'd been sitting on the edge of Lake Pontchatrain dangling her feet in the water. Apparently, her toes must've looked like teeny weenies, because the next thing she knew a seven-foot gar was dragging her in. She screamed and her thirteen-year-old brother ran to the rescue. He pulled her away and her leg was just a bloody stump."

Suddenly, we were at the spot, ready to git ourselves a garfish. The water, however, was down from the day before, leaving yesterday's eggs exposed to the sun, and the gar were out deeper, rippling on the surface. So I snuck out with my net, just in time to see a gar-tail rise. It slapped the water and they all shot off.

A fat lotta good all that book-learning did me!

We ended up chasing a bunch of retarded ducks on the shore, trying to get them with my special gar-net. They waddled and quacked while we stumbled after. Kevin went for one and conked it on the head, such that it went stumbling around like a drunken uncle.

It's a pathetic sight when grown men fail to git a garfish.

Colonel J.G. Burr of Texas was the Adolph Hitler of garfish. He was the Director of Research of the Game Fish and Oyster Commission in Austin in the '30s, where he tried his damnedest to destroy gar through electrocution, virtually sending thousands to the "chair."

Col. Burr's preferred method of execution was stringing a power-line across the bottom of a body of water, then dragging buoys across the surface connected to ground wires. He'd send

400 volts through the power line, and the fish within range would float to the surface, either knocked out or dead.

This shocking behavior on the part of the Colonel was encouraged by various bureaus of research and conservation which publicly called for inventors "to devise methods for gar control, since it is clear that this species is a real menace to many forms of fish and other wild life."

Col. Burr went on to construct a special boat meant for the massacre of gars: The Electrical Gar Destroyer. It was an 8- by 16-foot "barge" rigged with a 200-volt generator and an electric net that zapped the fish then scooped them up. There was a bright red floodlight hooked up to the bow to blind the garfish if they weren't quite dead, and lessen their struggle.

On the maiden voyage of the Electrical Gar Destroyer, Burr succeeded in wiping out seventy-five alligator gar and one-thousand turtles. After that, he went up and down bayous and canals ridding Texas of garfish (and whatever else happened to be there), even making excursions into saltwater to get gar that had fled the threat of his all-mighty net.

Mr. J.G. McGee of New Mexico then took a hint from the Colonel and rigged up something similar in the Pecos River in Roswell. He went to dams where gar had gathered and shocked them to death. Others followed suit, and soon, tons of garfish were floating belly up across the desert Southwest.

Meanwhile, Col. Burr was compiling all sorts of data on killing gar at various depths with various voltages in different degrees of salinity during different months of the summer. He exterminated millions, making a great dent in the American garfish population.

Following a massive gar-kill in Lake Caddo, this is what the great sportsman Col. Burr had to say:

> I saw one immense Gar, which seemed to be seven-feet long, spring entirely out of the water thirty-feet away. His jump was at an angle of forty-five degrees and I am sure he felt the current. This jumping of the Gars, whether they went into the net or not, produced a thrill which cannot be found in any other kind of fishing.

Contrary to claims that garflesh ain't fit for a dog to eat, there doesn't seem to be a shortage of gar-meat being sold in the South. I've seen steaks and filets at rinky-dink stores and gas stations all over Louisiana.

In Fishing Gear Online there's an article entitled "Gar in the Pan." The author, Keith Sutton, writes:

> Actually, gars are rather tasty, a fact that becomes obvious when you learn of the hundreds of thousands of pounds of gar meat being sold each year at Mom-and-Pop fish markets throughout the country. On a recent visit to a south Arkansas fish market, I watched as the proprietor sold hundreds of pounds of gar-meat in three hours, at three-dollars a pound. Catfish fillets, selling for two-dollars and fifty-cents per pound, were hardly touched by the customers.... "I can't get enough gars to meet the demand," the proprietor told me. "Once folks try it and find out how good it really is, they come back wanting more. The fish are difficult to dress, but the meat cooks up white and flaky, and tastes as good as any fish you ever put in your mouth."

Sutton goes on to tell about how he ate a freshly cut steak from a 190-pound gar, and how he was impressed with it. He compares the taste to crappie, before offering up this poem:

My pan at home it has been greased
For gar he is a tasty beast
I shall invite the local priest
To join me in this garish feast.

Whether the second to the last word in the poem is missing an "f," I can't say. But I can say what follows in the article: step by step instructions on how to prepare garfish. Basically, this is how it's done:

First, cut off the head and tail with an axe, leaving a big long tube of food. Secondly, use tin snips to split the bony hide open, right down the belly. Thirdly, peel the meat back from the armor using gloves to protect your fingers. After that, filet the meat along the backbone, then cut into smaller pieces.

Sutton goes on to list a multitude of recipes, including gar-stew, gar-cakes, stir-fried gar, gar boulettes, and garfish Mississippi. So far, this article is the best resource I've found on how to cook gar. It's available on-line.

After all that gar-study, I couldn't be held back. So I took off for the Gaspergou Bayou Oil and Gas Fields, where it's said the largest ancient gar in the state still seethe beneath the surface—some of them close to a century old. I was armed with a canoe full of milk jugs with guitar strings strung to treble hooks meant for lingcod up in Puget Sound, a bag of

rancid turkey necks, two gas cans filled with liquid chum, five cans of dog food, and my father's 9mm Luger captured off a Nazi soldier.

I also had one bearded Bulgarian with me, Plamen Arnoudov. Last time I took him fishing, he hooked an endangered paddlefish and I beat it to death with a hammer. We ate shovelnose for days, which is illegal in Louisiana.

But then again, so is fishing without a license. Which we intended to do—as almost every single Cajun does. And nobody tells Cajuns not to eat what they catch—that's what they've been doing since the 1600s, hunting and trapping and living off the land. So why should graduate students be any different? Just because the ancestors of Cajuns got abducted from Canada and dumped in a swamp, prompting Longfellow to write some poem about a tree—does that give them more right to fish for free than us? I don't think so.

It didn't really matter, though, because the place we were going was posted "OFF LIMITS" anyway. Gaspergou is owned by Texaco, who ran a big old petrochemical processing plant out there on a platform until just a few years ago when the State shut them down. Supposedly, they'd been dumping something that couldn't be mentioned in the papers. Now, however, the platform was abandoned, and that's where we heard the big ones lurked.

So we snuck through the cypresses. For miles and miles, great horned owls stared down at us while egrets nested all around. There were alligators lying on logs and copperheads winding through the duckweed. And when we got to the platform, there were vultures perched on giant pipes overgrown with poison ivy. But from a hundred yards away, we could see the surface rippling.

So we stayed where we were, baited up our floats, and tossed them out. The wind was with us, blowing toward the platform. Soon, twenty jugs were making their way toward the gar-swirls, each of them dangling a big honking turkey neck.

Then we broke out the chum. I'd bought a case of slicker (freshwater mullet) at a place called Breaux's in Henderson (one box, one dollar), then ground them up in the food-processor until it became an oily purée—which I put outside for three days in the sun. When the neighbors started complaining about the stench, that's when I poured it into the gas cans.

So Plamen and I, we put our spigots on and poured the soup into the swamp. A reeking red puddle began following the jugs, and that's when I saw a long armored back rise, then vanish. It was half the size of my canoe!

After that, drifting closer, we made some bait-bombs by pounding holes in the Alpo cans and hurling them out to smolder underwater and get the gar all up in a lather.

We waited. Suddenly a milk jug went under, then reappeared ten feet later. Then another one went down. Then another. The garfish were going nuts over there. We waited until all twenty were bobbing and bopping around the platform, and paddled over.

The first one we pulled up had a five-foot gar on it. It started splashing around in a frenzy. There was no way we were gonna get it in the boat without tipping over, so I leveled the Luger between its eyes and blasted a hole through its motherfucking head.

Then we saw the incredible. Its pals began attacking it, swarming it, right beneath us. We could see garbacks passing eight feet long, sometimes longer. They were ripping their fallen comrade to shreds and thrashing on the surface, roiling red with blood.

We gripped the canoe and tried to hold on. The buzzards above were screeching like the damned. A couple times the boat almost flipped—and we knew what would happen if we went into the drink. But then the ruckus ceased.

Under the platform, we saw nineteen milk jugs on the run. Something had spooked them. Something that made a tremendous splash, causing us to swivel and see a gar so huge that I'd lose all credibility as a garfish aficionado if I tried to describe the size of it. I will only say that some of those books weren't so far off, and that its entire chromy backside was cutting across the swamp, coming our way.

The next thing we knew, we were kicking up a rooster tail and paddling like lunatics. Our only thought was to make it to the Spanish moss and get up in those trees. And from that moment on, I no longer felt that burning urge (nor do I feel it today) to git myself a garfish.

TO A FATHER LONG GONE

Greg Keeler

Who could escape into the life of a sunfish
without becoming a slave to imagery? Green,
longear, pumpkinseed, bluegill, warmouth—wish
for the distant years where youth made these mean
little but joy, and you find yourself trapped behind
bars that come and go by instinct in the rushes
of fear or weather. Long to color a mind
long lost to abstraction, and a bright orange blushes
behind a turquoise so deep you could slip on a thought
and kill yourself. Better to stick with a father
and watch the bobber dive, on a deep life caught,
from red and white to dark green, than bother
to go there now, a father yourself, alone in a boat,
the sunfish a hidden mystery, colored by hope.

THE GRAND SLAM

Scott Bowen

Uncle seamus sat with Len on the patio, under the umbrella. They relaxed on chaise lounges. Seamus was quiet for a long time. He appeared to be remembering something. The sun was very bright and Len squinted at the reflections off the bright leaves of the rose bushes nearby. The whole property, with all its trees and bushes, was a chessboard of solid shadow and gleaming wedges of sunlit green. Len didn't wear sunglasses because Seamus didn't like people wearing sunglasses. The dark, goggly eyes confused him and he shouted, Look at me, when people in sunglasses looked at him.

Seamus was hoping for a grand slam as good or better than the one he had last week, or yesterday, whichever day. He drew his breath slowly and said slowly, People sometimes weren't sure the snook should have been a part of the grand slam, you know?

Snook should be, Seamus, Len said.

Seamus looked over his shoulder and down the long lawn to the hedge. His gaze wandered, slightly unclear, over the hedge to the woods beyond. Well, he said, the weather looks good.

Where'd you catch the snook, Uncle Seamus?

Seamus shook his head irritably then looked squarely at Len. Yeah, snook. Some people thought snook shouldn't be part.

Len said, How many snook yesterday?

Three. Then the tarpon, Seamus said. That tarpon was good.

I'll bet, Len said, sipping lemonade. Any permit?

There's a secret to them.

What's the secret?

Seamus held his clenched hands up against his chest and nodded, then slowly returned his hands to his lap. The gesture was setting the hook.

Len smiled at his uncle but Seamus didn't smile back. He blinked at Len, somewhat fazed. Len said, What's the secret?

Seamus looked down at his hands where they rested. They did not seem to him that they were his hands; though he felt their weight, the flesh seemed dense and insensitive. Len asked again about the secret and Seamus had to think before he spoke, saying, It's the hands.

Len nodded. He leaned back and closed his eyes. He was glad everyone else was gone: his sister, Leigh, his mother, Peg, Aunt Janine, who was Seamus's sister, and both Seamus's daughters, Kelly and Beth. They had all gone shopping. Every time one of them had come out to check on Seamus throughout the morning, they put their hands on his shoulders and stood behind him, as if to push him out of the chaise, or sat very close and leaned into his face as if to measure the light in his cataracted eyes. They talked to the old man in queries and polite cautions when he spouted off about something. Len hated to watch it.

Len's mother had called him at school before the end of the semester. She said that Uncle Seamus was "starting to slip" and that if Len wanted to talk with him while he was

lucid he should come home for a visit. Len said he needed five days for exams and then he could get away.

Seamus was Len's favorite great uncle—favorite because he had been the one to give him his first twelve-weight rod, a big heavy Sage. His other uncles and great uncles had all set fine examples, given him good things and a lot of advice. But when Len was too bashful to ask his father for such an expensive piece of equipment that he would not use as often as other rods, and did not have enough cash himself, Seamus somehow sensed his nephew's want and delivered the goods as a college graduation present. That uncanny sense Seamus once had about wants, those of people and fish, was now swallowed and divided by his problematic mind.

When Seamus had begun casting a line around the gardens and trees, Len's mother again called her son at school. Len was turning in grades, handing in his own papers, and wondering how to make it through without a summer assistantship when she called. She said, Len, come home for a little while and see Seamus.

Is he worse?

Yes. He wants to go fishing.

Well, let him.

He wants to go to Florida.

Put him on an airplane then. Send one of his daughters with him.

Len, don't be insipid, please. Uncle Seamus can't go anywhere.

Len held his breath a moment. He said, You're not going to put him in a home, are you?

I think between myself, Aunt Janine, and either Kelly or Beth, we can keep him here for a while, she said. But eventually we'll have to move him to either Kelly's or Beth's house and get home care, I think.

Why not our house?

It's just a stop over. They have to decide who's going to take him from here.

Why not his sister?

She's getting old too.

But Aunt Janine said she'd take him, didn't she?

Yes, she did, and she's only two years younger than Seamus. It would be too much for her.

Len shrugged when he hung up the phone. The next day he put his rent check in the mail and got in his truck. He drove the scenic route through North Carolina and Virginia, and managed to stay awake to cross half of the very long state of Pennsylvania. He arrived at his childhood home in the boonies by midnight. Everyone was in bed. His father was away on business. The house was utterly silent and made Len mindful that somewhere in the dark was a very weary, heavy head.

—⊢—⊣—

Len looked at the old man. Seamus had lost most of his grey-

brown hair and large, thick freckles covered his head. His face was tan and leathery, his eyebrows shaggy. His hazel eyes were discolored by the cataracts but still intense, darker than they once were. The most sure indication of his state was that he was dressed simply and a bit disheveled, for Seamus in his day had been a sharp, precise dresser and had reached the point in his fifties when he had enough money to have several tailored suits and numerous tailored shirts. In front of Len he wore a gray sweatshirt half tucked into worn-out khakis, and flip-flops. His unshaven face looked wrong.

Len had awakened that morning to distant shouts and as he wandered into the living room he looked out the big bay window to see his mother, Aunt Janine, and cousin Kelly standing around the old man who was blathering and shaking his fist. His right hand held an old fiberglass twelve-weight fitted with a big black Pflueger reel. Seamus's back cast of a tarpon fly caught in a huge blue spruce too high to reach with the rod tip. He jangled the line, shouted curses, and was in a fretful state.

Len wandered down the lawn in his bathrobe, went up to Seamus, and said, Hello, Seamus. Snagged?

Seamus turned with a start, began to turn away, then recognized Len and said, Hey. It's a good day. Then bellowed, Goddamn it!

Len brought the ladder, plucked the big Apte fly off the pine bough, and tossed it down. Kelly and Len's mother coaxed

Seamus up to the patio and sat him down. They talked him into breakfast and he acquiesced because he was hungry.

As Len poured himself coffee in the kitchen, his sister, Leigh, came in. What was Seamus doing? she said.

Fishing, Len said.

He was doing that yesterday and the day before.

Where?

Here. Across the lawns. Old Mister Waylan led him back yesterday afternoon. We went crazy looking for him. I don't know how he does it, Len, but you'll turn your back and he'll be gone. He's like a ghost.

What did Waylan say?

Seamus was casting at Mister Waylan's bushes, she said. Then he shouted at Mister Waylan to get out of the water.

Len laughed.

Why did mom bring him here? Leigh whispered.

She's trying to preserve the peace during negotiations.

No one wants him, huh? Poor old widower.

Aunt Janine will get him, which I think is right. She wants him with her.

Such a burden.

All she has to do is put a fly-rod in his hands and he'll be fine.

You're nuts like him, Leigh said, and went back to her room with a banana.

After breakfast, Len sat with Seamus in the shade of the umbrella. His mother asked if he would watch the old man for the day because, she said, everyone needed a break. He watched all the women leave en masse. He waved as they drove away, then sat back and sighed.

Looking at his uncle, he guessed that this was the way he would go himself, this or cancer. Senility and cancer were the family killers. Those sicknesses had ended the lives of his grandparents and some of their many siblings. Len was down to two great uncles and three great aunts, all in their seventies. He did not know if he preferred cancer or senility. He had seen senility in its last stages with a few other relatives and he wondered if its mental storm was worse than the bodily wracking of the Big C, as his own father called it.

Come on, Seamus, we're going fishing, Len said.

The old man said nothing. Len repeated himself until Seamus said, Where?

We'll go over to the South Branch.

South Key?

The Raritan, Seamus. South Branch. The Gorge.

Key West, Seamus said. Get a boat. The Marquesas.

We'll go there later. Let's get in some trout.

Seamus shook his head. Braddy, he said, you know I hate trout. "Braddy" was Bradley, Len's father.

Since when do you hate trout?

Since the first grand slam, Seamus said.

Len smiled to himself. He remembered that Seamus had

a grand slam back in the late seventies when Len himself was a young boy. Seamus must have had a few more around the neighborhood, casting to forsythia and patches of ivy.

It's not that long a boat ride from here, Braddy, Seamus said. We can make it.

When should we go?

Now, Seamus said with urgency.

Len would have put old furniture around the backyard and let Seamus blast the settees and chairs with a .12-gauge if the old man asked for it. As a matter of fact, that sounded pretty good, and there was an attic full of furniture. But how could he find a way to get to the Marquesas?

Seamus whispered to himself. Then he turned and looked at his grand nephew, his eyes cloudy but focused on Len. Yes? he said expectantly.

Do you know where you are, Seamus? Are we in the Keys? Len asked sincerely, and with sincere curiosity, because he did not want to invent a charade the old man did not already possess himself.

Seamus said, Are we?

Len considered what he wanted to say. He wanted to entertain Seamus, and give him some emotional adventure; not hurt him or make a monkey out of him. He rubbed his temples.

Are there fish out there, Seamus? he said. He pointed to the huge front lawn. Along that bank? Do you see fish? Tell

me if you do.

Seamus peered into the distance. Slowly he nodded. I see 'em, he said. Tarpon. They're swimming on the other side of that bank. Seamus pointed to the very edge of the property where stood a long pile of mulberry bushes. Len went to his room and found some old flies, then went back outside and took the old twelve-weight from where his mother had hidden it in the garage. He tied a ratty old Cockroach to the heavy leader then handed the rod to Seamus and said, I'll get the wagon.

Seamus faced the far mulberry bushes, his face wan but his eyes locked on the spot where the tarpon's dark backs showed. He nodded.

Len went around the back of the house. He hoped to give Seamus a nice morning of casting, and was pleased to find what he wanted—a battered wooden flatbed wagon mounted on a heavy chassis with big lawn mower tires. It had been used years before by one of the caretakers before the adjoining properties were sold to real estate developers. It was still used for hauling away leaves in the autumn. Len grabbed the handle on the end of the steel arm and pulled it out of the tall grass and steered it around the corner of the house. The wagon wasn't hard to drive backwards by pushing and steering with the heavy arm.

Halfway around the house, Len stopped. He wanted to know if this was wrong. No one was there to tell him if it was or wasn't. Was it patronizing to indulge the fantasy of someone half out of his mind? Then, stubbornly, he shoved the wagon along. Sometimes in life all one has is fantasy.

Seamus was standing on the edge of the flagstones as Len approached and when he saw his nephew he caught his breath and pointed. His hand trembled slightly at the end of his long arm. Len helped Seamus into the wagon. Seamus crouched unsteadily on one knee and held the side panel with both hands. The big rod stuck over the front panel. Len pushed the wagon from behind, going slowly, the fat tires sinking into the thick grass as they went until they were about sixty feet off the end of the bushes. Len held the wagon side, standing on the grass below Seamus. Seamus breathed hoarsely and said, There are two big ones. Just coming onto the edge, see?

In the crystal green water, two thick, bluish bars angled against the grain of the water.

The wind's with you, Len said.

Seamus rested against the wooden panel, legs aside like a soldier fallen after a long march. The long rod wagged with vibration. Seamus said nothing. He faced the water ahead. The tarpon there lolled at the surface, their silver scales turning the water to opal around them. Seamus watched the brown fly sail and snap with a false cast and he flexed his arm just as the rod loaded.

Len looked to where Seamus looked. He saw the black

dots of big bees that moved among the thick branches of the bushes and shoved themselves into the flowers, entering and wriggling with ecstasy. Robins called in the distance.

A tarpon swallowed the fly and Seamus's entire body stiffened when he saw the huge dark hole of its open mouth. He waited, letting the fish pull back and turn a few feet, then struck, bouncing where he sat, setting the hook. He let out a gout of breath as the big tarpon exploded out of the water and flung itself through the air. He cupped his line hand, cinching it until the line shot through with minimal burn. His arms jerked. There was little line to clear and soon the tarpon was on the reel. Seamus let out a happy groan and held on. The fish jumped again and Seamus strained to bow with the rod. The fish's violence felt as if it would pull his body off like a glove, leaving him sitting with just his mind in the boat. The tarpon leapt a third time and threw the hook. It was a lovely fish. Seamus smiled.

Len said, Seamus? The old man hadn't moved.

Seamus looked at the young man and smiled.

Still see them? Len said.

Seamus nodded. Len rolled Seamus down the lawn a short distance. Here Seamus cast to a lone tarpon lolling next to a grass bank. This one wasn't as big, maybe thirty pounds. The fish nosed into the fly and Seamus let it drift, sink, and then gave it an expert twitch that did not pull it away. The tarpon turned at an angle to the fly, its big eye studying the prey.

Seamus twitched it again and pulled it an inch and the tarpon turned and gobbled the fly. The fish came forward to deeper water, its mouth closing, the water rushing out its gills, the fly sandwiched against its upper plate. Seamus stripped slack madly then set the hook with a hard whip of the rod. The fish leapt forward, clear of the water, ran past the bow, and the reel sang.

Len watched the old man hold both hands to his chest, his mouth open. Len looked out where the tarpon ran away from the bank toward open water. Seamus turned to Len with wide eyes. Len got behind the wagon and pushed.

The tarpon made four great runs and ran Seamus into his backing. He slowly gained line as the boat motored over the widening, deeper water. The fish changed direction, turning toward a further flat. He fought the fish with his heart as much as his arms, back, and legs. His heart pounded against the pounding heartbeat coming across the line. When that heart slackened his did not, the pleasure and excitement driving his pulse as he brought the fish beside the boat.

He held the rod over his head and looked down at the long, lovely fish, the fly sticking out of its mouth. Braddy reached down and had the fish by the tail and pulled it over the gunwale. Flashes of sun off its scales filled Seamus's eyes. He laid back.

When he opened his eyes and saw where he was, he said, That way, and pointed. His arm was aimed at the pines near the road. Len pictured the map in his mind, saying, Woman Key?

The Marquesas?

Seamus talked to himself, whispering the words and thinking them over before he said, Yes. The Marquesas. He thought to himself: At the Marquesas there might be permit. No, there must be permit there.

Len pushed the wagon past the dogwoods and Japanese maples. Jays screeched in the upper boughs lit by the hot sun. Len went through the pines, over the shallow ditch and past the big blue mailbox. He looked right then left, then crossed the quiet road. The wagon bounced over the other ditch and down a mowed trail between the old forest and a field of planted pines.

Seamus watched the pelicans come out of the distance and sail by. He watched the water. The boat shot over turtle grass that gave way to deeper water. He didn't know how he was there or for how long, but he had caught and let go one good fish and felt that there had to be more. When he looked ahead the sun lit the water and the far key seemed to be elongated like some kind of mirage. The water browned. He thought his eyes were troubled and that he had been burned by the sun. He held his breath a moment, unsure that the boat was right. He felt as if he were being dragged bodily through the water. He closed his eyes and held his hand over his mouth. He thought about how a permit appeared when it noticed a fly, how it turned and nosed in. The way it held its body and whether it stiffened its fins or not told if it would take. Then there was the way to strike them, a sure strip-strike that should not be too soft but could yank the fly out of the permit's mouth if done too hard. He was not able to remember if Braddy was with him or not when he hooked and lost a big permit many years ago.

Len envisioned the edge of Woman Key in the line of beech trees at the bottom of a small mown field ahead. He turned the wagon to move with the grain of the mown grass and pushed Seamus slowly. See any? he shouted

Seamus saw that they were moving with the out-going tide. He looked back at Braddy and gave him a strange look because he crouched by the motor. The young man was not doing much sighting at all. Get up, Seamus said. They both stood in the boat. Seamus wiped the sweat out of his eyes with his shirt, felt his head and cursed because his hat had blown off. He put his bandanna on his head. He looked out along the expanse of sand-bottomed flat that extended off the key.

Len thought he saw something—a blackbird feather? A vulture feather waving in the grass?

Seamus saw it too and quickly bent to the fly box and found a nice Nasty Charlie. He took up the rod and tied the fly to the leader. He pointed and nodded, trying to force the words out his dry mouth. Where's the rod? Which one am I using? he said.

You've got it. Right there, Len said. Where are they?

Just there. Three bones. See?

The dark fingers waving in the green-olive flat were the bonefish, the edges of their tails sticking up in the sunlit ridges of water.

Seamus rose to cast. For the first time, he had the rod in his hands, so Len sat on Seamus's left. The wagon was stable enough that it did not lurch on its axles as Seamus's body motion set up a big false cast then rocked off his feet a bit as he went back then forward with the intended cast. The black feather blew up in the breeze. Seamus huffed because the bones had jumped forward as his cast unrolled so the fly fell behind them. He let it go down and jerked it a few times. He did not see the fly but he saw the top of the leader and he twitched the line with his stripping hand so the pink gleam of sunlight on the leader slid up and back. One of the bones turned, then the other two did, their bodies level.

The interested bonefish advanced. Seamus pulled the line easily but smartly then stopped. The bone tailed. Seamus pulled again and the bonefish pecked, pecked again and pounded the fly then turned to the side. He did not know if the fish had the fly. He carefully stripped six-inches of line and struck with the rod. A star of green-gold exploded on the surface and out of that came the fly shooting toward the boat until it slowed and fell.

Seamus huffed with disappointment. He sat down. The fly line was strewn on the field.

Reel up and we'll go further down the flat, Len said.

Seamus sat still, looking at the trees. Len reached over and squeezed his uncle's hand. Seamus stared at his nephew then looked down at his hands. He saw the line and reeled it back, then took off the bandanna, wiped his face, and tied the bandanna clumsily on his head again. Len shoved the wagon along.

Further down the line of beech trees were more bonefish. Seamus said clearly, Bones, when he saw them and Len stopped pushing and looked where Seamus pointed with the rod.

The rod was like a vector on a chart, a shiny brown line that led to the few odd-angled, darker lines that were bonefish in the clear, green water. Seamus was connected to them, feeling himself like a line drawn with one motion of a pen down the rod, over the line, to the fish. He wasn't afraid of the sensation, his body, vision, and mind cinched and fitted so he slipped through and out his right arm and down the rod and went sliding down the line to the fish. He was directly over them, their bodies oblong gray ingots amid the glitter of the water. Seamus hovered happily in thin air, the fly turning over below him.

A bonefish turned on its side, its big eye looking up at the man's face, the fly stuck in its jaw. Seamus braced himself with his arms, forcing himself back down the rod, feeling his legs fitting through the bottom of the rod, his insteps bouncing over the cork handle. He was back in the boat, the rod part of

his arms and ribs, and he pulled on the weight of the bonefish. He had this one hooked. It dashed through the flat.

Len sat with Seamus in the wagon as his uncle gripped the side panel, his arms shuddering now and then and he lowered and raised his torso, his jaw jutting. The bonefish was making a big run. Len looked out where the fish was and wondered how it felt and how hard it pulled. He waited until Seamus looked directly over the side of the wagon. He knelt beside his uncle, reached down, and pulled in all the loose line until he had the Nasty Charlie in his hand. Seamus looked at him, his eyebrows hooded over his eyes, his mouth slack. Suddenly he put his head back, his eyebrows raised to reveal his eyes and for the first time Seamus appeared to know just what he had done. Good one, he said.

Len smiled. How many bonefish have you caught, Seamus, ever? Did you keep track? he said.

Seamus looked at Len and said, Braddy, is this your boat?

Yes, Seamus, he said. What do you think of that sky?

The old man squinted at his nephew, shaping some unspoken utterance, then caught sight of Len's finger pointing skyward. He looked up. The sky was hazy but the sun shone through brightly. Seamus said, Let's go.

Len spun the wagon around and hoped that Seamus had no map in his head and did not know which way west was, or else Seamus realized that Len had just driven the boat into and over the mangrove. Seamus made no protest. Len pushed the wagon along the line of beech trees then broke through them to another field and went along an old tractor lane. He was going north.

Seamus watched the water go by as they crossed the Boca Grande channel. A group of frigate birds flew away in the distance like a handful of black sparks drifting in the air. The channel was calm and the wind was near dead, coming in sighs from the west. Way up in the sky were pinkish white clouds like cotton candy that oozed out of the haze. Seamus thought about his house and the fields where he lived.

Len skirted the base of a small hill, aiming for a stand of tulip trees. He went through the trees to a wooden fence. Here was the border of a horse farm. It used to be a regular farm, but thoroughbreds had replaced corn and cows. Len moved along the fence until he came to the corner and went through the saplings there, coming into a wide circular clearing in a thick woods of sumac, beech, and tulip trees.

Len imagined that this was a lagoon in the interior of the Marquesas. He stepped up into the wagon and said, All right, Seamus, we're here.

Look at all those frigate birds, Seamus said.

Len watched the tops of the distant trees swish in the breeze. A storm was building.

We're in the lower part of the Marquesas, Seamus. Let's try up along the edge here. Len pointed at the trees on his right.

Seamus sat up and looked around. A beautiful, wide

circular pool extended before him, the water green, then azure, then blue as the light changed the water with distance. Alongside and from beyond, he heard the rustle of the mangroves and smelled the broken-leaf odor that carried in the air. The breeze came now and then, very slight, from the west; good for a right-hander.

They did not go far when Seamus raised his hand, catching his breath. In maybe four feet of water directly in front of the boat were three big motes tipped with black: permit. Seamus stripped line, looked again at the fish and rose to cast. The Nasty Charlie hit the water and the fish disappeared. Seamus sighed. He stripped in the fly, held it in his hand, and watched the water.

Len watched his uncle leaning over the front panel of the wagon, staring at the long grass. The old man had not yet touched the rod. Len pushed the wagon slowly. The breeze was dying and the humidity rising.

Seamus turned and crept back to Len. He nodded and wheezed, putting his face in his nephew's face. He said, There are permit all over this flat. I'm going to get one.

I'll keep my eyes peeled, Len said.

Seamus turned and took the rod in his hands. He looked at the fly at the end of the line, the Nasty Charlie, and looked around for the other rod. He said, Where's the other rod? He did not understand what Braddy said in reply. He no longer wondered why Braddy wasn't helping sight more fish, because obviously the boy was no good at it. Seamus squinted at the water as his nephew poled along. When he again saw shapes tipped with black quills, he raised his hand and gave a low grunt. There they were, at ten o'clock, two permit as big as welcome mats. Seamus cast the fly to them and it landed too far away. He tried again and the lead fish flared its fins and the two of them raced off. Seamus watched them go, wondering how such bright silver animals were capable of disappearing so quickly in clear water.

———

The afternoon dragged on this way. As Len moved all around the edge of the clearing, Seamus spotted permit, cast to them, and either missed or flushed them. Once Seamus was so exasperated he let go the rod with a jerk and seethed through gritted teeth. Len wondered if permit populated the Marquesas like this, and if Seamus had been there once when they had; or were they were swimming in some flat in Seamus's mind, along some ideal, absolute key west of everything.

Len got in the wagon and said, What's going wrong?

Seamus looked at him and shook his head.

What aren't we getting it right?

Seamus studied his hands. Whatever was wrong with him was centered in his hands because they were heavier than he had ever known them to be. When he cast he was unable to have just enough touch to match the power of his stroke, and when he stripped the line, he pulled without crispness or

delicacy. He had been fine for the tarpon and the bonefish, but now, wearying under the sun and the effort to cast, a leaden fluid filled his hands. The fluid was in his shoulders too, and behind his eyes.

He looked at Braddy. Damned permit, he said.

What's the secret? Is there something you're forgetting to do? Len said.

Seamus did not know what Braddy meant. There was no secret to permit, none that Seamus knew. If there was, it was the secret that the fish kept itself, for when it did like your fly, it gave no high sign. The fish simply swam over, dipped, and ate it. Beyond that, there had to be the excellent draw of the stripping hand coordinated with the rod hand. Yet the motion was no secret. It was simply a very fine physical act not easily entered or completed, like bending a note on a guitar.

It's wrong. In my hands, Seamus said.

Let's try a little more. We can't give up, Len said.

You cast for a while, Seamus said. He sat in the stern of the wagon, hands in his lap, staring blankly.

Len stood with the rod. He picked out a few spots along the edge of the trees, a root here or twig there, and cast to them. He managed eighty feet pretty well, surprising himself. He was happy to be casting in Seamus's secret key, wondering what it was about permit that was so impossible.

After half-an-hour's practice, Len looked at the sky. A pile of brown-grey sat in the west. He looked at his watch: three-thirty. He figured his mother, cousins, and great aunt were by then in an immeasurable tizzy because he and Seamus were gone, without leaving a note. Len had not expected the trip to the Marquesas would take so long.

He looked around and realized they had made a whole circuit of the clearing. He pushed the wagon and the catatonic Seamus back to the entrance, near the trees. He knelt next to Seamus and pointed down the tree line. Seamus, he said. I see one. A nice permit, just there.

Seamus shifted and craned his neck. I don't see 'em, he said.

Watch. Just beyond the dark patch.

Seamus watched the water for several minutes. Yes, he said to himself. His breath hissed over his lips. Yes, yes.

Len watched his uncle lean over the panel, face forward, straining.

Seamus made the cast. The fly landed just ahead of the fish, the permit facing the fly. Seamus saw the fly as it sank. The permit rushed over, halted, then tipped its head down, tail up. Tension came through the line and rod. Seamus waited an extra second then moved both hands apart, and the line came taut in his hand, the rod bowed. He took a deep, uneasy breath as the permit ran fast directly away from the boat. He got the fish on the reel and the line sizzled away until the fish stopped abruptly.

Seamus wound the reel madly for a moment, then pulled

back on the rod. The fish was still there. It seemed to kick the line a few times before it ran side-long to the boat, far out into the middle of the flat. Seamus moved along the edge of boat, rod up, squeezing his hands reflexively to keep a sense of touch in them because he was afraid they would go completely dead and he would have to fight the fish without any feel at all.

Seamus knelt in the middle of the wagon. Len said nothing. He braced the wagon from the front so it did not roll as Seamus moved.

The permit was just into the backing. Seamus slowly wound the reel and pumped the rod, fighting the fish through vigorous turns of its wide body as it attempted further runs. It made a dash this way, then went further, sat, then went away into the middle of the big flat. It pulled hardily and sprinted this way, then that. This was a fine fish. Slowly, Seamus brought it back. He whispered, Just leader. Just close enough.

The permit was on the surface twenty feet away. It broke through the water then dove. Seamus wound it up again. He looked at the tiptop. He had maybe ten turns of the reel to go before he got to the leader.

The permit made a strong dive and then turned in a wide arc. As the old man turned the rod to follow the run his hands seized. He was unable to grip the reel knurl and his rod hand feebly clenched the handle. He moaned and spat, his left hand tapping at the side of the reel. He hooked his index finger on the knurl and tried to jerk the spool around. The permit nosed down hard and buzzed away from the boat, and the rod bowed in his hand then began slipping away. He wrapped the rod with his other forearm and fell forward on the gunwale, trying to trap the rod. Where was Braddy? He sensed the young man moving behind him and he tried to lift himself off the rod so Braddy could grab it.

As Seamus got to his knees and pulled the rod high, he looked at its bowed, quivering shape. He was so upset, so disgusted. Braddy did not take the rod from him. The permit did not stop running. God did not help him. With all he had left in his hands he held the rod handle and pulled in an attempt to turn the fish.

The line gave without any loud twang, and the rod went soft. Seamus reeled clumsily, furiously until he found the cut end of the leader. The permit had finned it.

Seamus groaned, Oh, so loudly Len asked if he was all right. The old man bowed down in the wagon, his face in the crook of his elbow.

Len panicked for a moment. He cried his uncle's name then pulled the old man's arms until he turned Seamus over and rested him on his back. Seamus's eyes were open but doped. Beads of sweat and tears ran off his face. His sweatshirt was stained dark across his chest.

Seamus, can't you hear me? Len said. He took Seamus's

pulse. We'll go home now. It's going to rain.

Seamus said nothing.

Len pulled the wagon as fast as he could back up the slope along the horse pasture, back to the narrow, mown lane and then up past the pine tree field to the road. They went up the front lawn and around the side to the patio. Len picked Seamus up and pulled him over the side and walked him into the house. When everyone in the kitchen saw them coming in, and saw Seamus appearing so wrung-out, with his red bandanna on his head, they immediately separated uncle from nephew.

Len weathered a blistering round of questions and harangues from his mother and great aunt over Seamus's absence. While Len sat in the living room, cornered, Seamus sat in the kitchen, forlorn and tired, as his daughters rubbed wet, cool cloths over his face and arms. His horror at the loss of the permit was not diverted by a large piece of pie put before him by Leigh. He did not want to eat. The fish was still with him but was gone.

⊢—⊣

After the storm came through and cleared the humidity and heat, Len sat in the living room in the dark. The electricity had been knocked out, but not the telephone. He sat in the light of a Coleman lamp, drinking a beer and talking to his father on the telephone.

He calls me Braddy, Len said.

Mmm, that's understandable, his father said. But please don't run off with him again. Neither one of us needs to get another earful from your mother or anyone else.

Do you know what the secret to permit is, dad?

Don't go after them and you won't suffer.

Seamus said he knew the secret of catching permit.

I doubt that.

Did Seamus ever have more than one grand slam? Len said.

Who said he had a grand slam?

He did, himself.

Len's father sniffed. He said, One time while I was down there with your mother's parents, Seamus went out and caught a bonefish, then a small tarpon, and then all he took were snook the rest of the day. I don't think he ever seriously fished for permit.

He was talking about snook today, Len said.

When did he say he had a grand slam?

Today.

Well, today wasn't his best day, was it?

He never said to you that he had a slam? Len said.

I don't ever remember, and that's something you wouldn't forget, his father said.

Maybe he was explaining it once to me when I was a kid and I thought he'd actually done it.

Memory plays tricks.

They said good night and hung up. Len rubbed the cold, wet beer bottle on his cheeks then wiped his face with his hand. He leaned back and said, Damn, wondering what terrible things he had forced upon his uncle.

Asleep in another room, Seamus dreamt of putting his heavy hands in the bright water to saturate them, and draw out the corrosive fluid. Then his blood took its saltiness from the sea and flowed freely again in his hands. The sense of touch returned to his fingers and palms. He felt the line between his fingers as lightly as if touching his wife's hair.

PART IV

Landing Net

BROWN TROUT *Salmo trutta dentix*
(Voidomatis River, Greece)

THE ODYSSEY

BOOK XII, LINES 294–305

Homer, Translated by Robert Fitzgerald

Then Skylla made her strike,
whisking six of my best men from the ship.
I happened to glance aft at ship and oarsmen
and caught sight of their arms and legs, dangling
high overhead. Voices came down to me
in anguish, calling my name for the last time.

A man surfcasting on a point of rock
for bass or mackerel, whipping his long rod
to drop the sinker and the bait far out,
will hook a fish and rip it from the surface
to dangle wriggling through the air.

JETTIES

Tim Weed

THERE IS A theory that America was discovered by Europeans long before Columbus. Apparently, by 1492 Basque fishermen had already cruised up and down the coast of New England for centuries, loading their ships with dried cod to trade back in Europe. The theory goes that they didn't tell anyone about it because the fishing was so good: cod is a sluggish and gullible ground fish, and it was so plentiful back then that it must have been exceedingly easy to catch. If the theory is true, the Basques deserve a great deal of credit, first for braving the transatlantic crossing in their tiny boats, and then, even more impressive, for keeping their secret so long.

There is a certain string of ballast rocks—a jetty—somewhere on the same coast where I too can usually count on fishing alone. It is a forbidding spot, and it would seem an unlikely place to catch a fish, especially with a fly-rod. The ocean is so vast, and the surrounding water is usually rough: you would think a little bucktail fly would get lost out there. Yet the big, beautiful predators of this part of the Atlantic: stripers, bluefish, the occasional false albacore or bonito like to patrol the edges of the jetty for bait fish on the incoming tide, and they can definitely be taken on a fly. Landing one of these game fish while standing on a pile of rocks jutting out into the ocean is no ordinary experience. There is something miraculous about it, something altogether beyond explanation.

Getting out across the rocks is treacherous. There is an

edginess to it: just enough danger to keep you sharp, but not so much that it seems foolhardy. On a cool mid-September day a walk along the jetty is a foray into a marine wilderness, a stark natural playing field with its own rules and its own rewards. When the northwesterly wind kicks off the fall striper season the water starts to swell and heave in a kind of ferocious, joyful dance. There is a pervasive feeling of freshness and renewal in the hours leading up to high tide: the shifting pressure of the wind on your waders, the crash and spray of white water against the fragmented stone and, as the flood gains momentum, the seawater beginning to pour over the jetty, from high side to low side. There is a short period, maybe twenty minutes, when it is still possible to spring from rock to rock even in the lower-lying parts. Then the jetty becomes fully submerged, marked only by a string of churning rips. Often I keep fishing until the very last minute, taking advantage of this narrow window of opportunity to scramble back, heart pounding, to the safety of dry land.

Today, casting into the wind as high tide approaches, I find myself wondering what would happen if I got stuck out here. Say I slipped, and in the struggle to regain my footing my ankle got jammed between two rocks, and the inexorable tide came in, immersing my head little by little, wave by wave. There would be time to think.

I decide to hold myself to three more casts: there's always another day, and the half-formed images of my own slow

drowning are ruining my concentration. The lower-lying rocks are already under water.

And then there is a tug on the line. Two tugs. A sensation of tremendous force, a fast run through my reel and down to the backing, then the line goes limp and the fly-rod springs back in my hand. That was quick: either a very big fish or a faulty knot, or maybe my leader was crimped from scraping over barnacles. I pick another fly out of the box in my chest pack and tie it on. With the next cast I spot a small boil on the surface near where my fly landed, a few deceptively light tugs and then—*wizzzz*—right down to the backing again. I press the bottom of my reel with my palm to slow the powerful run, but it's not enough. Almost to the end of the backing, and then a final tug and the line goes limp. This time the disappointment is almost crushing, but on its heels there rises a flush of triumphant expectation, the soaring joyous rage of battle joined. That had to be an albie, part of a patrolling school, or maybe a large striper. If I'm quick about it, I still have time. Hands shaking, I tie on another Clouser.

The ballast rocks are already nearly submerged. The water rushing in from the ocean side forms increasingly defined rips; the dull roar of flooding water is a steady background noise to the high-pitched screech of the wind. To move along the line of boulders I now have to wade in places, aiming my feet as I step for the bone-colored patches of barnacle visible through the seaweed. The bait-fish glow green as they dash across the jetty; sometimes they bump against my shins like a tattoo of soft bullets. As the water deepens it blurs the shape and incline of the rocks—every step is like a leap of faith. I know that the ocean is a force not to be trifled with, and I'm wearing waders; if I miss my footing I may not have time to kick them off before they fill up and drag me under.

Why am I still out here? It's not only the possibility of catching a big fish. There's something sublime about this, a terrible beauty in the moment. The greens of the water, the yellows and rusty browns of the seaweed, the luminescence of light and shadow playing on the swells and curling rips. And—inescapably—I'm part of it, immersed in it, playing an active role, probing for the living pulsing heart of the ocean. Almost without thinking about the meaning of what I'm doing, I unhook the straps of my chest pack to make it easier to release my suspenders should it become necessary.

The wind picks up and the spray peels off the tops of the swells, forming whitecaps all around; the water is now so stirred up that to a long-time trout fisherman it would seem unlikely, verging on impossible, that I will catch anything else. But I have reason to believe the rules are different out here.

I find solid footing and start casting again, stripping the line in periodic bursts to imitate a fleeing minnow. A flock of terns scouting along the jetty wheels and forms up, congregating over a rip just out of casting distance. A few of the precise white birds rocket down and hit the surface, coming up with bait fish. Then they all start to dive, one after the other, plummeting down like delicate origami kamikazes. My heart is pounding. The rocks are effectively underwater now, their jagged wet tips poking out only in the valleys of the swells. But I think I can still keep my balance and wade out the jetty, if I take it one submerged boulder at a time. If I could just get close enough to cast…

I clip the fly to the base of the rod and start wading toward the diving birds. Every step feels risky, my purchase on the barnacles tentative in the strengthening current. I know I'm pushing the limits; I should be heading toward shore, not out to sea. But it's not that much farther, and below the diving birds something big is breaking the surface. The splashing of game fish is distinct from the whitecaps, although it is hard to define why: more alive, more substantive, quicker to form and recede. Those are definitely fish, big ones, corralling and chasing down bait-fish in a frenzy of savage glee.

It's a long shot, but I think I can reach it. I brace myself against the current and unclip the fly. It looks panicked with its bugged out eyes and sweeping flume of chartreuse hair. I start to cast—the wind is strong so I have to double-haul. My first effort falls short of the fray. On the second cast there is an explosion of spray as the fly hits the water, and I'm on to a big one. Down to the backing again, almost all of it, then the run stops and I can spool some line. The fish is solidly on: if

I can keep the leader from scraping over barnacles or getting tangled in a lobster trap I know I can bring this one in.

The fight lasts a long time—it feels like twenty minutes, but it's probably closer to five. Several times the fish runs and dives, and each time I worry that I'll lose it. But finally I muscle it in close enough to see its outlines under the wind-tossed surface: a big striped bass, probably thirty-five or forty-inches long, well above the legal minimum for a keeper. Even before bringing it to hand I begin considering what to do. It's not every day that a striper fisherman catches a keeper. The buttery flesh takes exceedingly well to the grill, which is why local fish markets sell it so dear.

Should I keep it or release it?

When I lift it gently out of the water the fish is trembling, exhausted from the fight. It looks surprised and annoyed, but resigned to its fate. It is a beautiful creature, golden against the green water, the black stripes for which it is named running down the length of its powerful fuselage, the whole bathed in an aura of strength and vitality. It is a direct and magical connection to the wilderness, as noble as an elk, as ferocious, in its medium, as a grizzly.

If I kill it, I realize, I'll also be adding to my own survival risk, because it will weigh me down and unsettle my balance on the treacherous walk back over the submerged rocks. If I release it, I will have the satisfaction of knowing that this noble creature is still abroad in the ocean. Yet killing

it somehow seems the more honest action. I'm not a catch-and-release purist, because it seems to me that keeping and eating the occasional catch is an essential acknowledgement of our place in the food chain, a ritual recognition that the act of fishing is more than just "sport." It's a way to take responsibility for being alive.

A big wave crashes right in front of me, soaking me up to my hat and yanking me out of my spiritual reverie. With a sinking feeling, I realize I have stayed out too long. It is high tide, and the way back to shore is marked only by rips and white water. I release my grip on the striper and watch it hesitate for a moment, then accelerate back into deep water as the unexpected fact of its freedom dawns.

The walk back is terrifying. What had been a pleasantly thrilling excursion is now a scrambling, panicked retreat. I no longer feel like I belong out here. The current is strong, like a big western river in spring, and in places the water is chest deep, licking at the tops of my waders. Several times I lose my balance and have to catch myself on the rocks, cutting my hands on the sharp barnacles, but I hardly feel the pain. I'm breathing in short gulping breaths, bracing myself, keeping a low center of gravity to avoid being swept off. The realization of what I've done hangs in my stomach like a lead weight. I've laughed in the face of nature, put my life at grave risk.

Fervently, I try to convince myself that a quid pro quo

has been effected: the striper's life for mine. But I can't believe it, because I know nature doesn't work that way. Like black smoke the panic billows into the recesses of my brain, choking out any thoughts other than the dull, raw, reptilian urge to survive.

I can still see that striper clearly in my mind's eye. He's patrolling the rocks and rips at the edge of the Atlantic, hunting down minnows and sand eels with remorseless hunger, perhaps seeking out a brackish river delta to spawn millions of little stripers, all of them destined for a violent death of one kind or another. I've learned a great deal from that fish. I've learned that I'm not invincible, and the ocean is not a playground. And like a Basque sailor shipwrecked on a foreign shore, I think I know why my favorite spot is never crowded with other fishermen.

SELECTIONS FROM YEATS

William Butler Yeats

THE MEDITATION OF THE OLD FISHERMAN

You waves, though you dance by my feet like children at play,
Though you glow and you glance, though you purr and you
    dart:
In the Junes that were warmer than these are, the waves were
    more gay,
When I was a boy with never a crack in my heart.

The herring are not in the tides as they were of old;
My sorrow! for many a creak gave the creel in the cart
That carried the take to Sligo town to be sold,
When I was a boy with never a crack in my heart.

And ah, you proud maiden, you are not so fair when his oar
Is heard on the water, as they were, the proud and apart,
Who paced in the eve by the nets on the pebbly shore,
When I was a boy with never a crack in my heart.

THE FISHERMAN

Although I can see him still,
The freckled man who goes
To a grey place on a hill
In grey Connemara clothes
At dawn to cast his flies,
It's long since I began
To call up to the eyes
This wise and simple man.
All day I'd looked in the face
What I had hoped 't would be
To write for my own race
And the reality;
The living men that I hate,
The dead man that I loved,
The craven man in the seat,
The insolent unreproved,
And no knave brought to book
Who has won a drunken cheer,
The witty man and his joke
Aimed at the commonest ear,

The clever man who cries
The catch-cries of the clown,
The beating down of the wise
And great Art beaten down.

Maybe a twelvemonth since
Suddenly I began,
In scorn of this audience,
Imagining a man,
And his sun-freckled face,
And grey Connemara cloth,
Climbing up to a place
Where stone is dark under froth,
And the down-turn of his wrist
When the flies drop in the stream;
A man who does not exist,
A man who is but a dream;
And cried, 'Before I am old
I shall have written him one
Poem maybe as cold
And passionate as the dawn.'

THE FISH

Although you hide in the ebb and flow
Of the pale tide when the moon has set,
The people of coming days will know
About the casting out of my net,
And how you have leaped times out of mind
Over the little silver cords,
And think that you were hard and unkind,
And blame you with many bitter words.

THE ANGLER'S STORY

John Hollander

I let down my long line; it went falling; I pulled. Up came
A bucket of bad sleep in which tongues were sloshing about
Like frogs and dark fish, breaking the surface of silence, the
Forgetfulness, with what would have been brightness in any
Other element, flash of wave, residual bubbling,
But were here belches of shadow churned up by the jostling
Tongues from the imageless thick bottom of the heavy pail.
I could not reach into that fell stuff after them, nor fling
Them back into night like inadequate fish; nor would they
Lie flat and silent like sogged leaves that had been flung
    under
Mud, but burbled of language too heavy to be borne, of
Drowned inflections and smashed predications, exactness
    pulped
Into an ooze of the mere desire to utter. It was
My bucket, and I have had to continue to listen.

CLOSING DAY

James Rossbach

THE STATION WAGON, loaded, was idling in the driveway under the towering hemlocks in front of the Club. On the bottom step of the veranda, buttoned up for the long trip home, stood the old man. In back of him friends—both young and no longer young, murmured their farewells. It had been a glorious weekend, the last of the season. Already the maples were beginning to turn, and one could feel in the September sunshine a hint of colder weather to come.

Yes, the weekend had been marvelous—and unusual. It was without a doubt because of the old man's presence. Once an angler of extraordinary skills, he now was crippled with arthritis and could no longer fish. Yet it had been he, the non-fisherman at a fishing club, who had been the center of attraction, the focus of the enjoyment they had all felt. Assembling from the stream at lunch or at a late cocktail-hour before dinner, they had gathered around this former editor, as acolytes around a high priest, to share with him their triumphs and defeats of the day, to revel in his colorful recollections of streams of another era and to cherish the barbs of his sharp wit. His wife, some years younger than he, had fished successfully, and one sensed that he identified with her tales of trout risen, hooked and landed or lost.

Now, in the late-September setting sun, the whole bittersweet experience seemed to come together : the old man on the bottom step of a club he probably would never revisit, the season drawing to an end, the friendships of summer interrupted until another year. The old man seemed to sense this as he gazed out toward the stream through cataract-clouded eyes. His wife took him gently by the hand. "Come on, Doc," she said, "It's time to go."

"You're right, Mother," he answered. "You're right, as usual. Take me home."

RE-LAX-NESS

Jim Murphy

The floating stones once held by the fire
Drift down now to the sea.
Working up the river,
Lax makes memory from strong desire,
As I make mine of me.

A land, its blinds half drawn
Sleeps against the mist grey night.
The villagers lay face up,
Content to store the soft long light.

The glacier melts in the summer sun
I'm lying in the grass undone.
The land is moving, not the river,
Fire's now the steam it does deliver.

STEELHEAD TROUT *Oncorhynchus mykiss irideus*

LATE SEPTEMBER ON THE RUSSIAN RIVER

John E. Smelcer

The trees turn, suddenly,
as dawn rolls up what night unwound—
their slender necks
like tundra swans in shallow ponds.

There is no comforting chill
in the gray air,
only a screed of birds
scrawled on a bare sky.

Fog arrives in the narrow valley,
gray wings cupped like snow geese
landing between deserted stars
in morning's porcelainlight.

A trout waves in a shadow
contemplating my fly,
and while I watch, a bear—sleek and black—
crosses the river and fades off winterward.

PART V

A Necessary Passion

AMARE O PESCARE

Howell Raines

THREE OR FOUR weeks after Susan and I got married, I got up before daylight and drove a hundred miles to fish all day in nasty weather at a place called Okomo on the Coosa River. Years later, just before we divorced, Susan told me that she remembered waking up alone around ten with the rain beating romantically against the window and our orange cat curled up at the foot of the bed and thinking, "What kind of marriage is this going to be?"

Quite recently, I was on vacation on a tropical island with a voluptuous and passionate woman. Our room overlooked a fabulously landscaped pond bordered by boulders imported from the neighborhood of Mount Fuji and stocked with the large Japanese carp called koi. I spent many hours on our ninth-floor balcony. My companion said she wished I would look at her with the longing gaze I directed at the koi. She observed that I watched these fish with such devotion that I must be in the throes of interspecies male bonding. Had I failed to notice, she asked, that when viewed from above, swimming fish looks exactly like those magnified sperm you see in sex education films? She had a point, especially when scores of koi were swimming madly toward the bread balls fashioned from the toast I saved each morning from the room-service tray.

On the last morning of our trip, I got up early so I could keep an appointment to meet the keeper of the fish ponds. I had managed to introduce myself to him, and he promised to let me go on his feeding rounds, so I could get a close look at his koi. He was very proud of these fish and eager to share their history.

Koi are carp that have been bred in Japan for hundreds of years for decorative purposes. Some are gold. Some are the soft gray of good flannel. Some are orange and black, as garishly spotted as leopards. Depending on the pattern and brilliance of its pigmentation, a garden-variety koi can fetch five-hundred dollars or more. As I stood on a rock beside a palm-shaded pool and photographed these extravagantly colored fish while my lover slumbered in our bed, I thought this: "My God! I am doing it again."

In this case, I was not even fishing. I was looking at fish. Here is a fact I have had to face about myself. I am a person who needs to be near fish pretty often in order to be happy. Usually this involves fishing. Sometimes it may involve simply being in the same vicinity with them or handling objects that are associated with their capture. When I am home alone I like to scatter my tackle across the floor and play with it. I may pretend I am working on it, performing preventive maintenance, but it is really playing.

Through study and personal experience, I have learned that in our culture there is traditional tension between men and women over the issue of fishing and over sports in general. I do not claim that one side or the other is right. I simply retort that this exists.

These conflicts extend across class lines. The "golf widows"

at the country club feel just as aggrieved as women left behind on bowling night. Bowling leagues and tennis ladders do not exist solely because of an innate human need to compete. They are designed to enable men to say they have to be somewhere other than at home or the shopping mall. There is a reason, by the way, why men behave badly and start fights when they are shopping with their wives. One recent survey found that shopping is the least favorite activity of American men.

Even so, fishing seems to be a particularly contentious issue. I can cite many examples. Twenty-years-ago, just after the first generation of bass boats was introduced in the South, my friend Charles Salter, a fishing writer in Atlanta, told me that these boats had spawned a rash of divorces throughout the region. By 1992, one manufacturer, Skeeter, was running an ad in which an attractive woman in tight blue jeans faced the camera and offered some comments about her husband's affection for bass fishing. "Six-months-ago, we bought a new Skeeter fishing boat, and if he'd ever drag his buns out of it," she added, as the camera slowly pulled back to show a smiling fellow beside her, "I might introduce him to my new boyfriend, Bob, here."

The message intended by the boat manufacturer is clear. Fishing is so much fun and our boat is such a fine one that some men—maybe you—would be smart to give up this handsome, sexy woman for the pleasures they represent.

Hunting, spectator sports, even playground basketball all

carry an aura of male exclusivity. In the movie *White Men Can't Jump*, the wife and girlfriend of Wesley Snipes and Woody Harrelson rarely get to accompany them to the games that represent the primary incomes of two families. There is also a men-only flavor to the watching of professional football, although in this case the physical body of the absent husband may still be present in front of the television set. But fishing is different, according to Maureen Dowd, the brilliant *New York Times* writer who has long threatened to write a feminist tract under a title suggested by her friends, "Man: Beast or Burden?" "Fishing is not like tennis, where you can play doubles or he's gone for an hour or two," she says. "It's more than a sport. It's an escape mechanism akin to the leathery male preserve of the English men's club."

On the White House beat, Maureen Dowd spent what she describes as "torturous" days following George Bush and his buddies as they fished, hunted, golfed, played horseshoes, and tennis. Along the way, she established herself as an expert observer of that gender labeled by our *Times* colleague Anna Quindlen as "bears with furniture." "The playing fields are one of the fault lines in the battle of the sexes," Dowd wrote after observing a round of Bush's hyperactive "golf polo." In that article, she went on to record the First Lady's attempt to penetrate the Presidential buddy system.

"Earlier this summer, Barbara Bush confided in a group of reporters lunching at the White House that she was taking golf lessons. Her husband had suggested she do so, she said proudly, so that they could play together in Kennebunkport. The First Lady is always eager to find ways to spend more time with her husband.

"But the Bush vacation has provided a sad tableau of the rejection that every woman of average sporting abilities has faced in her life: Men, by and large, prefer to play competitive games with other men.

"Mrs. Bush has been seen tagging behind the President's foursomes, playing her own fledgling game with her friend from Kennebunkport, Betsy Heminway.

"The President took devilish delight, on Mrs. Bush's first outing at the Cape Arundel Golf Club, in stopping his own game and urging reporters to watch Mrs. Bush and Mrs. Heminway take their wobbly shots on the eighteenth green.

"'We'll make her nervous,' the President said mischievously. Asked why he did not play with his wife, Mr. Bush replied: 'We're going down life's path hand-in-hand for many years, but golf—we go our separate ways.'

"Mrs. Bush was clearly annoyed at her husband for putting her in the glare of network cameras. 'That's so mean,' she muttered, adding that the reporters were 'lucky' not to be married to Mr. Bush.

"When the President, pressed by journalists, finally agreed to play with his wife, the disillusioned First Lady shot back: 'When? Just like he's going to garden with me one day.'"

As Mrs. Bush's sarcasm suggests, Bush often seemed to be frantic to get out with the fellows. It did not matter whether he was going to play horseshoes on the South Lawn or shoot quail at a rich friend's ranch in Beeville, Texas.

Do men behave this way simply because they want to avoid the company of women? There may be a more subtle and charitable explanation. Whatever their romantic attachments, men and women need some degree of intimacy with people of their own gender. Women seem to achieve this naturally in the course of daily events, and when they ask one another how they are doing, it seems to be a real question rather than a ritual prelude to some bit of business. Men seem to need an excuse for intimacy, such as drunkenness, or a formal structure in which to achieve it—an athletic competition of some sort, a lodge meeting or, better still, a hunting or fishing expedition. Setting intimacy aside, some men may need this structure to communicate at all, and the often tongue-tied Bush may be a case in point.

According to George Bush, he and his 1988 campaign manager, James A. Baker III, shared their most intimate moments in duck blinds over the years. They had been friends for two decades when, in the spring of 1992, it became apparent to everyone in Washington, D.C., that Mr. Bush would lose the 1992 election unless Baker left his post as Secretary of State and returned to take charge of Bush's stumbling campaign. But it was several months before Bush and Baker could get away on one of the outings where they traditionally have their heart-to-hearts and decide what they are going to do. The scene of their 1992 retreat was a trout stream near Pinedale, Wyoming, and it was there that President Bush finally told his closest friend that he needed him at the White House. This happened in July, by which time Bush was far behind in the polls. He might still be President if he had been able to pick up the phone and pop the question to Jim Baker in April.

Leslie Fiedler, the literary critic, caused a storm of scholarly debate and no small amount of private anxiety by suggesting that there is a homoerotic element in male expeditions. Our literature is full of what he saw as latently homosexual bondings—Huck and Jim on the raft, Ishmael and Queequeg aboard the *Pequod*, Isaac McCaslin and Boon Hogganbeck and Major de Spain at their camp in the big woods where it was possible to hear what Faulkner called "the best of all talking." Fiedler's famous essay "Come Back to the Raft Ag'in, Huck Honey" and the subsequent publication of his book *Love and Death in the American Novel* in 1960 terrified a lot of men, including me. Around that time, I was writing my first long fiction, a hunting story highly derivative of "The Bear." After reading Fiedler, I spent days poring anxiously over my novella, trying to figure out if what I thought was a story about a boy and a dog was really a story about a boy and a boy.

Over the years, I decided I ran into fewer hints of repressed homosexuality around hunting and fishing camps than I did in hanging around high school football coaches, priests, Army sergeants, and those Brits who get overly nostalgic about boarding school. Still, heterosexual males are confused about why they want to go off by themselves and play. In this light, it is possible to see the men's movement, with its thunderdrums and wildman retreats, for what it really is: a support group for guys who want to get out of the house but are afraid their wives and girlfriends will either deny them permission or taunt them, as the feminist comedian Carol Montgomery did on a television talk show devoted to male-bashing. "How many guys over here male bond?" she asked the audience. A few fellows timidly signaled her. "Three of these guys raised their hands," she hooted. "The rest are going, 'Is that a homosexual question?'"

According to some recent books by women, the roots of male bonding and male exclusivity have more to do with male selfishness than sexual preference. Cris Evatt explored these issues in her book *He and She: 60 Significant Differences Between Men and Women.* "I wanted women to know and believe that men are self-centered, and I also wanted men to know how self-forgetful women can be," she said in a newspaper interview about the book.

It causes men stress that women do not want them to go off by themselves, she added. That is why they seem to ignore women's complaints. "Actually, men are not ignoring us. They are just trying not to have a panic attack. Some men can handle women better than others, and the confirmed bachelor is someone who can't handle women at all. I know a man like this who can't live with a man or a woman. He lives with a very placid male golden retriever. This dog is not dead, but he is very quiet."

I do not endorse male self-absorption. Again, I simply report it. Actually, I am not so sure that women really mind men going off so much as they object to what we might call the Cult of Macho Bullshit. I suspect this is why so many women detest the writing—or more precisely the thought and cultural fallout—of Ernest Hemingway. His work depicts the most desirable part of life as what men do with other men. The celebration of a man or men alone reaches its most extreme form in *The Old Man and the Sea*, where even the fantasies have to do with Joe DiMaggio's body parts and the only prominent female figure is the Virgin Mary.

Even in the less segregated Hemingway works, the main activities—fishing, hunting, fighting wars or bulls—are undertaken by men. The female characters are secondary, but usually described in a way that caused casting directors to think of the appearance and libido of the young Ava Gardner.

Hemingway's world was not unlike that which reached its most extreme expression in the gymnasia of ancient Athens. There the games, the conversations, even the most psychologically complex sexual relationships all took place among men. Like the Greeks, Hemingway tried to invent what his biographer James R. Mellow called a "masculine Eden" free of women, specifically Hemingway's tiresome mother, Grace, who liked to put Ernest in dainty dresses when he was a toddler.

For what it is worth, Mellow concludes that Hemingway was not gay, although his book includes an intriguing photograph of the author and a group of naked matadors at an all-boy picnic in Spain in 1931. Papa was worried that he might be homosexual or that other people might interpret his erotically charged celebrations of maleness and book titles such as *Men Without Women* as evidence that he was. In his review of Mellow's book, *Hemingway: A Life Without Consequences*, Philip Caputo concluded that Hemingway's "masculinism" did not represent "forbidden desire but a motif or theme squarely in an old American literary tradition. The male hero must escape society—usually associated with women, marriage, domesticity—for the wilderness, the sea, the road, the battlefield."

Clearly, Philip Caputo and Leslie Fiedler differ on whether this lighting out for the territory represents boys being boys or the pursuit of a homoerotic paradise. But either interpretation rests on the existence of masculine worlds that women simply do not understand. This interests me because when it comes to fishing, the assumption that women just

don't get it is manifestly untrue. All writing about fishing stems from Dame Juliana Berners and *The Treatise of Fishing with an Angle*, published in 1496. Scholars, mostly male, have recently called her authorship into doubt. Perhaps we can attribute that to jealousy, as few writers have better expressed the primal joy of the sport:

> It will be a true pleasure to see the fair, bright, shining-scaled fishes outwitted by your crafty means and drawn out on the land.

For good measure, Dame Juliana also issued the first written instructions in Britain on fly tying. The first American to explore the importance of imitating aquatic insects to fly typing and to make flies based on the study of nymphs in a home aquarium was Sara J. McBride, who lived near Rochester, New York. She wrote about her experiments in 1876, thirteen years before Theodore Gordon, the "father" of American fly-fishing, caught his first brown trout, and three-quarters of a century before Ernest Schwiebert pioneered "matching the hatch." C.F. Orvis invented the prototype of the modern fly reel and gave his name to the most famous firm in fly-fishing. But his daughter, Mary Orvis Marbury, handled the firm's fly-tying business and published a landmark book, *Favorite Flies and Their Histories*, in 1892. It is credited with standardizing the names and patterns of American flies, and when she died in 1914, Britain's *Fishing Gazette* said she ranked second only to Dame Juliana among women in the sport.

So much for the masculine provenance of fly-fishing. But if women were present at the creation of the sport, male writers gradually masculinized it. No one bothered to declare Mary Orvis Marbury the "mother" of American fly-fishing. In *Trout Magic*, Robert Traver said that you did not run into many women on the trout streams because men did not want them there. Even so, there are eighteen-million women who fish. Scientific Anglers, a tackle company, estimated in 1992 that there are over two-hundred-thousand American women who fly-fish regularly. Thirty-percent of the people enrolling in Orvis's weekend fly-fishing schools were women. That alone comes to twelve-hundred women a year who are learning the basics of fly-fishing. What amounts to a refeminization of the sport has brought a few troglodytes out of the bushes.

Fly Fisherman published an essay entitled "The Yuppie Invasion" that decried the growing popularity of fly-fishing among the affluent young of both genders, but its author's ire seemed focused on the presence of women in the temples of the sport—in this case the spring creeks near Livingston, Montana:

One of the pleasures of that [spring creek] fishing is the chance to compare notes with the serious anglers who have traveled from all over America and the world to fish there.

Four of us were discussing the relative merits of the Henry's Fork and the Bighorn over lunch on Armstrong's Spring Creek when a procession including a Porsche, an Audi, a BMW, a Volvo and a Saab pulled into the parking lot. Five women and one man emerged and suited up. They headed off upstream, presumably to fish. For the remainder of the day I kept coming across the women in the party, none of whom were fishing. They were sitting on the bank holding expensive rods, discussing life, sipping white wine and nibbling from a wheel of Brie.

I engaged in conversation with one of the encounter groups and learned that it was the man's birthday and the five women had traveled to Montana for the event. Armstrong's Spring Creek, the Valhalla of fly-fishermen, being used to stage a scene from *The Big Chill*. Does fly-fishing really need people who think *Pteronarcys californica* is a new type of varietal wine?

For my money, the women's use of the setting was admirable. To start with, it left more water for the dyspeptic author, and it is hard to think of a famous male fisherman who has not spent a fair share of his time sitting on the bank and drinking. But it put the writer, one Gerald P. Lenzen, in a bad mood.

"A year later, I was back on Armstrong's," he continued:

A woman fishing the riffle below me was playing a good fish. I walked down and offered to net it for her, hoping to get a photo of what was obviously a large trout. She declined my offer and told me that she would call her husband to net the fish. Reaching into her vest, she removed a whistle and deafened me with an earsplitting blast. Her hapless husband, who had no doubt flunked obedience school, failed to appear. After ten more minutes, a twenty-one-inch brown trout surfaced, firmly hooked through the base of the dorsal fin.

"Oh my, I foul-played him," she announced.

Foul play, indeed. It is time to get these people back into the lofts, sushi bars, and aerobics classes where they belong. If we don't, what will be next?

I found this a hugely, even nakedly informative piece of writing. What could be worse to a man like Gerald P. Lenzen than women sitting around on the bank of a sacred stream talking about life? The answer turned out to be a woman in the stream, hooked into a big fish and declining to be helped. Like racism, this kind of bigotry involves making a fault out of behavior common to all people. For example, foul-hooking a fish is a routine occurrence. You often see it on the television fishing shows. As for whistles, I used one when my boys were small to stay in touch when we were spread out along a stream. I have even seen whistles in the fly-fishing catalogs. They are usually in the section that has flasks for people who like to sit on the bank and take a nip while visiting with their friends.

I suppose there are gender differences between the approaches of male and female fly-fishers, but a clever essay by Mary S. Kuss entitled "Jesus, Pete, It's a Woman Fly-fishing" made me wonder how firmly rooted in fact they are. Kuss has turned all the standard clichés on their heads in telling of her experience as an addicted fisherperson since childhood. It started when, as a six-year-old, she pestered an uncle into taking her fishing and saw a sunfish take her bait, provoking shouts of "Pull, pull, pull!" from her instructor:

> When I finally did, it was too late, the sunnie had spit out the baited hook. I think I've spent the rest of my life searching for that fish, catching many others but never the one that got away on that fine spring day.

In adolescence, she turned to a friend's father for fly-fishing instruction. Later, she sharpened her skills on a trout stream near her Pennsylvania college. "Then I fell in love with, of all people, a nonfisherman." During courtship, he learned to fly cast and went fishing with her. Then after the marriage, he went less and less. "One day I asked him why," Mary Kuss reports, "and he looked me right in the eye and said, 'Why should I go fishing? I caught the fish I was after.'"

Mary Kuss's husband meant to flatter her by saying she was the only "fish" he needed to catch. But he touched on an important point. Most of us, like Kuss, are struggling to reconnect with something we glimpsed long ago. "One of the most remarkable characteristics of fly-fishing," she concludes, "is its capacity to become an obsession."

Here, I think, we may encounter a true gender difference among people who fish. Although Kuss seems an exception, men are generally more susceptible than women to obsessions with inconsequential pursuits, I believe. So are a lot of writers, according to any number of stories from

Moby-Dick right on through *The Bridge on the River Kwai*. The reason may lie in the masculine capacity for self-indulgence defined by Cris Evatt. The "masculine Eden" that Hemingway imagined was, after all, a place where men could do whatever they wanted to for as long as they wanted without regard for the preferences or claims of women.

It took me a long time to confess to my self-centeredness and even longer to relax about it. A couple of years after Susan and I divorced, I had a dream in which she said to me, more in resignation than anger, "You're just looking for an excuse to go fishing." And I answered. "I don't need one." When I awakened, I realized, happily, that this was true.

For the record, I want to say that most of the women I have known, including my former wife, were as reasonable and tolerant about my fishing as anyone could be expected to be. The problem is that I often felt an unreasonable need to go fishing.

I would not argue if you called this a childish need. Indeed, it is a yearning that I first felt on the morning after the trip to South Sauty and wished that instead of going to school I was going back to the bridge where I caught the crappies. I doubt I felt anything so powerful until the day I saw Pattie Wright on the beach at Panama City when I was sixteen. Since then my life has been blessed with a thematic question: *Amare o pescare?* To love or to fish?

It was on the shores of Lake Como in northern Italy, a place where both loving and fishing are woven deeply into the traditional culture, that I discovered an arresting linguistic fact. In Italian, *pescare* has two meanings. The second is "to try to find the meaning of." In Italian, the word for "fishhook" is *amo*, which links it to the noun for love, *amore*. Clearly, I am not the first to fish in these mysterious waters where we try to hook out the meanings of sport and love.

And I guess I have discovered the truth of what Mary S. Kuss discovered. When couples in which only one partner fishes have a conflict, the real issue is usually the amount of time that is spent and the degree of obsession exhibited. The Skeeter commercial was saying the same thing, in its rough-hewn way. Something has to give.

John N. Cole, in his autobiography, *Fishing Came First*, put his cards on the table concerning this conflict over priorities by recounting the following conversation with his father:

> "I don't know what's going to become of you, John." My father shook his head, his eyes angry, his fists in knots. "The only two things you care about are fishing and women. Nothing else means a damn thing to you."
>
> "Well, you got them in the right order," I said.

It is possible to argue that in the matter of fishing and women, John Cole and I come out at the same place and that he simply expresses it more honestly. Susan would have liked me better if I had spent more time in art galleries and the garden. After the divorce, a woman I had been seeing happily for some months said the time had come for us to compare our calendars to determine when I would be around and when I would be fishing. Things trailed off after that.

But let this testament show that I do not want to line up with Mr. Cole in believing a fishing life has to have separate compartments. My mother and my aunt Grace and the granny woman who taught me about limit on crappie were beside me the first day I fished. Between my father and mother, she is by far the more avid and more skilled fisher. She has caught bigger bass than anyone else in the family, and over the past twenty years, I have spent more time fishing with her than with my father. As a girl growing up in Alabama, Susan fished with her grandfather, and part of the magic of our courtship was that it took place on waters she had known since childhood and that I could not have fished those private lakes without her. My girlfriend in college was at home on the waters from the Tennessee River to the Gulf of Mexico. The biggest fight we ever had was when I told her that a snapper trip out of Destin, Florida, was going to be for men only. Fortunately, my brother and his wife overruled me.

So I have learned not to regard fishing as a male preserve. The fact that thousands of women are taking up fly-fishing is historically apt, flowing from a tradition that dates back to Berners, McBride and Marbury. It is also inevitable, I think, since fly-fishing is the most feminine branch of fishing,

relying as it does on touch, intuition and a more relaxed, nurturing and uncompetitive feeling for the quarry and its home. Perhaps that is why men discover fly-fishing when they age past the point where, as Tom McGuane puts it, they are simply "running on testosterone."

Mary S. Kuss says that many of the women coming into fly-fishing "do it as a way to spend time with a boyfriend or spouse." But I am not sure that is the norm. For every woman I know who fly-fishes with her husband, I have met a single woman who fly-fishes on her own or with a mixed group of male and female friends. This, like the enrollment figures at the Orvis school, suggests there may be a deeper trend in play here, and it is beginning to show up in the demographic studies.

Divorce is increasing in every age group, but most rapidly among people aged forty to fifty-four. Divorcées in this age group increased from 1.5 million in 1970 to 6.1 million in 1991. The numbers are increasing because people who get divorced are staying single. Digging into these figures, Jane Gross, a *New York Times* reporter, found that women are staying single in greater numbers and more happily than men.

She interviewed a forty-six-year-old woman in Kalamazoo who "comes and goes as she pleases and spends the money she earns without reproach," much of it on her horse. Jane Gross also found a fifty-five-year-old man near Detroit who complained: "Some of these women, it's an ego trip for them. It's hooray for me and the heck with the other guy. They don't know how to share. Fine and dandy. Let them do their own thing."

How long will it take this wave of role reversal to overtake the traditional stereotype of the clinging woman? A very long time, I would guess, because it is deeply embedded in our culture, as evidenced in a pivotal scene in the movie *Out of Africa*. In that scene, the character based on Denys Finch-Hatton is the mouthpiece for the traditional male view. He and his lover, Karen Blixen, the Danish woman who wrote under the name Isak Dinesen, are sitting by a campfire. Her desire to be married and his desire to follow the freebooting life of the African hunter are in collision.

> She: "When you go away you don't always go on safari, do you?"
> He: "No."
> She: "You just want to be away."
> He: "It's not meant to hurt you."
> She: "It does."
> He: "Karen, I'm with you because I choose to be with you. I don't want to live someone else's idea of how to live. Don't ask me to do that. I don't want to find out one day that I'm at the end of someone else's life. I'm willing to pay for mine, to be lonely sometimes, to die alone if I have to. I think that's fair."
> She: "Not quite. You want me to pay for it as well."

The real Denys Finch-Hatton was a charismatic, emotionally distant man who was apparently able to sustain the life of radical freedom that he described. We will never know how he would have emerged from the midlife passage, because he died at forty-four, alone, in a plane crash at Voi, Kenya, in 1931. But in today's America, women know what Jane Gross found in her reporting among the fourteen percent of the middle-aged population that is divorced. Most men talk a good game of a-man's-got-to-do-what-a-man's-got-to-do, but when they get a little bit lonely they get clingy and pitiful. The Finch-Hatton model is valuable for men of my age group because it suggests that it is important to be honest about your selfishness and not to talk the talk unless you can walk the walk.

So here is where I came out as I entered my fiftieth year. We are not on this earth for long. Part of what a midlife crisis is about is figuring out what gives you pleasure and doing more of that in the time you have left without asking for permission or a financial or emotional subsidy from anyone else. I believe in a balanced life. I do not want to fish all the time. I am extremely fond of people in general and women in particular. In fact, as I get older I more and more prefer their friendship and company to that of men. But I have learned that I am also a person who has to be able to go fishing whenever I can and for as long as I want to go. It is a silly thing, but there it is.

The day may come when I do not care to fish anymore. That day is not here yet, but it could happen. Just as I outgrew the Redneck Way, I find that I do not much like to go to the streams in Pennsylvania and Maryland where Dick introduced me to trout fishing. I prefer the rivers out West or the saltwater flats in the Keys or on the Gulf Coast. And sometimes when I am in the West or on the coast, I feel like I have had enough after a day or two. Anything is possible in the life of a man if he lives long enough. Even maturity.

A FISHING TALK
GIVEN AT YALE

Ernest Schwiebert

"I don't know why I fish, or why others fish, except that it makes us think and feel." —Roderick Haig-Brown, 1946

*W*HAT A WONDERFUL party. And what a wonderful purpose for a party, to say nothing of its magnificent setting: the Presidents' Rotunda at Yale. The portraits of Yale's historic leaders are a bit unsettling tonight. I am reminded, as I see them watching us in their academic robes and colorful hoods, of John Fitzgerald Kennedy's remark on the occasion of his celebration of Nobel Prize winners at the White House.

"I believe there has not been such an assemblage of intelligence in this room," the young president deadpanned, "since Thomas Jefferson dined alone."

The Presidents' Rotunda at Yale. It is a bit intimidating, and Allan Poole and I were a bit nervous, given our allegiance to Old Nassau, until we finally got to the bar. We were not entirely sure of ourselves. We decided to sit together, until we could decide on a strategy. We were clearly outnumbered in this coven of Old Bulldogs.

I intend to speak seriously of fishing tonight. What better place for serious fishing talk than Yale.

But before such serious matters, I believe that Alan and I are forced to agree that the *Yale Anglers' Journal* is a splendid idea, wonderfully executed and brought to life. We have long been aware of the unique fishing books in the jewel-box reliquary of the Beinecke Library, and the remarkable collection of David Wagstaff.

Princeton cannot quite match this astonishing plentitude

203

of riches, although it has the collection of Carl Otto von Kienbusch, the books and manuscripts and papers of Eugene Virginius Connett, and the open-stack treasures of the Rockey Collection. And the parade of Princeton anglers and fishing authors is a bit unusual: William Cowper Prime, Henry Van Dyke, Grover Cleveland, Edward Ringwood Hewitt, Doctor Edgar Burke, Eugene Connett, Russell MacGregor , Otto von Kienbusch, Manning Barr, Philip Nash, Walter Steel, Victor Coty, Dana Storrs Lamb, and Austin Francis. It is only a partial list, but with all of its talent, these men never thought of anything like the *Yale Anglers' Journal*. And we salute you tonight.

It was a pleasure to see James Prosek again, and it was intriguing to learn of his new book project. But I must salute his *Compleat Angler*, not only for its subtle watercolors and its contribution to Waltonia, but also for his manipulative skills in convincing Yale that a two-year travelling fellowship to fish was legitimate.

I have a grudging admiration for his success, since I once made a similar proposal to *National Geographic*, while a fellow member of the Anglers' Club of New York, Luis Marden, was its international editor .

Jonathan Trumbull Wright was a promising photographer with *Geographic* in those days, and we suggested a poetic picture essay, visiting the haunts and rivers that inspired the great British fishermen and their

books. Wright was a skilled fisherman and alpinist himself, and I had known him since his boyhood in Aspen. We had worked together on magazine shoots before, including one in which Wright did his shooting with a helicopter harness under his armpits, and his boots planted on the skid. The starboard hatch had been removed, and he was shooting our MacKenzie boats as the helicopter hovered under the rim of the gorge, while we attempted to negotiate the wild chutes of the Black Canyon of the Gunnison.

We lost a boat in the first rapids below the Morrow Point boat access. No one was hurt, but the really dangerous stuff was overhead, as Wright worked outside the cockpit, with his boots braced on the skid.

And he became a great photographer.

Wright did the still photography for the American Bicentennial Expedition on Everest in 1976, reached its summit on a later television climb, and took cameras to the pinnacle of Ama Oablam in 1979. He was killed in Tibet a year later, in an avalanche on Minya Konka, which rises 24,790 feet above the Sichuan Province.[1] We would share no trip to Europe.

I can picture what we might have gotten there, on the rivers of England and Scotland, something like the little poem that James Prosek has achieved in *The Compleat Angler*, but with more characters. He has written a lovely book.

While still a graduate student in architecture and art

history at Princeton, under Jean Labatut and Donald Drew Egbert, I spent considerable time filling out my dance card in undergraduate courses, and that moonlighting was spent at McCosh Hall. My mentors there included Alan Downer, who taught courses in theater; Carlos Heard Baker, the Hemingway biographer; and Gerald Eades Bentley, who was Murray Professor of English Literature. I knew Bentley and Baker quite well.

Their yardsticks were austere, and had they lived to witness the constructivist excesses of recent years, I am convinced that much subjective nonsense (like much post-modern architecture) would have been dismissed as doubtful conjecture. All disciplines are plagued with reiterations of the doubtful and the obvious. The story of Walton is straightforward and lovely, and the evocation of his landscapes and his rivers is a worthy purpose in itself.

I suspect *The Compleat Angler* was a lyric madrigal to fishing the gentle rivers of Middlesex and Derbyshire, and little more, other than its glimpses of a diverse and interesting life well-lived. Walton's fishing friends form a remarkable list, and a testimony to his education and wit, whatever their source. His little prose pastorale was not a clandestine allegory, a subversive document in a strife-torn England oppressed by Cromwell and his henchmen although Walton clearly supported Charles II.

Sometimes things are merely what they seem, and

that remains enough. Sigmund Freud and Kenneth Starr notwithstanding, the cigar may only be a cigar. But our roots are wonderfully old.

We are here to celebrate an ancient and honorable sport, with roots reaching deep into antiquity. There are Egyptian sources as old as two-thousand years before Christ, which depict rod fishing in the tomb murals of Beni Hasan. Chinese texts also describe rod fishing in those centuries. There are glazed tiles from the lost temple ruins of Nineveh, a thousand years later, depicting our sport in a flowing spring-fed pond. Such anglers may have caught trout, since there are such fish in the headwaters of the Tigris and Euphrates.

The Roman scholar and poet, Claudius Aelianus, tells of fly-fishing and fly-making in the Second Century, in his *De Natura Animalium*.

Joseph Needham writes in his remarkable *History of Chinese Science*, which includes several shelves of scholarly and densely reasoned volumes, and more than a thousand pages of astonishing bibliographic material and notes, that brightly feathered lures were fashioned by Chinese artisans, four centuries before *De Natura Animalium*.

Needham includes an illustration from a scroll painting by the celebrated twelfth-century landscape painter, Ma Yuan, which clearly depicts a fishing reel, four centuries before its first appearance in English, in the little handbook published by Thomas Barker in 1651. There is no mistaking the device or its purpose, and Needham speculates that the reel may have logically evolved from Chinese gadgets used for preparing fibers and spinning cloth.

It would seem that Marco Polo might have brought more than spaghetti and silk and gunpowder in his baggage when he returned to Venice in 1295.

Our first mention of fly-fishing in English, including descriptions of fly-making, is found in *The Boke of Saint Albans*, an artifact published by Wynken de Worde in 1496. There are contemporary writers who would like to discount the existence of its purported author, Dame Juliana Berners, the prioress of Sopwell nunnery at Saint Albans. Her *Treatyse of Fysshynge Wythe an Angle* was apparently written about 1420. There is an incomplete manuscript copy in the Wagstaff collection at Yale, the work of an unknown calligrapher of about 1450, when Berners was alive.

Despite the revisionists, I support the thesis of the late John MacDonald, the senior editor at *Fortune* who remains the finest American fishing historian. MacDonald was fascinated with Berners, and examined a number of copies of her *Treatyse* in the United Kingdom. He also explored the comments of the antiquarian, John Bale, who included the prioress in the literary biographies of his *Scriptorum Illustria Majoris Britanniae* of 1559.

Bale remains a bit controversial, since he was a Carmelite who turned against Rome, and campaigned bitterly for the principles of Martin Luther. He apparently participated in the theological quarrels of the sixteenth century, in which many British reformers were forced to leave the United Kingdom as Marian Exiles. Such exiles settled in English colonies at Geneva and Frankfurt-am-Main. But there is no evidence that Bale's strong religious convictions have prejudiced his observations on Bemers, since they are laudatory and judicious. His *Scriptorum Illustria Majoris Britanniae* comments begin with a few expository facts:

> Juliana Barnes, illustris faemina, corporis et animis dotibus abundans, ac formae elegantia spectabilis, inter alia humanae uitae folatia, venationes et aucupia in magnis habebat delicis.[2]

MacDonald further tells us that Bale used a colleague as his principal firsthand source, and the biographical treatise *De Viris Illustribus, Sive de Scriptoribus Britannicus*. It was the work of John Leland, who had served as court librarian and antiquarian to Henry VIII, and had died in 1552. But MacDonald did not stop there.

William Burton was another British antiquarian who was familiar with Leland and Bale, and was actually in possession of Leland's notes and papers. Burton presented these notes and papers to the Bodeleian Library at Oxford in 1632. Burton lived within a century of Leland, and spent decades pouring over the collated books and manuscripts that Leland had discovered in his investigations, which had

included most of the castles, manorhouses, monasteries, convents, universities, and private libraries throughout the British realm, at the orders and authorization of Henry VIII.

Among the books and manuscripts in the possession of the Bishop of Ely, Doctor John Moore, was included a complete copy of *The Boke of Saint Albans*. His gracefully embellished church suffered great damage at the hands of Cromwellian troops, and the angling fraternity is fortunate that this book was not lost when most of its religious sculpture and icons were wantonly smashed.

There are handwritten annotations in this copy of Berners, which is still found at Cambridge University, a few miles south of Ely. MacDonald explored the book in great detail, and his paleographic studies confirm that they are in the hand of William Burton.

The opening handwritten notes are based upon Burton's thorough knowledge of Leland's entire library, as well as his notes and papers, with the help of Burton's own scholarly perceptions of the fifteenth-century:

> This book was made by the Lady Julian Berners, daughter of Sir James Berners of Berners Roding in Essex; Knight; and sister to Richard Lord Berners. She was the Lady Prioresse of Sopewelle, a nunnery neare Saint Albans; in which Abbey of Saint Albans, this was first printed in 1486. She was still living in 1460, according to John Bale.

The disciplines of history do not rest merely on the printed word. Both oral histories and contemporaneous accounts have often proved correct, and I believe we should trust witnesses who lived in or near the period in contention, unless they had some obvious axe to grind. It is usually quite easy to identify the furtive undertones of malice. John Leland was highly regarded in his time, and in the century that followed. His access to the finest libraries of the United Kingdom was unique, and Leland died only sixty-odd years after the publication of *The Boke of Saint Albans*. And I rest my case.

We must remain skeptical and wary of revisionism, as

well as its ulterior purposes, since dissenting opinions make waves, and attract more attention, than scholarly affirmations of our heritage. Few readers seem to see the temptations implicit in willful dissent, since it draws the historian himself into the limelight. Thomas Steams Eliot understood these sins in *Murder in the Cathedral*:

> The last temptation is the greatest treason;
> To do the right deed, for the wrong reason.

I was among the few who were privileged to know the British expatriate, Roderick Haig-Brown, and I treasure our encounters in New York, Sun Valley , Jackson Hole, and Aspen. I first met him through Ed Zern, at a dinner party in Scarsdale, which lasted long after midnight. The photographer Dan Callaghan and I once drove from Portland to Campbell River, and we spent a four-day weekend with the writer, in the book-filled atelier where he worked. It was late winter and there were migrating grosbeaks in the orchard, which lay just beyond his writing desk. Fitful February sun danced on the dark river. We recorded our conversations and Callaghan took pictures, and we got to see the poet in his British Columbia landscapes. Haig-Brown cherished our sport, with its alchemy of history, tradition, literature, athletic grace, science, and art. Such convictions are obvious in the beautiful closing paragraph of *A River Never Sleeps*.

He confesses that he does not fully understand why he chooses to fish, or why others fish, except that it makes us think and feel. I cannot think of two better reasons for anything. Haig-Brown later tells us that everything involved in our sport is beautiful, like the rivers themselves, and everything they nurture. He concludes that were it not for the swift poetry of rivers, with their pewtery light in the rain, the trembling pull of their currents, and the feel of their cobble under his feet, he would fish less often.

And he closes *A River Never Sleeps* with the observation that he fishes simply to be near rivers, and concludes that if that sweet epiphany is true, he is grateful that he finally thought of it. All lives have epiphanies of sorts, sudden insights both large and small, and the trick is simply not to miss their meanings. I think that I fish for beauty.

My first epiphany came more than sixty-years-ago, on an unpaved country road in southern Michigan. I saw a man fishing, and asked my mother to stop. The little river was crystalline and smooth, with a pea-gravel bottom, and its currents slipped past cedar roots and sweepers. The flow was relatively swift, and tumbled past his legs. His golden line was working back and forth in the sun, in a noiseless ballet of lazy rhythms, before dropping his flies tight against the fallen logs. There was a splash and he tightened. It was not a large fish.

But it fought splashily against his dancing rod before

it finally came to net. I scrambled down from the bridge, and the man held it in the net until I reached him. My fishing had been limited to bullheads in muddy creeks, and pumpkinseeds and perch off our Michigan dock, but this fish was a revelation, and in the words of my favorite New Zealand fisherman, the colorful Hughie MacDowell, it seemed like a fish straight from God's own mold.

It was a brook trout of six-inches. But its flanks were like a jeweler's tray of opals and moonstones and rubies, its bright tangerine fins edged in ebony and alabaster, and its olive back and shoulders like the vermiculated endpapers of a rare French edition. It was an epiphany, a bright potshard of living poetry, and I have never been happy with anything else. It was beautiful.

Such beauty is increasingly important, perhaps our only antidote to the brash cacophonies that plague these demotic times. Trout fishing is quite beautiful. Its skills offer an equilibrium between history, tradition, physical dexterity and grace, strength, logic, problem solving, esthetics, science, our powers of observation and diagnosis, perceptions, and the full spectrum of our experience. Our tackle and fly boxes are quite beautiful too, and the serial chess games of tactics and entomology and fly-making remain unique.

Beauty. The sport is filled with beauty. We share the passion for bright rivers tumbling toward the salt, the deft choreography of swifts and swallows working to a hatch of

fly, and the quicksilver poetry of the fish themselves. And in seeking such beauty, in the crystalline magic of trout water, we may discover that beauty is the most endangered thing of all.

NOTES

[1] The alpinist Rick Ridgeway led the Minya Konka expedition, which included Yvon Chouinard. Ridgeway and I delivered eulogies for Wright, at the Aspen Institute for Humanistic Studies. Ridgeway recounts his death in *Below Another Sky* which was recently published by Henry Holt.

[2] There are a number of translations of these words, each seeming to reflect the prejudices of the author in question. Neither Joseph Haslewood in 1810, nor William Blades in 1881, could quite bring himself to admit that a beautiful woman could possess both a thorough knowledge of the field sports, and also be prioress of a nunnery. But as MacDonald points out, the knowledge of sport obtained from her beginnings as a noblewoman of Bemers Roding was quite plausible, and such expertise would not be lost after her subsequent vows as a nun. I believe the best translation of Bale's description of Bemers might be the following:

> Julian Barnes, illustrious woman, eminently abounding in gifts of body and spirit, and remarkable for her physical form and elegance; among the solaces of human life she venerated the field sports in the highest estimation.

SOUL TO SOUL

Thomas Robert Barnes

These clouds slipped by me
when I wasn't paying attention.
Too many not to notice collective brooding.
Some huddle, sit on heels waiting for tears to fall.

Evening begins to topple
by the time I've worked above them,
pulling shadows tighter,
leaving room for elbows of light.

I bring my father's list.
Three fish he had not caught:
Dolly Varden, Arctic Grayling, Golden Trout.
My brother finished it for him.

I am stuck on the last,
chase its name across my tongue,
Golden Trout,
who swims higher than clouds.

Each time I climb this crater
I think of those first fingerlings
and who must have carried them
from water to water to put their fire here.

What I bring of my father,
his bristled face on Saturday mornings,
food of his breath winnowing years on earth,
more than killing catching them.

Though he would never know
the slash of scarlet behind their gills,
warriors emblazoned by their own bleeding,
golden thrums come back to pocket,

he would know their slime,
same smell of it on coats and hands
for days or weeks
or all these missing years,

and though his lungs, his heart
would never make it here
to this held-high cup,
hole of water carved in sky

I bring the thought of him in my hands
to touch his blood to their blood
and then only
to hold and to release.

IN TWO DAYS THE LEAVES WILL COAT

Elaine Bleakney

The surface of this pond. The radiant
dark will disappear. You cast. I lose
the hook until it gets closer to the rocks and drags
steeped green shallows. It must
be cooler where they are, it must be fine. You
cast again and the repetition is not for

remembering, not for anything but asking
please give me the most furtive beauty.
Please arrest me in time.

And he comes, a male so bright and ready.
You hold him over the rocks. His pale jaw. His
impossible, fevered body
fights. Relaxes. Do leaves swim
over us, am I in the century to hear you slip
apart from the world, inside
the world always?

SALUDA PROBABILITY

Juaquín Hernàndez Canegato

Today, I went looking for twenty trout
That I heard hovered near the interstate bridge.
Almost there, an owl and I met suddenly.
He stopped to glance and listen, from his tree,
To my bare chest and shy clumsy paddle,
Which was digging, filling, digging, filling
Small wet graves with each careful, mechanically perfect,
Locked, stroke. Or more correctly, rotation.
The wing paddle, they say, does not slip sideways
Like a conventional paddle can.
My owl's glance is like those caddisflies—
That slip up to the surface and are sipped down
By the dog-food trout that were stocked last week
By my state's Department of Natural Resources.
Good lads. Great guys, for giving the rednecks the fortune
Of throwing chartreuse roostertails and drinking beer
And keeping every single fucking fish they catch:
"Well, thank you, Billy Sunday"—So fleeting that before I
    had the chance
To pencil him in my memory, the old unkempt owl
Fell swiftly toward a finger mullet
That simply did not know what hit him.
I, for one, was happier than a dog with two peters

To see the river run and the owl toil,
To know that splashes are shooting stars,
That the making from start to finish is special,
That the hoi polloi is familiar with ripples,
But hardly ever that strigene driving force.
Juaquín, as I rotate my right wing
Over this pellet of owl-shit, I will tell you:
"I have still never ever seen a hover of trout.
Unplanned motion is an unfettered soul,
Beautiful, beautied fuel, (et tu) Brute Fu(lano).
Stars burn out bright.
Small fish meals are enough.
We can only remember what we see,
And know that beauty is probability."

FLATHEAD TROUT *Salmo platycephalus*
(Soğuksu River, Turkey)

RUMMAGING THROUGH THE BASEMENT FINDING PISCATORIAL AUDUBONS

Robert Behnke

*T*WENTY-FIVE YEARS AGO the College of Veterinary Medicine vacated a WPA era building on campus and it was turned over to our expanding Department of Fishery and Wildlife Biology. At the time, I was in need of space for my collection of trout specimens and for a great volume of books, journals, literature, notes and files I had accumulated over many years. I was allotted a large area of the basement where I unloaded my goods and set up shop.

Over the years the Fishery and Wildlife Department continued to grow and more space for faculty and graduate students was needed. The old basement would be torn out and reconstructed. All of my possessions would have to be removed. A worst nightmare became a reality.

A large part of my time in recent months has been devoted to sorting through boxes, shelves and file cabinets to decide what to save and what to dispose of—separating wheat from chaff. Sorting through the files turns up some interesting bits of historical miscellany.

A newspaper clipping from 1974 reported that the first Atlantic salmon had returned to the Connecticut River. The story included a prediction that 30,000 salmon would be returning to the Connecticut River in thirty years. With this clipping was a copy of a special supplement to the Greenfield, Massachusetts *Recorder* of June 8, 1990. A new $17 million anadromous fish research laboratory on the Connecticut River at Turners Falls, Massachusetts was to be dedicated.

The new research lab would be operated by the U.S. Fish and Wildlife Service with an annual budget of $1.7 million. The main emphasis of research would be Atlantic salmon, especially the restoration of salmon to the Connecticut River. A sophisticated computer model predicted that by the year 2021, returns of Atlantic salmon to the Connecticut River would reach 38,000. This reminded me of what I have written about the "illusion of technique" where sophisticated but simplistic models are often a poor substitute for knowledge and a deeper understanding of the subject matter.

The greatest number of Atlantic salmon counted in the Connecticut River since the first one was recorded in 1974 was 529 in 1981 followed by 70 in 1982 and 39 in 1983. Since then, despite great increases in hatchery production and stocking, salmon returns to the Connecticut River have run between one-hundred and three-hundred in most years.

A file drawer contained correspondence, notes and photos covering many years of communicating with some dedicated people, who like myself developed a passion, almost an obsession, to find and learn about rare and vanishing forms of trout.

I first met Bob Smith in 1975. At that time Bob was a recently retired waterfowl biologist with the U.S. Fish and Wildlife Service. He was an avid angler who had attained a stage of angling satisfaction whereby his greatest pleasure was derived from catching and photographing all of the species, subspecies, and distinct races of North American trout. This passion for wild, native trout culminated in Bob's book: *Native Trout of North America* (Frank Amato Publications, Portland, Oregon: first edition 1983, second, revised edition 1994). Bob Smith did an excellent job of interpreting my publications on trout evolution, until then largely confined to the scientific literature, and making them available to the angling public. He became an effective crusader for the preservation of wild, native trout.

Bob Smith's book encouraged others to develop similar interest in native trout. Kyle McNeilly of Calgary, Alberta made contact with both Bob Smith and me to further his interests in putting together a museum-quality exhibit of realistic taxidermy models of all the forms of trout covered in Bob Smith's book. In return, Kyle helped Bob Smith to find and catch the "Sunapee golden trout" from an Idaho lake. The "golden trout" of Sunapee Lake, New Hampshire was an Arctic char left over from the last glacial retreat. It has been long extinct in Sunapee Lake, but some eggs had been shipped to Idaho in the 1920s and stocked into a few cold mountain lakes. Bob Smith was elated to learn he now had an opportunity to catch a true Sunapee trout to add to his life list of rare trout and include in the second edition of his book. By the time Bob had arranged his Idaho trip in search of the Sunapee trout, Kyle McNeilly had already been there and filmed the Sunapee trout. Later, Kyle made a return trip, coming down from Canada to meet Bob at the Idaho lake where Smith caught, photographed and released the Sunapee trout to fulfill his dream.

I had the opportunity to see Kyle McNeilly's exhibition of trout replicas at a trout conference in Alberta in 1999. It is an amazing one-of-a-kind exhibit. Truly a labor of love.

Glen McFaul of Arizona is another angler with a deep fascination for rare, native trout. Glen carries a portable aquarium to photograph live fish. Glen has traveled much of the western U.S. checking on sites where I found rare trout from 25 to 40 years ago. His photographs and observations on the current status of many rare trout have been a help to me in keeping up-to-date on extinction threats. Page 142 of my 1992 monograph on western trout mentions that the known natural distribution of the rare Colorado River subspecies of cutthroat trout was extended to the Escalante River drainage based on Glen's finding a population there in 1991.

Perhaps the most unusual of these modern day trout Audubons is Johannes Schöffmann of Austria. Although Johannes is not an angler, he lives out his obsession for rare trout in his far-flung travels from China to North Africa. He dons a wet suit and enters the fish's domain. He makes observations and captures specimens for further study with a net.

In the winter 1986 issue of *Trout* I wrote about brown trout, I mentioned a relative of the brown trout that I named as a new species, *Salmo platycephalus*. The new species was known only from three specimens collected from a river in Turkey in 1966. I also discussed a peculiar trout described in 1924 as *Salmo pallaryi* from Lake Algueman, Morocco. I made a request for anyone who might have any information on the status of *S. platycephalus* or *S. pallaryi* to please let me know.

Johannes went to Turkey and sent me photographs and detailed notes on *platycephalus* that he found in a spring-stream. Its distribution is restricted to a small area of the river drainage and its continued existence is threatened by sediment loading from agriculture and road-building. Johannes went to Morocco and verified that *pallaryi* is extinct, but found that the diversity of the native brown trout of North Africa has its origins in at least two separate invasions of two distinct ancestors. (Johannes preserved tissue samples from the trout he collected for use in molecular genetic research.)

Johannes also made surveys and collections to determine the status of some peculiar trouts of Adriatic drainages: the marble trout, *S. marmoratus* and the "soft mouth" trout of the genus *Salmothymus*. He found that both are now very rare; their original distributions have been greatly reduced.

After returning home from his expeditions, Johannes writes up a report of his findings including detailed taxonomic descriptions, life history observations and an analysis of the threats to continued existence of the rare forms of trout. He publishes the reports in an Austrian fisheries journal. When I read Johannes' scientific papers, the range and depth of knowledge displayed indicates formal training in ichthyology. When I later learned that Johannes is a baker by profession and a pure amateur ichthyologist, I was all the more impressed by his level of expertise. Johannes exemplifies the true meaning of amateur: one whose interest and enthusiasm for a subject is driven by love of the subject, not because it is part of their profession.

In 1995 I received a letter from a Yale student, James Prosek. James was then putting together a text to go with his paintings of trout in what was to become a highly popular book: *Trout, An Illustrated History* published by Alfred Knopf in 1996.

James inquired about trout in the Tigres-Euphrates basin. Did a trout stream run through the Garden of Eden? Johannes Schöffmann had recently sent me a paper on his expedition to record the characteristics of trout native to the Tigres drainage of Turkey (this was the first description of Tigres trout in the world literature).

James Prosek was planning a trip to Europe and I suggested he contact Johannes Schöffmann. With two such passionate trout lovers getting together, wonderful adventures were bound to be forthcoming. In the first two trips, James and Johannes sampled the historical trout waters of Slovenia, Serbia, Bosnia, Croatia, Greece and Turkey. James wrote the story of their adventures including his portraits of the diverse forms of trout they encountered and published it, most appropriately, in *Audubon* magazine (January–February, 1999).

In the summer 1992 issue of *Trout*, I wrote about grayling. I mentioned a specimen of a grayling-like fish in the fish collection of the British Museum. This specimen was brought back to England in 1897 by St. George Littledale. The specimen was considered so distinct that a new genus and species was described for it. The collection locality is stated to be: "South slopes Altai Mountains on Chinese territory" (Mongolia). This species has not been found since and there is no other record of a salmonid fish in south slope Altai drainages in China (drainages toward the Gobi Desert). The mystery of the south slope Altai grayling set the stage for the next wonderful adventure of Johannes and James in search of the mystery fish. James and Johannes met in Ulan Bator, Mongolia, rented a Russian jeep and began their quest. I received a postcard from Mongolia relating that the jeep had four flat tires in the Gobi Desert. They failed to find the south slope grayling but encountered a known species of Mongolian grayling, *Thymallus brevirostris*, in north slope Altai drainages, part of a large internal basin. No other salmonid fish exists in the internal basin and the Mongolian grayling evolved as a predator on the several species of minnows it lives with. It attains the largest size of any species of grayling but is so little known that there is no official world record for Mongolian grayling. The most up-to-date account of the Mongolian grayling can be found in a paper authored by Johannes in the Austrian fisheries journal.

Last summer, James and Johannes traveled to Kyrgyzstan to find the easternmost natural distribution of brown trout—*Salmo trutta oxianus* of the Aral sea basin.

The small fraternity of piscatorial Audubons are composed of a disparate group whose common interest is their passion for learning about trout that goes well beyond the ordinary. How many potential new members might there be? Anyone out there interested in taking another look at the south side of the Altai Mountains?

MARCEL PROUST AND THE ART OF FLY-FISHING

R. Howard Bloch

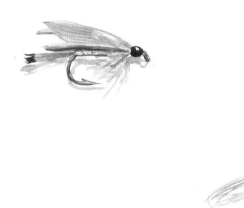

For a long time I used to take what the British call a reading vacation. I would sleep until nine, read until two or three, then fish until dark in the pocket water of the Madison as it calmed, rich in oxygen and bugs, from the desperate tumble out of Earthquake Lake. The excitement of the feeding frenzy that accompanies the last rays of light pouring down the great valley from Ennis to Raynold's Pass, bringing the fish out from under the cut banks, left no other passion in its wake. On the good fishing nights you felt like a fellow deep into a detective novel, unable to put it down until you discovered who did it and how.

I used to think that my life in New York and in Montana was the stuff of two different worlds connected only by Delta Airlines and Hertz. The ideas that ruled my professional existence—ideas about the status of the referent, the difference between language and speech, and gender as a social construct—belonged to a higher sphere having little to do with fishing's close observation of nature and careful looking about. Gradually, however, I came to realize that the yearly stepping out of the city and into the streams of the Rockies was merely a process of changing perspectives upon the thing I loved the most—reading itself. The reading that I did during the winter and the fishing I did during the summer were communicating vases that met somewhere deep in my psyche, intractable, untreatable, inaccessible, the mainspring of my biological clock.

Fishing is a kind of reading, which is why so many fisherman, when they are not fishing and not tying flies, like to read about fishing. They indulge winter fantasies with articles about perfected streamers and new material for the belly of a jassid and with river stories—the classics of Hemingway and Grey, those of the modern masters Schwiebert, Chatham, and Lyons. Indeed, beyond reading as a form of self-help or of escape, fishing may not only be a kind of reading, but the most intense form of reading there is.

Descending upon an unknown stream has always been like encountering a book for the first time. You hold it in your hand, you examine the cover, you try to situate it among the books you have read in terms of type—a novel, poetry, a play from the English or French tradition. So too, before thinking about fish, one takes in the terrain, one begins to read the water. Is it one of the silvery sluiced pocket-waters laced with boulders like an action packed mystery à la Stephen King? Or is it a slow meandering meditative crisscross of a meadow, like a novel by Austen or James? Is it a steamy cauldron like the Firehole, one of the deep circles of Dante's *Inferno*? An oily-slick dark water like the Madison in the Park, which evokes the exotic perfumes of a Baudelaire poem? Or is it one of the clear chalky trickles like the Upper Ruby, with the clean lines of an O'Henry story? Rivers, like books, fall into genres, and our generic expectations determine how we begin to read them. For this much is true, and Faulkner

knew it when he began *The Sound and the Fury* with a discourse on the trout of the Charles River and the process of forgetting time: stepping into the river involves reading the river and everything that surrounds it.

I look at the water's surface in order to get a read upon how the fish may be feeding. One little break, one tell-tale ring, and I think dries. I've met a lot of fisherman on the rivers of Montana, and of these only a few—usually young and impatient—prefer to fish a nymph underneath when he could fish a dry on top. That's because the magic of fishing lies in making a fish rise to your fly, something that Marcel Proust, a man who spent 18 years in bed writing the greatest novel of the twentieth century, a man who was once photographed with a tennis racket but who certainly never fished, articulated better than anyone else. Proust compares the effect of metaphor upon the reader to the sudden appearance of fish on the unbroken surface of water—the Vivonne of his childhood—where the instant before there was no life. The rise of a fish participates in the miraculousness of creation. This is why both Proust and Joyce took the river as prime metaphor, a channel of our consciousness whose branches lead upstream to the roots of our being.

When the fish are feeding on the top we look around to see what's hatching or what's floating on the surface. Is it big or small, drowned fly or spinner? Are they taking it with a gusto or sipping it just under the slick? When we can't see the fish feeding, we think wet or nymph, and, turning a couple of rocks, become like ancient divines reading the future in the entrails of animals or the shape of clouds. I haven't kept a trout for as long as I can remember, and I have often wondered what it is that attracts me so to connecting with a fish. Perhaps connecting is not the right word. What really excites me is not catching a fish, it's not even hooking one. The thrill lies, as for Proust, in producing a fish from water where just an instant before there was none. It lies literally in making contact with the trout which rises to take a good look and perhaps even to snap at my fly. A well presented #14 elk hair caddis floating dragless from the bump at the end of a perfect cast carries all the charm of a conversation and the terror of a seduction.

Fishing for me is a way of communicating with trout, and my flybox holds the vocabulary of the tongues we speak. Will I speak a language which will please the fish by reproducing a bug found in nature? The flies that imitate what we observe around us—a green drake with its long braided tail pitched at just the right angle, a pale morning dun with gossamer wings, a callabatis with speckled spines—are like the natural tropes that, according to the classical rhetoricians Cicero and Quintilian, do not make us question our understanding of how words work to make sense of the world. We imagine, of course, that fish love the naturals because they cannot tell the difference between artifice and reality. Or can they? Sometimes I think that the fish I catch year after year are my pets, my friends. They know the difference between a real bug and my imitation, but they rise to a perfectly presented Hemingway caddis in order to greet me or to compliment me on the ease of my cast. Such moments recall, in fact, Hemingway's dictum about writing as a process of making what one knows felt in one's writing rather than seen: the false effortlessness of true art. Other times, however, I use lures that I know very well do not exist in nature and that are said to produce a strike by exciting the fish's anger. These are like the artificial rhetorical tropes that transfer a word's meaning from a proper sense to another, as when we speak of the arms of a mill or of laughing fields. Indeed, there is something a tad lewd, against nature, in the strips of silver vinyl running down the back of a maraboo muddler or in the fluffy-dancing black down of a Yellowstone leech. I like to think that my fish friends strike at one of these as if to say "How dare you insult us with such a monstrosity!"

Flies—wet or dry, terrestrial or water-born, nymph, pupa, or emerger, streamer or spinner—are so many different foreign tongues, and the infinite variety of sizes, colors, and patterns belonging to each are the words we use to communicate with a trout. I hate to think how many times I have felt like Gustave Flaubert, who claimed to have spent whole days looking for just one perfect word, which in my terms means taking all morning or afternoon in pursuit of just the right piece of feather tied to a hook. I remember spending the better part of a day whipping the water on one of the spring creeks south of Livingston trying to figure out what the big browns were slurping just under the bubbly-rich emerald surface. I had tried everything in my box when a couple of old timers arrived for the evening hatch. John MacDonald, the man who discovered Theodore Gordon and who also edited the oldest treatise on fishing from a manuscript in Yale's Beinecke Library, plucked a #24 white cahill from under the lid of his box and fastened it to my tippit with a piece of 7×. I never landed one of the slurpers, but, having found just the right word, I did communicate with several trout as the sun lay down dappled across the hills of Paradise Valley.

Fishing, like writing, has to do with finding just the right word, and, like reading, it has to do with understanding the signs of a river as we move up it looking for the characters that punctuate its continuous flow and that are the signs of fish. Fishing is about moving in one direction along a trajectory that contains its own dramatic stops and starts. Where the swift water meets the ebb, an undercut bank, the calm wake on either side of a protruding boulder, the riffle caused by the aftercurrent of an invisible big bottom rock are the river's breathing points. Like commas, semicolons, periods, paragraphs, and chapters, they indicate the spots where fish like to feed and rest. Sometimes, even, I imagine the canny rainbows as the finicky readers of the food floating past, and I wonder if they have a way of commenting to each other—perhaps with the swish of a tail—on the quality of the fare.

When you begin to wonder what the trout are thinking and what they are saying to each other chances are that you're under the spell of a special kind of mania which has always made me wonder whether it is the fisherman who hooks the fish or the fish which catches us. Rather, just about anyone who has tasted the streams of the Rocky Mountain states has been hooked on fishing, a state of mind which resembles nothing so much as Proust's description of a man in love. Obsessed, jealous, abject in his projections, he imagines that other people are catching his fish and communicating with them in his absence. He suffers from a condition that renders him at once helpless and inoperable. Proust's man eventually falls out of love, realizing that he had been obsessed all along with a woman who wasn't even his type. My case, however, is more serious still, for I am in love with something that is not even of my species. There is, of course, always the possibility of settling down with a good book and waiting for the madness to subside, but there is also the possibility of taking what the British call a reading vacation.

PART VI

Hook, Line, and Sinker

JEALOUS FISHERMAN BARES SOUL

Steven Rinella

O F ALL MY flaws, the worst is that I can't stand to see other people catch fish. I like to watch myself catching fish on home video, and there's nothing better than looking at photographs of me posing with my latest catch, but something strange and out of my control happens—my blood pressure soars, my collar feels tight, my fists clench—when I have to watch some guy I don't know reel in a big one.

My therapist suggests, rather simplistically, that I suffer from garden-variety jealousy. But what does she know? If I'm out fishing and I get skunked, while the guy next to me is raking them in, then how can I go home and blame getting skunked on poor conditions? Or let's say I'm standing in a nice, comfortable fishing spot in the shade of a willow with an ice-cold beer; I'm not catching anything, but I'm thoroughly enjoying myself. Then I look across the lake, only to see some guy pulling in bass left and right. How do you think that makes me feel? What am I supposed to do, move into the lip-blistering sun?

My old girlfriend, Sandra, is the only person I've ever met who actually likes to see other anglers catch fish. We'd be fishing and she'd yell something like, "Oh, wow! Steve, look at that guy's fish! Awesome!" Which was embarrassing. For a while I thought Sandra simply needed some kind of confirmation that there were fish in the water. In an attempt to quiet her down, I took to saying things like, "Baby, there're a lot of fish in this lake. No sense in getting excited if you see someone catch one." But no sooner would I speak than she'd be jumping and shouting about some dude across the way battling what looked to me like a dinky little minnow. Especially irksome were her mindless impulses to introduce herself to other fishermen and cheer them on. In hindsight, I can't help but think there was a direct correlation between her poor behavior and our eventual breakup. My therapist disagrees.

I recognize that the road to recovery is never a straight one, so I'm trying to gradually change my ways. Not that I aim to emulate Sandra's cheerleader routine; I just aim to stop wishing hellfire on every man who hooks a fish in my presence. For now, my strategy is the art of Zen. I don't have to notice the trout on the end of someone's line as it tail-skips across my limp monofilament, because who's to say that the trout really exists? And if it does, it's obviously part of the dominant paradigm that the media dupes me into believing. So chew on that.

My efforts at curing the world of jealous insanity do not stop at my own sacrifices. Because I feel that all fishermen are responsible for changing their ways, I make a point of screaming and hollering a whole lot every time I hook a fish. When I'm fishing my old home stretch in the Saint Mary's River, between Michigan's Upper Peninsula and the Canadian province of Ontario, I stand in the middle of the river so everyone on shore can see me, then every time I

hook into something, I make coyote-like yipping noises and announce the species—Pink salmon! Chinook!—along with an estimated, perhaps slightly exaggerated, weight. I'm only trying to help my fellow fishermen; it toughens their skins.

Of course, my battle isn't fought on water alone. I take my message of reform everywhere I go. If I get to talking to some guys at a river access or in a bait shop, I tell them about catching a lot of fish that maybe I didn't actually catch. Some folks might call this bragging, or worse, lying, but that's because they don't detect my subliminal message: if I pad the numbers a little, it's only to expose my fellow anglers to the successes of others (me). Sufficient exposure, I'm convinced, will replace their envy with sportsman-like joy. After all, we're a team. So if a man tells me about catching a nice fish, I might just declare him a bald-faced liar. Not to embarrass or harass him, but to teach him that catching fish is not necessarily the name of the game. By the same token, I'll tell people that I didn't catch fish where I actually did, and vice-versa.

We can win this war, slowly and steadily. I see change happening all the time. The other day I was so fed up with someone catching fish in front of my face that I decided to snap his rod in half. As I conjured up some Arnold Schwarzenegger-type statement to accompany my attack, he yelled over to see if I wanted half of his sandwich. I was suddenly freed of my violent impulse. The rod was spared.

I'm always a little shocked at how damned nice people can be if you know how to play your cards. Together, that fisherman and I made a great stride. But you can only give him so much credit. If I was cranking in fish, I'd share my sandwich, too. Not that I wouldn't rub a little fish slime on his half, but what do you expect from a free sandwich? The way I see it, fishing is all part of the Big Circle of Life. Think of the Big Circle of Life as a gigantic fishing reel. When I'm doing the reeling, life is good. When you're doing the reeling, you might be wreaking serious havoc on the Circle, so keep it to a minimum and we'll all be better off.

FLY-FISHING WITH JESUS

Dennis Sipe

I knew it was Him because He didn't wear waders.
He didn't wade, He walked on the water,
and cast no shadow, and made no ripples.
He was almost clear, really.
but you could tell it was Him.
Like a kid's plastic statue holding candy,
but He held the reflected trees and sky.
He wore the perfect fishing hat
that you could look for all you life
and only find in Heaven.
His casting was perfect.
I think He ties His own flies,
because I never saw one refused.
Or maybe Mark slipped Jesus a few of his,
tied at God's bench on Heaven's only vise.
Jesus was fishing upstream ahead of me.
So I just watched His presentation
and learned a few tricks,
until He turned to me and asked:
Did you see that last rise?
I said, "sure Jesus what a trout."
He backed out and stood beside me,
and He wasn't clear anymore.

He wore a green waxed-cotton robe
with lots of pockets.
He said, "that is your fish, buddy."
(I felt pretty good when Jesus called me buddy)
"Here try one of these angel wing caddis."
He handed me a size sixteen.
It was all I could do to tie it on.
"I've always liked your knots," Jesus said.
"Thank you," I said,
and I looked into his fig colored eyes.
"I guess you don't need polarized sunglasses,"
"No," He said and smiled,
and I felt warm and light,
better than after a shot of my friend Elwood's
165-dollar-a-bottle scotch whiskey,
every other Friday on poker night.
I worked into position while Jesus spotted
for me from the bank.
The big rainbow rose two more times.
Then, I worked out some line and laid out the fly
and got a good drift over its feeding lie.
It rose and sipped the angel wing
and I raised my Winston four-weight rod

quick and smooth enough to make the line tight.
It felt like a good set.
"Thank you Jesus," I yelled.
With such a fine tippet I had to let him
have more of his way than I liked,
and I followed him down through the tail
of the pool and into the rifles.
I played him perfectly, I palmed my reel just right.
And Jesus was with me
and I lead that rainbow to His net.
"Five-pounds, one-and-half ounces," Jesus said.
"Thanks buddy," I said before I thought.
Jesus smiled.
And even though I forgot about the camera in my vest,
so Jesus could take a picture
before I released that beautiful trout.
It was probably the best day of my life.

THE NEW FLY-FISHING BOOKS

Christopher Buckley

EXTREME FLY-FISHING
By Budd Revill

The author, Budd Revill, a former Navy SEAL who used to assassinate Vietcong cadres (he includes a perhaps too-graphic chapter on this period of his life), argues that fly-fishing has been "pussified" by an over-reliance on expensive, high-tech equipment, packaged fishing trips, and especially, "high-priced lodges where you eat off china." His solution is probably not for everyone: he dispenses with waders, preferring to insulate his legs by greasing them with the fat from "whatever animal is handy—a cat will do." He uses only barbless—and hairless—dry flies and, instead of a modern carbon-fiber rod, a four-foot rattan cane of the kind used on American teenagers in Singapore. "It's got a nice feel to it," he observes, "and once the fish is exhausted, you can use it like a club." *First serial, Esquire.*

WHITE BEADS, BROWN TROUT
By J. H. Wells

The title of this collection of somewhat obscure essays on trout fishing by Wells, a lay Zen monk in upstate New York, comes from a saying of Hakuin, the eighteenth-century Japanese Zen master: "Should you desire the great tranquillity, prepare to sweat white beads." One day, while casting for a humongous brown trout in the Beaverkill River, near Roscoe, New York, Wells found himself asking, "What is the point?"

(Some readers may ask the same question.) He suddenly flung his rod into the river and "began to bark like a dog." The reaction of the trout is not recorded, but the reader may find himself asking, What is the sound of one trout yawning?

GILLS
By Peter Benchley

The celebrated author of *Jaws* is at the top of his form in this gripping tale of a vengeful Dolly Varden trout that terrorizes a fishing camp in British Columbia. Trouble starts when the fearsome, sixteen-inch monster attacks a female wildlife biologist. The trout will not rise to normal flies, and eventually Game Warden Willie (Mac) Shaughnessy and his half-Jewish sidekick, Hamish Cohen, must engage the trout-battling skills of the grizzled half-Inuit, half-Scots poacher, Angus Nook. The harrowing ending, involving a squadron of Canadian Air Command F18s and a canoe paddle, is a page-turner that will leave the reader reluctant to go near running water for months. *Book-of-the-Month Club main selection; movie rights to Columbia.*

BASSHOLES
By Ed Weiler

Trout fly-fishermen have always thought of themselves as the pure heirs of Izaak Walton, and of spin-casting bass fishermen as Neanderthal throwbacks. This book, by an

English professor at the University of Vermont, leaves no doubt as to where the author stands. "Bass fishermen watch *Monday Night Football*, drink beer, drive pickup trucks, and prefer noisy women with big breasts," he writes. "Trout fishermen watch *MacNeil-Lehrer*, drink white wine, drive foreign cars with passenger-side air bags, and hardly think about women at all." The last characteristic, he suggests, may have something to do with the fact that trout fishermen spend most of the time immersed up to the thighs in ice-cold water. *First serial, Atlantic Monthly.*

THE APOSTLE AND THE NYMPH
By Edgar Cole, PH.D.

The author, a biblical archeologist, challenges Norman Maclean's famous asseveration in *A River Runs Through It* that the Apostle John was a dry-fly-fisherman. He draws on his excavation of Ut-Ekmek 2, in modern-day Israel, where, he says, John and the other apostles used to go wet-fly-fishing during the annual landlocked-salmon run. Cole provides impressive evidence in the form of an almost perfectly preserved #6 woolly bugger that closely corresponds with a nymph-type fly made out of chenille which John mentions in a blistering letter to Peter. (Peter had chided John and the other apostles for fishing when they should have been spreading the gospel.) Cole writes about the moment he discovered the woolly bugger with the excitement of Howard

Carter peering for the first time into the tomb of King Tut: "When I saw the telltale chenille body, I thought, Maclean's going to pass bricks when he sees this." But before Cole could communicate his discovery to the world he was arrested by Israeli authorities, charged with trespassing on a top-secret military installation, and held incommunicado for more than a year, during which Dr. Maclean died. Cole claims, convincingly, "The Israelis were then trying to improve relations with the Vatican, which didn't want it to get out that John used wet flies. They had too much invested in the dry-fly myth."

THE GAON
OF BOZEMAN

Peter Just

"*In our family, there was no clear line between religion and fly-fishing.*"
—Norman Maclean

A STORY IS TOLD of the great Hasidic rabbi, Reb Schmuel Bupkiss-Fischman, the Master of the Good Fly, the Gaon of Bozeman. One evening after the Sabbath meal, Reb Schmuel was sitting at the table, surrounded by his students and disciples. He stroked his full, grizzled beard, opened a button of his black gabardine fly vest, and, sighing with contentment, he took a sip of wine from his cup.

One of his prize students, Art Flickovitch, asked him a question: "Rebbe," said Flickovitch, "under what circumstances is it permitted to fish an emerger as a dropper on a dry fly?" The room quickly fell silent as every ear bent to hear the Bozemaner's answer, for this was among the most vexing questions surrounding the elaborate code of law and ritual governing fly-fishing, calling for the most erudite and discerning Talmudic reasoning.

Some held their breath awaiting the answer, for the Rabbi had long declined to declare his position on this thorny matter of theology.

A faint smile graced the Bozemaner's lips as he nodded slowly. "A difficult and subtle question, my son." He leaned back and closed his eyes in contemplation as the congregants waited with bated breath. After an almost unbearable pause, during which some of those present claim to have heard the soft sound of snores emanating from the Master's direction, the Rabbi opened his eyes and spoke.

"As you know," he began, "according to the school of Rabbi Ray Bergman, it is never permitted to fish an emerger and a dry together, unless the emerger is also a floating fly. Reb Ray—who, for some reason, always liked to wear a tartan tallis—held that a dry fly is unto meat, while a wet fly is like unto milk and it is strictly not kosher to mix meat and milk." Some of the Bozemaner's students squirmed in their seats to hear this, having themselves on occasion switched from a dry to a wet without changing leaders.

"On the other hand," continued the Rabbi, "the Letorter Rebbe, Vince Marinarovitch, took the position that, since the account of Creation makes mention of the 'fish of the sea' but not of the streams (as it is written 'have dominion over the fish of the sea, and over the fowl of the air' {Genesis 1:28}) the rules against mixing flies apply to anadromous fish, but not to those which are strictly freshwater. Thus, according to the Letorter, it is permitted to fish a wet fly as a dropper on a dry to stream trout and landlocked salmon, but never to steelhead, searun browns, or, heaven forbid it, to Atlantic salmon. This would be almost as bad as fishing with worms, something only gentiles do." Many in the room gasped to even hear mention of such practices from the lips of this holy man, and Pinky Abramovitz, the youngest student in the Bozemaner's yeshiva, fainted dead away.

"And how are we to know which school of thought to follow, Rabbi?" asked Flickovitch.

"I will tell you, my yingling," answered Reb Schmuel. "It is written 'I will send both the early rain and the later rain,' thus establishing the Almighty's regulation over these natural phenomena. The 'early rain' is the rain of Spring that comes after Passover, which marks the beginning of trout season, that much is clear. But what could be meant by 'the later rain?' I interpret this 'later rain' to be a reference to spinner falls, which dapple the waters like rain, and causeth the trout to rise. Therefore, from now on, my followers are permitted to fish wet droppers off dry flies to non-anadromous salmonids—leave the bass to the gentiles, please—but only between Passover and the Shemini Azereth, and never during a spinner fall. And if you think about this, it is another proof of the Almighty's love for us, for it would be meshugeh to fish a wet during a spinner fall."

All around the room there were murmurs of awe. "Such a Rebbe we have!" they rejoiced. "Who is like unto him for wisdom and subtlety?"

"Of course," said the Bozemaner as he rose and buttoned his black gabardine fly vest, "you must never tie the dropper on the bend of the dry fly's hook. That's what that mamzer, Reb Pincus, in Livingston does. And now, my children, the sun has set, the Sabbath is over, and something tells me there is a blue-wing olive hatch about to come off. Let us go to the river."

ANOTHER POEM FOR PSYCHOANALYSIS

M.J. Trease

I want to fight like Ernest Hemingway,
Like Jacob wrestling 'gainst his nameless foe,
To beat my phrases down and make them say,
"I give!" so that they tell me what they know.
These secrets of my tongue unlock a door
That opens to a lake beneath the hills,
A place, secure, it bears no scars of war,
Where water shines so clear it gives me chills.
To my surprise, I find Nick Adams there.
He's wading, casting where the water's deep,
And waiting, hooks some words that look so fair,
But hard to swallow when it's time to eat.
 We cast. We catch. We clean. We carve. We cook.
 I wake my sleepy leg and close the book.

ABOUT THE AUTHORS

AARON ALTER is currently an undergraduate at Yale University, where he is editor-in-chief of the *Yale Anglers' Journal* and vice-president of the Yale Fishing Club. Since he was a teenager, Aaron has traveled throughout Asia and Africa working as a guide and translator for groups of all ages. His experiences in Senegal as a fisherman are truly unique, and include extensive exploration of never-before-fished stretches of the Gambia River.

DANE BARCA spent two years as a commercial lobster fisherman in Maine, but now lives a far more quotidian life about a hundred-feet from the San Francisco Bay. He can be reached at DANEBARCA@GMAIL.COM.

THOMAS ROBERT BARNES is a screenwriter and backcountry skier by trade. His writing tends to follow his interests in sports and history, but like any good dog, it has a mind of its own. His work has appeared in many small magazines, mostly in New York.

ROBERT J. BEHNKE is professor emeritus of Fisheries Conservation and Wildlife Biology at Colorado State University in Fort Collins, Colorado. He is the author of more than 200 articles and papers regarding fish and fisheries and has served on numerous advisory boards for state and federal agencies. He is the author of several books including the seminal *Trout of North America*. He began writing the quarterly "About Trout" column for Trout

Unlimited's *Trout* magazine in 1983. He lives in Fort Collins, Colorado with his wife, Sally.

ELAINE BLEAKNEY lives in New York City. Her poems have appeared in *Crab Orchard Review*, *Hotel Amerika*, and *The Konundrum Engine Literary Review*. Her favorite angling poem is "King of the River" by Stanley Kunitz.

HOWARD BLOCH, Sterling Professor of French, is a graduate of Amherst College and Stanford. He taught at the University of California Berkeley and Columbia before joining the Yale faculty in 1997. He is a scholar of the French Middle Ages whose work spans the subjects of literature, law, economics, social history, and the visual arts. He teaches in the Department of French and in Medieval Studies, has served as Director of the Division of the Humanities, and is currently Chair of the Humanities Program. He has published numerous books, including *A Needle in the Right Hand of God: The Norman Conquest of 1066* and the *Making and Meaning of the Bayeux Tapestry*. Bloch is a Fellow of the American Academy of Arts and Sciences.

SUSAN BORDEN lives in St. Paul and fishes in nearby waters: Lake Phalen, White Bear Lake, the St. Croix River, and the Cascade River. She also travels gladly to the Boundary Waters Canoe Wilderness Area in northern Minnesota for paddling, camping, and fishing every year or so.

SCOTT BOWEN grew up on the Delaware River, where he began fishing when he was five-years-old. He is the author of a short story collection, *The Midnight Fish*, and a forthcoming novel. He lives and writes in Bucks County, Pennsylvania.

DOUGLAS BREWER (Abu Faruk) is a Professor of Anthropology at the University of Illinois and Director of the Spurlock Museum. He has written numerous books and articles on the archaeology and fauna of Ancient Egypt. Most of his early academic works focused on the fishes of the Nile and their archaeological significance. Although his present academic position is far from home, he still manages to fish the waters of Washington State for salmon and trout. His new delight is teaching his children, Joseph and Rachel, the art and love of fishing.

CHRISTOPHER BUCKLEY is the editor of *ForbesLife* and is the author of a dozen books including, *The White House Mess*, *Thank You for Smoking*, *Florence of Arabia*, and *Boomsday*.

JUAQUÍN HERNÀNDEZ CANEGATO is from Veracruz, Mexico and works full-time crafting and restoring stained glass windows. His work can be seen in buildings and churches from Brandon, Florida to Altoona, Pennsylvania. On the side, Juaquín enjoys to fly-fish, sip Argentinean wines, and read modern American poetry.

JIMMY CARTER was the thirty-ninth President of the United States serving from 1977 to 1981. He was awarded the Noble Peace Prize in 2002. He has been continually involved in world diplomacy and has founded the Carter Presidential Center, an institution dedicated to international aid and conflict resolution. He is the author of many books including *Keeping Faith*, *The Blood of Abraham*, and *Everything to Gain*, which he wrote with his wife Rosalynn.

PETER FONG is a seasoned fly-fisherman from Pray, Montana. His writing has appeared in *Fly Fisherman*, *Fly Rod and Reel*, *Gray's Sporting Journal*, *The New York Times Sophisticated Traveler*, and *Tumblewords: Writers Reading the West*.

KEITH ALEXANDER FRYER was born in Lismore, New South Wales, in 1950. He likes to be known as a "mad-keen fisherman." He has had short stories published in an Australian fishing magazine and was joint winner of Editors Choice, Writespot 2001 Summer Short Story Competition ("As Decreed").

JOSEPH A. FURIA was co-founder and the first editor-in-chief of the *Yale Anglers' Journal*. Joe designed the first issue while a freshman at Yale in 1996, recruiting the first literary contributors and staff and establishing the mission, tone and look of the publication, all of which survive to the present day. After college Joe worked for five years in marketing, sales, and business development for two technology companies. He has also worked for the U.S. Department of the Interior, U.S. Department of State, and CBS News. He is currently studying environmental and natural resources law at Lewis & Clark Law School in Portland, Oregon where he is the Online Managing Editor of the law review, *Environmental Law*. Furia received a BA with Distinction in Political Science from Yale College.

BENJAMIN GREEN is a native Californian who lives on and fishes the rivers of the North Coast. He is the author of nine books, including *The Sound of Fish Dreaming* and *Barbless Hooks and Anchorholds*.

CHRISTINE HEMP has had poems and essays featured periodically on National Public Radio's *Morning Edition*. Her essay and poem about sending a poem of hers into space on a NASA rocket won her a First Place Northwest Society of Professional Journalism Award. Her work has also appeared in such publications as *Harvard Review*, *Boston Review*, *ZYZZYVA*, *Christian Science Monitor*, *Maine Times*, *The Drunken Boat*, and in anthologies by Macmillan, Simon & Schuster, and Orchard Press. She lives in Port Townsend, Washington.

JIMMY HODGES is a longtime resident of Milton, Connecticut. He spends his days tying flies and dreaming up fishing stories, his evenings on the water or wooing women with bad puns.

JOHN HOLLANDER is a Sterling Professor of English at Yale University. He has written numerous books of poetry including *Reflections on Espionage* for which he won the 1976 Political Book Award given by *The Washington Monthly*. His book *Rhyme's Reason: A Guide to English Verse*, is a popular handbook for writers of verse.

PETER JUST grew up in the suburbs of Washington, D.C. He was educated at the University of Chicago and the University of Pennsylvania and has taught anthropology at Williams College since 1988. Stranded in western New England, he taught himself to fish with a fly, which he continues to do on the Deerfield, Hoosic, Battenkill, and other local waters.

GREG KEELER, a professor of English and Creative Writing at Montana State University in Bozeman, Montana, should probably be categorized as a subspecies of "renaissance man." As for the "sub," he mouth-breathes and knuckle-walks among the best. As for the "renaissance," he writes poetry, articles for magazines and scripts for plays. He paints, sings, and plays the guitar, harmonica, and kazoo. These are in addition to being an avid fisherman.

IVAN KERBEL grew up in Sofia, Bulgaria and was a fencer at Yale. He maintains that foil- fencing is like fly-casting, though he observes that fencers and fly-fishermen seem to be keeping this truth from each other. He is senior associate director of the MBA Career Management office at The Wharton School, University of Pennsylvania.

TAYLOR KITCHINGS teaches American Literature and Film at St. Andrew's Episcopal School in Ridgeland, Mississippi. His lyrics are included in the novel *The Road to Eden's Ridge* by M.L. Rose and he has played piano and sang in New York, Memphis, and Europe. His original album, *Clean Break*, has become a collector's item and is available on the Internet. He is married and has two wonderful children.

DANA LAMB, born in Brooklyn, New York, was an avid conservationist and angler throughout his life. He wrote nine books including *Bright Salmon and Brown Trout*, *Not Far From the River* and *Woodsmoke and Water Cress*. He died in 1986 at the age of eighty-six.

RON MCFARLAND teaches seventeenth-century and modern poetry, contemporary Northwest writers, and Hemingway seminars at the University of Idaho, where he directs the creative writing program.

ED MIGDALSKI, retired natural history museum scientist, ichthyologist, and outdoor educator at Yale University, is the author of nine books and more than 150 journal and magazine articles. Yale's Peabody Museum recently published his latest book, *Lure of the Wild: The Global Adventures of a Museum Naturalist.*

SKIP MORRIS is the author of many books on fly-fishing topics including *Morris on Tying Flies, Fly Tying Made Clear and Simple, The Art of Tying the Nymph, The Art of Tying the Bass Fly,* and *Morris & Chan on Fly-fishing Trout Lakes.* Skip also writes columns for *Fly Tyer* and *Fly Fishing and Fly Tying* and is a frequent contributor to many other American fly-fishing magazines. He lives with his wife, Carol, and their four cats on Washington's lush and sparsely populated Olympic Peninsula.

JIM MURPHY is a man of letters and former owner of numerous college bookstores. He is the founder and owner of the Redington Tackle & Apparel Co. and is an infamous and well-liked member of the fly-fishing community. He lives in Stuart, Florida, with his wife and four children.

JAMES PROSEK, co-founder of the *Yale Anglers' Journal,* began his writing career at the age of twenty with *Trout, An Illustrated History.* His other books include, *Joe and Me: An Education in Fishing and Friendship, The Complete Angler: A Connecticut Yankee Follows in the Footsteps of Walton, Fly-fishing the 41st: Around the World on the 41st Parallel, A Good Day's Fishing,* and *The Day My Mother Left.*

HOWELL RAINES was born and raised in Birmingham, Alabama. In 1992, he won the Pulitzer Prize for "Grady's Gift," a *New York Times Magazine* article about his friendship with Gradystein Williams Hutchinson. He is the author of *The One That Got Away: A Memoir, Fly Fishing Through the Midlife Crisis, Whiskey Man,* and *My Soul is Rested,* which is considered an essential work on the history of the civil rights movement. He was the political editor of both the *Atlanta Constitution* and the *St. Petersburg Times* and was the executive editor of the *New York Times.*

ELLIOT L. RICHARDSON was an avid fly-fisherman of Atlantic salmon, trout, steelhead and saltwater fish for over fifty years. He served four U.S. Presidents in senior policy and cabinet positions including: U.S. Secretary of Defense (1973), Attorney General of the United States (1973), U.S. Secretary of Commerce (1972–1973), U.S. Secretary of Health, Education and Welfare (1970–1972), and U.S. Under-Secretary of State (1969–1970). He died in 1999 at the age of seventy-nine.

STEVEN RINELLA grew up in Twin Lake, Michigan. His writing has appeared in many publications including *Outside, Field and Stream, Men's Journal, DoubleTake, Bowhunter, Fly Fisherman, The New Yorker, American Heritage, Big Sky Journal.* His new book is *The Scavenger's Guide to Haute Cuisine.*

JAMES ROSSBACH was an avid angler beginning on a small pond in White Plains, the Adirondacks, and northern Maine.

He later traveled for trout and salmon fishing trips to Alaska and much of the western and northwestern United States, as well as Canada, Europe, Iceland, New Zealand, and South America. His only prolonged interruptions were five years of active duty during World War II. He worked in the investment business for almost thirty-five years and was a general and, later, a limited partner of Ingalls & Snyder. He served on the boards of the Museum of the City of New York, Goodwill Industries, and the Miramichi Salmon Association. He was also the editor of *The Anglers' Club Bulletin.*

ERNEST SCHWIEBERT was a Princeton alumni, trout fisherman, and author of numerous books including *Death of A River Keeper, Trout, Nymphs,* and the *Compleat Schwiebert.* He died in 2005 at the age of seventy-four.

JOHN SMELCER is the author of the Pulitzer Prize nominated collections *Riversongs* and *Songs from an Outcast,* as well as *Kesugi Ridge* and *Changing Seasons.* He has written *The Raven and the Totem, In the Shadows of Mountains,* and an autobiographical essay, which appears in *Here First: Autobiographical Essays by Native American Writers.* His poetry has appeared in over 200 periodicals.

MARK SPITZER is a professor of writing at the University of Central Arkansas. His books include *Riding the Unit, The*

Pigs Drink from Infinity, Chum, Bottom Feeder, and five books of literary translation. See WWW.SPTZR.NET for more info.

RICHARD STOLL earned a BA from the University of Washington. During twenty-five years as an environmental scientist and engineer, he has managed large public and private environmental projects and programs, conducted baseline research, and taught at post-secondary institutions. He has also worked with governments, non-government organizations, and industry in the United States, Canada, South Korea, Malaysia, Tonga, and Fiji.

DANIEL STRANAHAN lives with his family in Seattle, Washington and he works with The Needmor Fund, a family foundation which funds grass-roots community organizing and advocates for social justice. He continues to chase steelhead where and whenever he can.

JOHN STRULOEFF is a former Stegner Fellow in creative writing at Stanford University and is currently the director of the creative writing program at Pepperdine University. His stories and poems have appeared recently in *The Atlantic Monthly, The Southern Review, The Literary Review, Other Voices, Prairie Schooner, ZYZZYVA,* and elsewhere. The manuscript for his short story collection, *Animals,* which includes "The Fish Garden," was a finalist for the Iowa

Short Fiction Award. His first book of poems, *The Man I Was Supposed to Be*, will be published in late fall 2007 by Loom Press.

ROBERT TISDALE, a Yale PH.D. in English, writes "I teach, but am most myself when writing or fishing—aspects of the same mystery—finding something significant in a place where at first nothing more than scenery appears to the eye." He enjoys fishing the dark, clear lakes of Northern Minnesota.

M.J. TREASE was born on Thanksgiving Day in Galion, Ohio, in 1976, and he grew up in Nashville, Tennessee. He graduated from Ohio State University in 2001.

CALE VAN VELKINBURGH grew up in the small ski town of Frisco, Colorado where he spent his summers ditching golf lessons for afternoons on the local creek, fishing for tiny brook trout. Many years later, Cale is still blowing off more popular activities and spends his summers guiding the big rivers of Montana. His new drift boat has built in speakers and a margarita blender, and he is sure to piss someone off on the river this summer with his vivacious antics, but he doesn't care. And he likes nymphing.

TIM WEED attended Middlebury College and earned degrees from the University of California and Warren Wilson College. His fiction has appeared in *Colorado Review*, *Gulf Coast*, *The Gihon River Review*, and numerous other magazines. His essays and feature articles have appeared in *Couloir*, *Middlebury*, *Northern Woodlands*, *Mountainfreak*, *Snowy Egret*, THEMORNINGNEWS.COM, *International Environmental Policy*, and elsewhere. His short fiction collection, *The Camp at Cutthroat Lake*, was a finalist for the Lewis-Clark Press Discovery Award. Tim has worked in restaurants and on construction sites, for investment firms, adventure travel companies, ski resorts and fish markets. In the course of his career as a director of international education programs, he has lived and worked in many foreign countries, most recently Argentina and Cuba. He is at work on a novel.

COLOPHON

The text of this book is set in Adobe Caslon,
designed by Carol Twombly in 1990,
based on the typefaces cut by English
typefounder William Caslon in the 1730s.

The titles and heads are set in Bookman,
designed by Ed Benguiat in 1975,
based on the typefaces cut by Scottish
punchcutter Alexander Phemister in the 1850s.

It was designed by Gary Robbins.